WHERE THE TREES TALKED

My Life in Africa

WHERE THE TREES TALKED

My Life in Africa

MAGDALENA MOS

(✳) **green**hill

https://greenhillpublishing.com.au/

Mos, Magdalena (author)
Where The Trees Talked
ISBN 978-1-922957-39-9
Memoir

Typeset Calluna 10/15

For my beloved children, Adalia and Chris.

You are my life.

INTRODUCTION

Sanity is relative

It was 1993. At twenty I had just finished my university degree, and after my graduation, I decided that the best thing I could do with my life was to go to Africa to join my boyfriend, Harry. I embarked on my perplexing journey in high spirits, which gradually evaporated as I touched down on three consecutive continents over three consecutive days. According to my travel agent, flying from Australia to Nigeria via London, Tokyo, and Egypt was *apparently* cheaper.

Two years before my departure, Harry resigned from a secure, well-paid engineering job in Australia, and accepted a position to work at a foam plant in a notoriously unsafe country in West Africa. It was a spontaneous decision. He said he would be back in two years. Yet there I was instead, two years later, disembarking from a plane loaded with home-coming locals in Lagos, Nigeria. The situation seemed like an incomprehensible paradox. It was not my first time in Nigeria. I had lived there ten years ago when my parents, sister Edyta, and I had come from Poland, and we had happily lived there for three years. We left when I was eleven years old.

Over the years, I wondered what strange winds of fortune drove me back to Nigeria. The fact was, I had missed it. I still remembered my school, my friends, and the aromas of the tropics, but my memories were that of a child. I had not been to Africa on my own. Was this why I needed to go back? I had only known Harry for a couple of years, yet there I was, risking everything on a whim. My comfort was that I had a return ticket, and the plan was for both of us to return to the security of Australia within twelve months. I was just there to speed things up a notch, and to revisit the place of my lingering childhood memories.

We stayed in Nigeria for ten years, which is where we got married. I returned to Australia soon after because I was pregnant, and I blatantly refused to have my first child in Africa. We had somehow, accidentally, survived all these years, despite everything life had thrown at us, and that was nothing short of a miracle. But I was beginning to think our luck was running out.

Harry stayed in Nigeria.

This book is about the ten years of delirious life, filled with laughter, tears, adversity, daily calamities, isolation, fascinating locals, amazing friendships, and my gradual descent into insanity. However, sanity is relative and depends on the perspective.

This is to the Africa I have always loved and will always miss.

CHAPTER 1

SNAPSHOTS FROM POLAND

My maternal grandmother, Helena Kolenda, was born in 1933, in a small Polish village called Zablocie. Her home was a white-washed timber hut covered by a cosy straw bonnet of thatch. It stood surrounded by a spiky wooden fence, which in the summer months was intricately veiled by cascades of rambling flowers and creeping vines. The cheerful little house was situated first or last — depending on which direction one came from — on a long, windy country road, gently nestled amongst fields, meadows, and forests.

Behind the houses and the outbuildings stretched the neatly ploughed fields and fruit trees. In the early spring, bees buzzed amid the intoxicating flower heaven, assiduously collecting pollen from the scented blooms. In summer, the orchard heaved with trees laden with succulent apples, sweet pears, and scarlet drops of cherries. Nearby, dairy cows contentedly chewed the abundance of lush grass from the fertile meadows, generously sprinkled with golden dandelions, and scarlet poppies. A refreshing stream murmured its way along a mossy bedrock a short distance away.

An ancient gnarly pine forest hedged the village from the other side. In late summer, women and children collected baskets of blueberries in its shaded undergrowth. With the onset of autumn, edible mushrooms were carefully picked from the rich forest floor by the savvy villagers. They were then preserved in vinegar or dried on long strings next to the tiled kitchen ovens, to be eaten in soups and hearty gravies during long frosty winter months. People in those remote parts of Poland had been living off the land and forest for centuries and little seemed to change over the years.

Peeping through her cottage window, little Helena would stare at the majestic ancestral pine forest spreading opposite her house in awe. In the evenings, its ethereal music of amaranthine whispers lulled her to sleep. When winter covered the surrounding countryside with its luminous blanket, hungry wolves howled mournfully into the night from deep within the snow-covered forest. By 1949, my grandmother was a beautiful dark haired sixteen-year-old girl. After the war, a dazzlingly handsome newcomer appeared in her town. He went by the name of Jozef Wegierek. Helena and Jozef were married within the year and my mother, Barbara, was born a few years later.

My parents met in 1968. At seventeen, Barbara was beautiful and enveloped by a veil of waist-long black hair. She was studying to be a teacher. My father Zygmunt, a serious blue-eyed young man, was twenty-three and in his final year of studying electrical engineering at university. His main hobby was photography. Zygmunt asked Barbara for a walk in the park under the pretext of a photoshoot, hoping it would turn into a promising date. The autumn walk exceeded his expectations, and my mother has been his muse ever since.

My parents married in 1970, and my sister Edyta and myself were born in the following two years. We lived in an ugly, grey apartment block, the likes of which covered the whole of Poland, courtesy of our omnipresent neighbour, the Soviet Union. We were in the midst of the Cold War and on the wrong side of the Iron Curtain. However, none of that mattered to me as a child. My life centred around the yearly summer holidays my sister and I spent at my grandparents' country farm.

My father's parents, Jan and Wladyslawa, were both born in Druzykowa, a small remote village in the southern Polish countryside. A five-minute walk from my grandparents' house led straight into a dense, shady forest filled with dignified evergreen spruce, hornbeams, and pines. The more sedate deciduous trees earnestly competed for light and space in the lower levels of the forest, where birches, aspens, hornbeams, and beeches created an elaborate medley of browns, greys, and greens in shadowy alcoves. An exquisite mosaic of pink heathen, translucent ferns and moss-covered rocks coated the rich forest floor and created the perfect breeding ground for the lowest level of this rich forest, the fungi. The resulting medley of edible mushrooms waiting to be picked every autumn was the source of an ongoing competition, not only in my grandparents' household but also among the two hundred Druzykowa villagers, all self-proclaimed mushroom gatherers and connoisseurs.

A few decades ago, Polish people were the source of a serious study by an enterprising foreign scientist, who tried to understand and analyse our fanatical mushroom fascination. The result of his detailed study proclaimed us as 'mycophillic,' synonymous with mushroom lovers. On the other side of the study, Anglo-Saxons were apparently 'mycophobic,' a self-explanatory word. Considering that the folkloric English names of mushrooms sound like a fairy tale gone sensationally wrong, with horrific names such as witch's hat, destroying angel, poison pie, witches' butter, devil's urn, or dead man's fingers, I could truly relate to British fungal anxiety.

My grandfather's greatest hobby was smoking foul-smelling, cheap Polish cigarettes; a big secret from my grandmother, who did not approve. The way my grandfather Jan went about it was not at all subtle. Several times a day he sat on an upturned rusty old bucket in full view of the kitchen window, where my grandmother invariably presided, and contentedly bellowed thick fumes of noxious smoke straight into his wife's sensitive nostrils. Once finished, still delectably shrouded in a white cloud of cigarette smog, he smiled and mischievously winked at us. We usually played in close vicinity, unknowingly receiving the full benefit of passive smoking.

'Don't tell grandma I smoke!' he warned us in a booming and gloomy whisper, which could be heard within a kilometre's range, as he was already quite hard of hearing. Jan would then inevitably convulse into a smoker's coughing fit.

We never did tell. We never had to, since grandma knew better than anyone that her husband smoked like a chimney. We children, however, always kept our mouths shut for two reasons. First, because then we would be in trouble with our dear old grandpa, whom we feared deeply and reverently. We had no wish to precipitate events that would eventuate in his bad temper. Secondly, we really did not give a hoot, as we had many more important things to do.

As if to compensate for her husband's obvious shortcomings, my grandmother's main passion in life was going to church. Like most Poles in those days, she was a fervent God-fearing Catholic, but Wladyslawa took this meaning to glorious new heights. After recovering from the heavy blow of my father, her son, not becoming a priest, she decided to become a live-in fixture of the village house of prayer instead. To her religious credit, Wladyslawa used the grandchildren left in her care to the best of her advantage. Being all girls, we were conveniently used as church decorations every Sunday mass, strategically positioned in the most visible locations for maximum effect. We made quite a sight; five city, God-fearing girls, dressed in freshly starched white frocks, hair carefully braided and adorned with gigantic white ribbons. The village populace, not used to such eccentricities, would stare at us, awestruck. We enjoyed the limelight, sweet smiles frozen on our angelic faces. The church was our stage, and we loved it.

The rest of the time, we were left to our own devices. Our favourite hideout at the farm was the barn. It was filled with fragrant fresh haystacks, brought from the nearby field on a horse-drawn carriage, with us precariously perched on top. We spent countless hours there, peeping through the holes in the wooden walls, gloriously invisible but seeing everyone. When not in hiding, we roamed amongst the farm animals.

The chicken coops were accessible only by a wooden ladder, and we made sure to check for eggs several times a day, driving the chickens to distraction.

When we got bored of the farm, we roamed the single gravel road of the village, where we were chased by the vigorous and spirited Druzykowa children. There were hordes of them and only five of us. We were girls, and they were mostly boys. Life was not easy for us 'city girls' as the village children offensively, yet justifiably, would call us. We tried to prove to them that we were just as fast, dirty, smelly, and foul-mouthed as they were. Quite naturally, we were never able to prove that.

One day, our all-girl cousin troop fell into a barbaric ambush somewhere on the curve on the single Druzykowa dirt road. The village boys attacked us with perfect stealth and without any warning. They suddenly appeared in front of us, jumping from the roadside bushes. Armed with long sticks which they brandished dangerously close to our faces, they smiled at us with cruel, winning smiles. The vigilantes' timing was perfect, as we were just coming back from an impromptu visit to the priest on an errand for our grandma. We were not dressed for guerrilla warfare. So, we did what girls do best under such circumstances; we did not engage in combat. We just screamed like damsels in distress, as befitted our dress code situation.

Help was as swift as it was unexpected and arrived in the form of a slightly more mature village boy, who happened to be our grandparents' next-door neighbour. He wasted no time in flying to our rescue, on the way slowing down just enough to pick himself a nice juicy bunch of prickly nettles, providentially growing on the side of the road.

8

What happened next is an endearing memory still as pleasurable today as it has been for the past forty years. Jacek — for this was our saviour's name — brandished an enormous nettle bunch like a sword-wielding knight, evenly and generously distributing his blows in quick succession to the half-naked stupefied village commandos. He missed no one, and the total surprise of the counterattack meant that before they recovered enough of their senses to run away, they all received generous second and third swipes. It was only then that the nettle stings began to activate, and mixed with the dirt and the sweat on their naked skins, the itching must have been excruciating. The vigilantes started scratching and howling as they decamped in a disorderly bunch.

We girls watched this humiliating retreat in total, glorified silence. All that remained of the bushy nettle sword were a few wilted stalks in the hand of our knight in shining armour. We knew how to be grateful and showed it by always thereafter running straight to our neighbour's house when we needed rescuing from the village vigilantes, and Jacek never failed to be gallant towards us. We never knew if he helped us that memorable day because he just wished to silence our deafening screams, or whether he had fallen helplessly in love with one of us, and chivalrously saved his lady love and her ladies in waiting from distress. This was a topic of wild speculation between us girls for the following weeks, and we finally all came to the same conclusion. Our knight was indeed desperately and deeply afflicted with love — for every single one of us.

I recall almost nothing of my first — and what proved to be the last — year of schooling in Poland. Most of my childhood memories from my birth city centred around the sandpit, centrally located amidst the tall apartment blocks where we lived. This was the children's hub. A totally child-owned, no-nonsense, no adults space, where friendships bloomed, sandcastles were painstakingly built by some only to be heartlessly smashed by others, and block wars ravaged our young and fearless ranks.

It was also the place where new pets were shown off triumphantly to the jealous and awe-struck block urchins. One day, a girl took her newly acquired boxer puppy for a stroll around the crowded sandpit. She certainly captured our instant attention and horrified stares. We immediately surrounded the pair in euphoric sympathy. After a one-minute silence to honour the tragedy unfolding in front of us, one of the urchins finally ventured a question.

'What's wrong with its face?' he asked, afraid to further precipitate the demise of the wrinkled hairy mess, looking at us balefully from half-closed watery eyes.

'Did it smash into a car?' came the helpful gory suggestion from another source.

'How long before it dies?' whispered a third, with thrilled anticipation.

'Look, its teeth are sticking out, they are about to fall out!' cried a mesmerised girl in horror.

We all watched in earnest and waited for the puppy to expire in front of us, teeth rocketing out of its mouth. Much to our disappointment, it did not. The girl turned on her heels and ran away crying, taking her dying puppy with her. After that, we never again saw the pedigree dog — or its owner. The thought that the poor canine was naturally endowed with such an ugly and creased appearance never crossed our minds. It was damaged goods to our expert eyes.

And so, our life followed a slow and predictable pattern. We went to school, played in the sandpit, spent our weekends at grandma Helena's house, and spent our summer holidays in Druzykowa. That normalcy, however, ended abruptly when in the year 1980, my parents made the most reckless decision of their lives. My father accepted a lecturer's job at a polytechnic, in a remote town called Auchi, in Nigeria. Only to be a two-year contract, my parents decided after a series of whispered nocturnal debates, that we would all go to Africa.

We never returned to live in Poland.

Chapter 2

AFRICAN BUSH RIDE

'So, Segun, what do armed robbers do...?'

I cannot remember much about what I felt or thought when we first landed in Nigeria. We did not know it at the time, but Lagos Airport was, and still is today, considered one of the busiest, dirtiest, most chaotic, and most corrupt airports in the world. That, coupled with dilapidating internal and external infrastructure, or lack of it in general, would explain why it is hailed as the most intimidating airport in the world. However, it was the first airport we ever landed in, so to us, it was all the same.

We were more preoccupied with the fact we had survived our first aerial flight. To this day I don't know if it was by chance or a miracle. We flew on a Russian Aeroflot plane, and since airline catastrophes were not publicly available yet, we did not know how harrowingly close we defied the statistics by arriving at our destination alive. Suffice it to say, a simple Google search nowadays would reveal that in the decade of 1980, 2,106 people perished in Aeroflot plane crashes. This is only counting the ones which Russia did admit to. It is also not counting the crashes which miraculously did not have casualties, yet crashed in the most horrendous circumstances all over Russia. The details of the incidents are pages long and read like a fantasy fiction story.

Just before take-off, the seats directly behind us were filled with excess luggage by the discourteous Russian flight attendants. We managed to stay in dignified, semi-upright positions because we strained against the onslaught with all our force. We did not complain.

Our neighbours across the aisle, with less forethought, spent the entirety of the six-hour-long flight bent over in emergency landing positions. They did not complain either. It must have been their first plane trip too. Perhaps, they thought that is how one travels on planes. Or perhaps, somehow, they knew the statistics and did not mind sitting in crash landing positions throughout the flight.

We got out of the plane in Lagos, still rubbing our painful backs, and were immediately taken aback by the intensity of the heavy, humid air. We felt like we had stepped into a gigantic, stagnant, breezeless bubble of heat, infused with new scents our senses were not accustomed to. We were smelling the quintessential essence of Africa; a strong, musty, pervasive bouquet of unforgettable aromas, which we felt engulfing our airways in successions of humid waves, the next more shocking to our offended senses than the one before.

One never forgets Africa's haunting smell, which over time you learn to love. Returning travellers breathe it in with joyous gulps of euphoria. We were not at that stage yet. In fact, we were extremely far from it.

'Try not to breathe!' was my mother's advice from between clenched teeth. By then we were unwillingly propelled forward by the forceful crowd of impatient passengers disembarking from the plane. We sailed through the airport arrival gates carried by the flood of humans, all united at storming the airport building, with a determination bordering on collective madness. Once inside the walls, the crowd dispersed in all directions, and the four of us, still miraculously together, were deposited back onto firm ground.

What did not help our situation was that we stood out like sore thumbs, as we seemed to be the only white people there. The friendly locals were now clamouring loudly in different dialects, profusely using their hands for emphasis, and running everywhere in a hurry. My mother looked at my father speechless. My father looked back at her clueless. I looked at my sister, and she stared blankly back at me. We all wanted to cry and go back to where we came from. We huddled closely together, my parents instinctively herding us in between themselves as a protective barrier. They eventually began to suspect that there must be some underlying logic to this stampede.

'Let's just wait and see what happens. Surely these people know what they are doing...' said my father, without much conviction in his voice.

Watch we did, and it slowly became apparent that the people indeed knew exactly what they were doing and where they were going. First, we noticed the big athletic young men, all potential Olympic gold medallists for the 100-metre sprint event. Or maybe *that* was the Nigerian Olympic team of 1980? Who knows? Legs like baobabs and arms to match, they easily breezed to the customs window, pushing everyone out of their way. As we watched their lightening progress across the airport in an entranced stupor, we noticed that the Dream Team were closely followed by less fit older Nigerians, who nevertheless showed incredible agility and grit for their age, and what they lost in speed, they made up in excellent hurdle techniques and commendable resourcefulness.

That group, totally unphased by the numerous prostrate casualties strewn haphazardly across the stampede path of the Olympic Team, nimbly somersaulted over the perils, not even slowing down for those injured. We watched mesmerised as whilst doing so, they simultaneously alternated the usage of their elegant leather briefcases as shields or swords, either protecting themselves from oncoming fists — or using them to pound people on their heads. Most of these men wore suits.

'These must be businessmen...' my father said in a faltering voice.

The businessmen group were closely tailgated by a strong troop of robust Nigerian ladies, who by virtue of their stout size, took a bit longer to reach the finishing line. However, once there, the voluminous dames utilised their mountainous body mass to violently crush through the male hurdle group. Next, with the tremendous momentum gathered in their charge, they pulverised the energetic mass of young Olympic athletes already wildly gesticulating at the passport check window.

Clamours of pain from crushed toes and broken ribs mixed with loud protests and curses followed the ladies earth-shaking homerun, but no one dared to protest when they pushed their way to the window first. We were to learn much later that no one messes with Nigerian women. They were a force to be reckoned with.

Last in the race were the mothers. They walked slowly, methodically picking up their crying children strewn all over the floor following the successive waves of sprinting passengers, and neither the mums nor their dishevelled tots minded too much the disgrace of what just happened to them.

As for us, we were left at the very bottom of the chain, behind the mothers of the last few crying children. Even the sick and the elderly were slowly gaining on us. As everything steadily slowed down, and everyone left to claim their baggage, we were the last to go through customs and made our way to the last stage of the airport process. Waiting for our luggage to arrive turned out to be our first lesson in Africa's legendary notion of time, patience, and forgiveness.

The baggage claim area was just a big dirty space with lots of missing walls. In the middle was the conveyer belt, or rather, what was left of it, as we immediately saw that it was in no working order. We wondered if it ever *did* work considering the sad state of collapse it was in. Picking our way amongst the crowd, now harmoniously camped around the space, we joined the athletes, the hurdle group, the voluminous women, the mamas with children, and the sick and elderly in what was to become a long and bonding wait. Looking around us, we were astounded at how quickly the mood of the crowd had changed from dangerous to friendly. The fast-paced events of the last hour seemed to have been forgotten and forgiven. Some of the passengers had already made new friends with their past adversaries, slapping each other on the shoulders, calling each other *broda* and *sista*, and laughing with pure African joy. Cascades of laughter erupted from place to place as jokes and food were shared.

We were just as amazed that no one was expressing any impatience at the fact that our luggage was delayed by what eventually would turn out to be a couple of hours. When it finally did arrive, it was hurled one suitcase at a time into the anticipating crowd, by a few sweaty and exhausted airport personnel. They had obviously been hired as conveyer belts, and by the looks of things, previously used to manually offload the plane's entire cargo hold; hence the few hours delay and their state of near collapse.

After we recovered our luggage, for which we had to scramble at top speed when it was thrown in the opposite direction, we were found at the arrival hall by a Pole sent to pick us up. He arrived five hours after the plane had landed; he was only half an hour late. He had no problems picking us from the crowd, and he apologised profusely for his lateness, but we were too bewildered to care and extremely relieved that we finally had someone to take care of us in that unknown place.

From the airport, we went straight to a guest house adjacent to the Polish Embassy in Lagos, where, as planned we were to wait for a representative from Auchi to arrive and drive us to our destination. Auchi is situated about five hundred kilometres from Lagos and is the second biggest city in the Nigerian Edo

State. My father was to start his two-year contract as a Principal Lecturer in the Department of Electronics and Engineering at Auchi Polytechnic. Back in the 1980s, it was a thriving multi-cultural education centre, renowned in the whole of Nigeria for its high academic standards, aimed at educating a skilled work-force in the areas of Business, Engineering, Applied Sciences, Technology, Art, and Environment. Till today, in 2023, Auchi Polytechnic has kept its high academic standards — and is hailed as one of the best Polytechnics in the whole of Africa. Our arrival there in 1980 coincided with a big influx of foreign lecturers, who provided internationally recognised levels of education along a wide range of pedagogical fields.

On the third day of our arrival, a driver arrived at the Polish Embassy guesthouse, introduced himself as Segun and politely announced that we would be leaving for Auchi early the next day. We were finally well and truly on the last leg of our long journey. After a quick breakfast the next morning, we piled ourselves into a rusty white Peugeot decorated with the Auchi Polytechnic logo on all four doors. To our family, the dubious-looking car was an utter luxury and we instantly felt like a delegation of foreign dignitaries, as opposed to a herd of terrified elephants from the airport.

We waved joyful goodbyes to our new Polish friends from the embassy, who from the onset of our arrival seemed bewil-dered to see our whole family together. According to them, normally the man of the family always arrived first, followed months later by his family. 'To prepare the groundwork, so to speak,' they tried to make clear to my parents, shaking their heads in disbelief. That was 'the customary way of doing things in Nigeria,' they added forcefully when my parents still chose to ignore the worried looks on their faces. After all, what could go wrong?

Everything went well while we were still in the traffic-congested city. Being stuck in the '*go-slow*,' Nigerian pidgin English for traffic, was an accepted part of life for all Lagosians. Destination times in Lagos were calculated by using complicated and elusive algorithms which accurately predicted the sizes of various *go-slows,* according to the time of the day and geographical location. Distance to the destination was an irrelevant variable, as depending on the time of the day, a three-kilometre distance could be covered in two minutes or two hours.

Our driver must have meticulously calculated the right time to leave in the morning, as we rolled steadily out of the city. Segun progressively developed higher velocity speeds when we left the city behind, where we inexplicably found ourselves on a narrow road, filled with potholes and no dividing lane.

'Segun, what is this side road?' asked my father anxiously, eyes peeled on the badly dilapidated road stretching endlessly into the horizon.

'This is the highway to Auchi, sa. It will take us straight there. Only 500 kilometres to go. We go arrive in no time at all, no worry, sa.'

My mother, who had been frantically fumbling between the car seats to locate the seatbelts, had finally arrived at a mortifying conclusion.

'There are no seatbelts at the back of this car,' she whispered to my father, panicked.

'Well darling, not to worry... there are none at the front either,' was my father's reassuring reply, his eyes firmly locked on the road in a hypnotic trance.

From his prime perspective in the front seat, there was certainly a lot to look at, and as my father was slowly taking it all in, he looked increasingly shell-shocked. The road was extremely narrow and barely wide enough to accommodate two cars passing in opposite directions. There were more potholes on the uneven surface than there was asphalt. Drivers in both directions expertly swerved off their lanes to avoid the cavernous potholes in their path, without bothering to check if there was a car approaching opposite. That meant that at any time, we had to swerve in avoidance of the incoming cars driving straight at us, without ever reducing their maddening speed.

In the back seats, my mother, sister and I had our eyes glued to the side windows. The sides of the road were tightly packed with burnt carcasses of cars and trucks. They lined the street in both directions, one horrifying crash after another. What was more staggering was that no one seemed to have learnt from those past mistakes.

Just like the roads, most of the cars were in an alarmingly bad state. Indicators were a luxury seldom possessed, so the drivers used intermittent honking to announce their intentions, often adding specific hand signals to clarify the point. That seemed like a very natural thing to do under the circumstances, as none of the cars had any windows either. To add to the chaos, there were no traffic signs or traffic lights, only very numerous checkpoints that appeared suddenly, and in the middle of nowhere.

As we approached our first such checkpoint, we were bewildered to see they were staffed by army men in full military camouflage gear, complete with walkie-talkies, helmets, and ammunition belts. We were yet to discover we had arrived in a country ruled by the military. As we came to a slow stop in front of the barrier blocking our road, a Herculean soldier-at-arms approached my father's window, a big fatherly smile on his sweaty face. His face was marked by an intricate pattern of tribal cuts and scars. My mother, my sister, and I instantly shrunk down in our back seats, terrified.

'*Oga, na how your dey? Everything ok sa? How is your dey sa?*'

It was our first real encounter with Nigerian pidgin English. It made little difference to us women, slouched at the back of the car, if it was Oxfordian English or pidgin — since we didn't speak a word of either. My father, however, was in a hugely different situation. He thought he spoke passable English, which we were led to believe was the official language in Nigeria. However, much to his bewilderment, he had not understood a word of what the imposing soldier had just said.

'*Oga, na waa o, wetin dey matta? How is your dey sa?*'

Feeling he had to say something, anything, my father tentatively opened his mouth. Nothing came out. All the English he thought he knew had evaporated from his dazed brain.

'*Sabi you no sabi sa? Na how is your family sa?*'

The soldier glanced at us cowering at the back.

'*How are you sa? How is your wife and shildren?*' asked the soldier again this time a bit slower, as if he was talking to a dimwit.

That seemed to work. Propelled into action by two words that sounded familiar, and following the direction of his curious gaze, my father sprang into verbal exertion. He ventured into his purest textbook English.

'*My family is fine. I am fine. Thank you. How are you?*'

'*I dey fine sa! I dey fine! How are you? How is your family? Everything good? Wey you dey go?*' the soldier was delighted he had established verbal communication with the strange imbecile.

'*I am fine. My family is fine.*'

'*It is a lovely day oh. A lovely day sa. Na where do you travel on dis very road, sa? Na fa?*'

'*We are going to Auchi.*' My father's frozen brain was quickly thawing in the heat of the acute mental exertion.

'*To Auchi! Na waa o! Dat be fah fah! How are you, sa? How is your family?*'

'*I am fine. My family is fine too. Thank you.*'

'*Na good oh. So how are you sa? Na how is your family, sa?*'

'*I am fine. My family is fine. How are you?*'

It was becoming painfully evident, even to us women flattened on the back seats, that the conversation was getting nowhere, and that the colossal soldier wanted something from my father. He was now half leaning inside the car, nonchalantly caressing his rifle, glints of happy anticipation in his eyes. They were met with glints of horror and total incomprehension in my father's. On the sixth round of niceties, when my father was one more time assuring the solicitous soldier that he and his family were fine, and '*how was he?*' our driver could stand it no more. He suddenly produced a twenty naira note from his pocket and gave it to the big army man in a practised covered gesture, almost too quick for our eyes to register. It was the equivalent of forty American dollars, a big sum of money.

Our shocked brains instantly registered what had just happened. We had never seen extortion practices before, but it seemed the most natural thing to do where we were. The soldier was not going to let us pass without a bribe because bribes were an entrenched part of life in Nigeria, a way of life that we soon learned to accept. We were also soon to discover that all expatriates were, by default, rich in the eyes of all Nigerians, no matter how poor they were. No wonder the lucky soldier looked so gleefully happy to see us.

We encountered many such checkpoints, all staffed with robust army men solicitously inquiring about our health, while nonchalantly caressing their rifles. My father had learnt his lesson and now had a stack of bribe money at the ready.

'Had I known there was going to be toll road costs with no change given, I would have changed the money into smaller denominations,' seethed my father, as he grudgingly gave away twenty-dollar notes without daring to ask for change. That journey on the African road proved to be more expensive than a luxurious limousine voyage on the smoothest tollways in Western Europe.

Later, we found out that Nigerian army men spent their holiday periods selflessly manning this type of illicit checkpoint. They rotated the staff in a synchronised manner, making sure they shared the profits between themselves. The roadblocks were by no means temporary affairs, but sturdy permanent structures, blocking traffic in both directions. The army worked only on the main roads. Spacious palm-leaved huts adjacent to the roadblocks provided welcome shade for a quick cat nap in the middle of the day, if toll business was slow. Right next to the military barricades, there were always a few women from nearby villages, bent over makeshift fires. They roasted corn and bushmeat for the hungry mercenaries, providing them with an abundance of bush fast food throughout the day. The symbiotic system worked both ways. The roadblocks boosted the local economy, and the soldiers protected the local village people. It all made total sense in Nigeria.

We were halfway on our journey to Auchi and stopped in a small town for a quick stretch and a toilet break. As we resumed the road, Segun looked nervous. He kept his eyes suspiciously on the thick bush surrounding us — as if expecting a wild animal to come charging at us at any moment. We enthusiastically expected that too and perked up in our back seats. Finally, the exotic part of the journey was about to begin. After all, were we not in the middle of Africa? Lions, elephants, and zebras should be making an appearance soon.

'So, what animals live in this forest? asked my father politely, following the driver's jittery sideways gaze. He winked at us in the back, as if to say, 'wait till you see your first lion behind that bush over there.' Segun looked at my father thinking he misheard. Then his worried face lit up in understanding.

'*Animals dey are! Ruthless animals, sa! You are right in calling dem so, sa! Dose army people at the checkpoints, dey nevah shoot innocent people like dese animals of armed robbers do!*' he enthused, throwing more nervous looks left and right, completely ignoring my father's question about local fauna.

'Armed robbers...?' asked by father surprised at hearing this new term. He racked his brain to try to remember if he had heard anything about armed robbers in Nigeria before. All he could suddenly remember with startling clarity were the worried looks of the Polish Embassy staff in Lagos as they were waving us dubious goodbyes. Things suddenly started to make a bit more sense.

'*Yes sa, dey patrol dis very very road we are driving on now, day and night!... Dey know where de army checkpoints are, and dey know better not to interfere with dem...*'

'So, Segun... what do these armed robbers do?' asked my father nervously.

Here I must digress slightly. It took us some time after we had settled in Auchi to comprehend the full extent of my parent's folly in deciding to come to a violent African country, rife with corruption, violence, criminal unrest, and an ongoing unsettled political situation. Unknowingly, we happened to have arrived in Nigeria during a new and very volatile political climate.

Nigeria gained its independence from the British in 1960. In 1963 a Prime Minister and President were elected by a parliamentary system of government, replacing the monarch, Queen Elizabeth, as the ceremonial head of state. In the resulting First Republic, Nigeria appointed Nnamdi Azikiwe as President. The First Republic lasted from 1963 to 1966. It was swiftly overthrown in a bloody military coup in 1966, which saw the ruthless decapitation of the Premier and the Prime Minister. The country's first military Head of State, Johnson Aguiyi-Ironsi took office on January 16, 1966. He was in turn assassinated a few months later in a counter-coup in July 1966.

General Yakubu Gowon took power in 1966 and managed to stay alive even after the 1975 coup, which left him deposed after a record eight years and 362 days in power. He was three days short of a whooping nine-year tenure, an impressively long time by Nigerian standards. Gowon was ousted from his coveted Head of State seat by another ambitious military man, Brigadier Murtala Mohammed in 1975. Unfortunately, Mohammed did not have his back covered, and he was in turn assassinated in another bloody coup in 1976. His successor was Lieutenant General Olusegun Obasanjo. After three years and 258 days in power, the wise man decided to resign, thus keeping himself alive.

The Second Republic — which lasted from 1979 to 1983 — under the democratically elected President Shehu Shagari, saw the interruption in the long-standing military regime. In 1983, Shagari was deposed. We just happened to be in the country in the short-lived return to democracy between our arrival in 1980 and our hurried departure in 1983 — when things had gone mad again. Corruption and unlawfulness were already rampant when we arrived 1980, and the political situation was electric. No one knew when the next government coup would be and who would strike. 'Armed robbers' were already a well organised criminal entity, renowned for its violence and brutality. They went largely unpunished due to the growing social unrest.

By the time we landed in Nigeria, everyone was terrified of armed robbers, especially the foreigners, who seemed to be their preferred target because of their perceived richness. The Nigerian armed robbery, a budding national crime organisation, would later develop into a worldwide crime syndicate, specialising in money swindles. Nigeria would become synonymous with phenomenal frauds on a global scale in early 2000.

Our family had the doubtful privilege of witnessing firsthand the birth of these organisations in their country of origin.

However, we were blissfully unaware of such future events, and so was Segun. I do not think anyone of us would have willingly agreed to this road trip had we had a little glimpse into the future. As it was, Segun looked extremely uncomfortable just talking about the subject, and following my father's question, was silent for a long time. After pondering about our sanity for a while, he graciously gave us the benefit of the doubt. He must have deduced that we were from another planet. He was not entirely wrong in that assumption. The comforts and safety of Europe were quickly becoming, even for us after barely a week in the tropics, a distant mirage.

'Well sa, first, dey have their special spots in the bush....dey wait for a car to pass by, sabi? Dey like to choose their cars well well. Dey will not attack a poor car, because dey know there is no mohney inside. It is only a waste of time for dem. But when dey see a rich car coming, a group of robbers, dey go throw nails on the road. Dat will cause a flat taya and when de car slows down enough, anoder armed group down de road runs out of the bush with machetes, knives, and guns. Der is no chance of escape, sabi?'

After that exhaustive explanation Segun grew ominously silent. He thought he had said enough and that my father's imagination would do the rest. It did not.

'So, what happens then?' asked my father dimly, still hoping for the best. Segun sighed. It was obvious he would rather not talk about the uncomfortable subject.

'Well, sa... dey ambush the car, and dey drag the people out.... and orda dem to give dem everything dey have on them. If you are *lucky, dey leave you naked at de side of the road with just a few machete cuts and bruises... but if you are not quick enough to give dem your watch or your wallet... well, dey chop your hand off and leave you to bleed to death. Or dey just kill you.'* He swallowed hard and looked in the rear mirror apprehensively.

'And oyinbos are their prime targets...' he added grimly under his breath.

'What are *oyinbos?'* asked my father quickly, a glimmer of hope in his fast-failing voice.

'White people!' answered Segun with a baleful look at his car full of pale, sweaty, glistening *oyinbos.*

It was only at that moment that my father finally understood that we were in a dangerous country, inhabited by people who had it in their heads that just because we were white, we were prime targets and fair game for assault, robbery, and murder. The value of life had a different meaning in Africa. Finally, and much too late, did my father realise what dangerous cargo we were, and how perilous this road trip in the Nigerian country-side really was.

The question of, how *'quickly'* was *'quickly enough'* for the lurking armed robbers, now became my father's main worry. Does one start throwing items of value through the window when hit with a hail of nails? Or does one politely wait for the vigilantes with the machetes to emerge from the bush a few metres down the road, and *then* quickly relieve oneself of said valuables and garments? Also, is one allowed to keep their undergarments if left to live? And what if the boot gets stuck (which we incidentally knew it would)? What if our best efforts at compliance failed because of such a glitch?

Now, in an anguished retrospect, my father was also beginning to understand why the man at the airport looked surprised to see all of us together, and why the Poles at the embassy tried to explain that it was not a good idea to bring everyone along for the trip to Africa. Indeed, who brings his whole family into a hell hole like this?

Fortunately, and unbeknown to us, Segun had a master plan. He probably had his own family to consider and was not going down without a fight. Still travelling at a breakneck speed of 120 kph on the ramshackle road, he suddenly swerved sharply into the surrounding bushland. There was no road, not even a dirt track. There was, however, a big steep hill.

Going up was no problem, but at the top, we glimpsed the unobstructed view of the descent route to the bottom, which was a big pool of muddy water. The depth was difficult to judge, but as we quickly approached it, we had no leisure time to speculate if we would float or sink. We splashed through it like a giant jet ski. As we sped through the bush, more hills with red muddy pools at the bottom would appear right in front of us, every one of them steeper, muddier and scarier than the one before. We tried not to squeal in terror as we came upon endless descents with potholes the size of miniature volcano craters. We spent more time airborne than in contact with the red dirt underneath us.

My father never lifted his eyes off the speedometer. Understandably, he chose the lesser of two evils. Looking directly in front of him as we flew through space was not an option for his shattered nerves. My father was a novice driver. He was used to straight, predictable European asphalt roads, with lots of orderly lights and road signs, and drove at a conservative speed of 50kph in a 60kph zone. Life had not prepared him for this African road trip.

Despite the unexpected bush detour, which in hindsight probably saved our lives or at least saved us a lot of money, we covered the five-hundred-kilometre distance from Lagos to Auchi in one day. We arrived at Auchi Hill Top Hotel, the only hotel in town, just after nightfall. The darkness had the advantage of sparing us the dismaying sights of the greatly decrepit establishment.

We disembarked from our car and unconvincingly thanked Segun for bringing us safely to Auchi — he was a tour de force of heroism which we only appreciated later. We were shown our two rooms which were directly opposite each other, on the second floor of the building. It seemed to be the more prestigious area of the hotel, although it was hard to tell as everything was quite shabby.

We were still rattled by the day's events, so by a silent consensus, we chose not to complain too much about anything. We all knew we were lucky to be alive in the first place. In brighter spirits, knowing that we were at the end of our journey, we took stock of our rooms, freshened up and made our way to the first floor for dinner. Despite our fatigue, we felt ready for whatever Africa had in store for us. How soon we were to discover just how wrong we were.

Much to our delight our food was served almost immediately. We were all famished as we hadn't had much to eat the entire day except for a few dried crackers and biscuits. However, the surprise discovery of a gigantic cockroach, flat on his back and under a piece of steak on my plate propelled my senseless father into action. It was driven by desperation, as he was in the final stages of emotional exhaustion. He immediately hailed the waiter and without a word — he had never seen a cockroach before, so was unsure as to the scientific name — pointed to the offending roach laying dramatically on its bed of rice. Not only was it almost as big as the piece of steak which steamed it, but the roach also had the audacity to be half alive, quivering its six spiky legs at us in an unconvincing show of defiance. Ignoring my screams, and that of my sister and mother, the waiter looked at the offending insect and swiftly administered a deadly *coup de grâce* with his big serving spoon. Satisfied at having pleased the customers, he then diligently removed my plate with the dead insect and smoothly replaced it with another. He then served me a generous portion of rice using the same utensil he had just used to terminate the cockroach.

'Enjoy your meal sir, madam,' he said, gallantly bowing, flashing a glistening white-toothed smile in our direction.

The three of us had stopped screaming and instead stared in shock. This is when the lights began to flicker ominously and then went out altogether, plunging the room into darkness. No one from our family was game enough to be flipping more steaks in the darkness, no matter how reassuring the waiter's smile was. We all stood in unison and exited the dining room in a desperate stampede. Running madly, we made our way along the dark corridors back to the safety of our rooms. On the way, we encountered a terrifying amount of live brown insects. Some were rustling on the floor, some were scuttling on the walls and ceilings, others were crunching under our feet, and more were buzzing excitedly right next to our faces. Our stampede through the corridors was accompanied by our terrified howls and screams.

'Hm... I think they are *cockroaches*, but for the word of me, I did not know they could grow to this size. Or that they could *fly...*' muttered my father, after finally recovering his speech in the safety of our room.

'And anyway, my girls, it makes no difference what they are as we are only here for the night, and we will probably never see those *cockroaches* again. Tomorrow we will be in our new house, as I have arranged with the Polytechnic, and I can assure you, there will be no flying cockroaches there,' he added, trying to sound cheerful and reassuring.

He was right. There were to be no flying cockroaches in our new house. However, how we almost wished there had been a few months down the road when we discovered a new species of bugs.

Chapter 3

TOMORROW

'By the Grace of God'

The first good thing we learnt, was that life in Africa followed its own special hypnotising rhythm, which had nothing in common with the Western concept of time and urgency. What supposedly was meant to happen '*tomorrow*' invariably happened a few days, weeks, months or sometimes even years later. Sometimes, it never happened. No one asked questions as to why. Things were simply forgotten, and life went on. The only definite time concept which would prove to be crushingly accurate, was that tomorrow *never* happened tomorrow. *Tomorrow* was a very abstract and much-loved term used by all Nigerians when faced with having to deal with an urgent matter. It really only signified that it would happen when it happened. '*By the grace of God,*' was added religiously, for added emphasis on the improbability of it happening at all.

We learned that patience, faith, belief in miracles and good humour would help to navigate the Nigerian bureaucracy with much less emotional scarring. We also learnt to reduce our expectations for anything to go as planned to zero. We were then positively rewarded when things did sometimes happen, most of the time long after we had forgotten we had once made a request in the first place. In our case, the *'tomorrow'* meant that we would stay at the Auchi Hill Top Hotel not overnight but for a few months, because, for some obscure reason, our promised bungalow was not ready. It would, *'be ready soon, by the grace of God,'* we were reassured daily by the friendly and deeply religious Nigerian staff in charge of our accommodation arrangements.

Coincidentally, the courses at the Auchi Polytechnic which were meant to resume '*in a few days,*' did not resume because the students and the teaching staff were on strike. *Intermittingly.* They would resume '*soon,*' said a staff member to my father, who was anxious to begin his lectures. After all, we had travelled across the globe for him to perform his professional duties. No one seemed phased by this turn of events, nor was anyone in a hurry to return to work or study. Eventually neither did we, as we slipped comfortably into a resigned but peaceful African philosophy.

My father did not begin his lecturing duties at Auchi Polytechnic until a few months later — when the teaching staff and students finally decided they were ready to come back. *Simultaneously.* The fact that their respective issues remained unresolved did not seem to bother anyone. In the meantime, our family was continuing to adjust to the African way of life. Slow-paced, happy, patient, relaxed, unpredictable...

To our credit, we adapted so well to our new lifestyle that we showed no surprise when endless unexplained complications kept further delaying our settling process. As a genuine credit to how seamlessly we assimilated with local customs and conditions, we showed great and genuine astonishment when months later we were finally able to move out of Auchi Hilltop Hotel into our new house. The term *new* is used in the loosest of terms here. First, for some unfathomable reason, we were given a bungalow in the Auchi Polytechnic Old Quarters, a set of houses built haphazardly around an oval and surrounded by a wide red dirt road. The houses, built a couple of decades before our family landed on the continent, were beginning to show alarming signs of dilapidation. Some were already crumbling.

All the other expatriates, ranging from Russian, German, Egyptian, Ukrainian, Hungarian, Austrian, Bulgarian, and Polish, lived in the new, custom-built, pristine, and aptly named Auchi Polytechnic New Quarters. Everything there was *new.* The New Quarters was a wonderful, resort-style hamlet in a picturesque location on prime Auchi Polytechnic estate grounds. It featured spacious new bungalows, majestically surrounded by beautiful gardens and magnificent tropical trees. The bungalows came fully furnished and all had functioning air conditioners — a technology we had not encountered before, hailing from one of the coldest countries in Europe. The New Quarters were specifically built to accommodate the numerous expatriates working in Auchi during the booming years of the early 1980s. They were lecturers, doctors, engineers, dentists, and architects, all there for a limited contract of about four years.

Our family had no such luxuries in our 'new' old bungalow. Its paint inside and out was peeling, revealing several layers of previous hues underneath, and it was encrusted with a generous layer of dirt and grime. It had cracks in the walls and ceiling, and the floors were a dirty laminate grey. For ventilation, our abode had one small fan in the imposingly big living room.

On the first night, we discovered that we were not the sole occupants of the house. Not even by a long stretch of the imagination. The residence had millions of termites already comfortably residing within its walls. They spent their daylight hours cosily sleeping off last night's binging, and methodically chomping through the remaining wooden foundations of the old bungalow after the sun went down. None of us slept that first night. The unnerving gnawing grew louder as the night evolved into dawn.

'What if the roof falls on us, mum?' I asked, listening to the creaking noise from above.

'It's ok, we will just stay awake to make sure everything is ok,' answered my mother soothingly, a lit torch in her hand pointing upwards, her unblinking eyes in a fixed stare on the circle of light reflected on the ceiling.

My father did not say anything. He just lay in bed with his eyes wide open, too scared to blink in case the whole roof fell in that millisecond. It was impossible for our inexperienced ears to know if the roof would last a few more minutes, hours, days, or months. Just in case, we kept an all-night vigil.

None of us relished the idea of waking up under a collapsed roof full of termites. In retrospect, the mobs of gigantic flying brown cockroaches from Auchi Hill Top Hotel seemed like a slight inconvenience.

The next day my father began the lengthy and complicated African parley process, to try to remedy the situation. He patiently and repeatedly explained our termite predicament to a long chain of officialdom, and to whomever he thought could be remotely in charge of the issue.

'Our new quarters are inhabitable,' he would begin politely.

No one really understood why. Even after he would explain about the termites.

'The house is still standing, is it not?' they asked, surprised at my father's plea. Everyone who looked at it could ascertain that fact without the slightest doubt. Even my father ran out of arguments after a while. We then had to wait a further few months for a more suitable bungalow to be assigned to us.

My sister and I had our own predicaments, which we thought were just as pressing. Aged eight and nine, we discovered that we were one of very few expatriate children in the whole of Auchi. Standing out like sore thumbs in a sea of chortling Nigerian children and being called '*oyinbo*,' or skinless, was now the new norm at our local Auchi Polytechnic school. We were promptly enrolled there by our parents, who worried that we had already missed so much schooling due to the unexpected African delays. As if that was not enough of an embarrassment, we did not speak a word of English.

Luckily, we were young enough to overcome adversity without too much psychological trauma. In a matter of months, we spoke English, and we made friends with the Nigerian children, who were very friendly and kind to our minority group. We learned to sing the Nigerian national anthem, standing at attention during daily morning assemblies. It was a new anthem back then and had only been officially inaugurated two years prior to our arrival. Nigerians never missed an occasion to sing it with unfaltering enthusiasm and the school grounds were as good a place as any to spread the proud nationalistic feelings. Following the anthem, we effortlessly recited 'Our Father.' After that, there was time for a nursery rhyme before we marched to our classes to begin our lessons.

Chapter 4

MADE IN BRAZIL, OF VINTAGE UNKNOWN

'I really don't think it's a good idea...'

It was not long before my parents realised that if we were to have a normal existence in Auchi, we would need to get a car. However, there were several complications, which became immediately apparent when my parents launched themselves into the task. The first drawback was that my father knew absolutely nothing about cars. His knowledge began and ended with the undisputed certainty that all cars have one steering wheel, four tyres and an engine. In retrospect, my then eight-year-old child's knowledge of the topic did not differ much from my father's.

The second impediment lay in the fact that my father barely knew how to drive, and he did not feel confident about starting his driving career in this part of the world. We had all discovered by then that Western traffic rules did not apply in Nigeria. As a matter of fact, there were no rules at all that we could identify or understand. The only local road practice was to keep to the right. Even that single rule did not apply if the road on the right was gone, as it very often was. The numerous potholes the size of miniature swimming pools also made driving in a straight line impossible, and drivers regularly swerved onto the opposing lane to avoid them.

'You stoopid idyyyot!'

'Your modar and your fodar are idyyyots!'

'Get off the road, who learn you how to drive? Na your moder?! Idyyyot!'

I never could understand why close family members were always brought up in the window conversations which inevitably accompanied such road acrobatics. The abuser never chastised just the driver of the offending car. His *modar*, or *fodar*, *sista*, and *broda* would always be thrown in for good measure too. Admittingly, the insult had the desired effect. Thus, the verbally assaulted driver would reel in fury and retaliate insults at his bully, in the process covering successive generations down the genealogical tree, including grandparents and grandchildren, aunties and uncles. No one ever got offended by the traffic-inspired insults and each driver went from being the victim to being the bully in quick alternating successions. No grudges were held. Ever.

Road crashes were the norm rather than the exception. They happened all the time. Cars were used to transport everything, including live goats for dinner, white baby zebu cows, and outraged cackling chickens squeezed by the dozen into small wicker cages. Bamboo poles and corrugated iron sheets stuck out for metres from the boots, and mattresses naturally fit on the spacious rooftops. The rooftops were generally used as trailers and were loaded with thick layers of mysterious packages and parcels, all different shapes and sizes, ingeniously piled up in an intricate puzzle on top of the car.

The rule of five passengers per car never made it to Nigeria. They just piled up on top of each other until there was no more space to move. Sometimes three people sat in the passenger seat next to the driver, limbs sticking out of the window. No one found it strange or out of place. This was the norm. Petrol was expensive, and every car trip was used to its full potential. Nothing was wasted.

Very shortly after our arrival, my father was told through the expat grapevine that a Polish couple were leaving Nigeria and had a car for sale. This was not an occasion to be missed. A car from an expatriate owner was a rare luxury as we could ill afford to risk buying a vehicle from an unknown source. As soon as he heard the news, my father asked a friend for a ride and rushed to Benin City to finalise the deal, before someone else snatched this beauty from him. He should not have worried. As it turned out, much to my father's surprise, he was the only interested party at the destination. Not only that, but when the owner saw him and to his horror realised that my father was a fellow Pole, he did everything he could to dissuade my father from buying the car.

'Yeah, no, you see, you really don't want to buy this car,' he said to my father as they were inspecting it.

'Oh, but I do, I do! I really need to buy this car,' insisted my father, passionately.

'It is not really such a good idea...' persisted the owner, trying to give my father some clue as to his good intentions.

'But this is a perfectly good car! It has no rust, the windows are working, the indicators are good, it looks great!' my father enthused, having covered all the things he knew about cars in this thorough inspection.

'I think this is not such a good deal,' pressed the nervous owner again.

'I really like this car!' declared my father firmly, seriously offended at the owner's sudden disinclination to part with his vehicle.

In a last desperate effort at solidarity towards a fellow Pole, the owner used his trump card.

'It's an old car, you know... and it's made in Brazil!'

He was seriously worried, and to emphasise the monumental admission he arched his eyebrows, winked one eye, dejectedly shook his head, sighed heavily, and made a series of disheartening sounds. Having thus exhausted his body language cues aimed at discouraging my father from pursuing the transaction, he tried to gently lead him away from the vehicle.

His pantomime, however, was useless, and his valiant efforts at chivalry fell on deaf ears. My father's knowledge of cars was

limited, and the least of his concerns was where the car origi-
nated from, or what vintage it was.

'Now, you listen to me! I will take it! I have travelled
a hundred kilometres to buy this car and I am not going
back empty-handed!'

'Look here... hmm... it may have a few minor issues with it...
hmm... which I should perhaps mention.'

'I'm telling you, I travelled all the way from Auchi to
get this car and I am not leaving without it! You cannot just
change your mind about selling it now! Do you even know how
much trouble I went to organise to come all this way? Here is
your money!'

My father grandly handed the owner the lofty sum of three
thousand dollars. It was a walloping amount even then for
a second-hand car. He had to take a loan to accumulate all the
money. But reliable cars in Nigeria were expensive and this was
the price paid for safety. In retrospect, it would have been much
more reliable and considerably cheaper to have purchased an
obstinate local old donkey for twenty dollars. At least occasionally it would have been mobile and perhaps partially predictable.

'As you wish.'

The owner had run out of well-intentioned arguments
and gave up trying to talk sense to my father. He pocketed
the money regretfully, and sighed heavily. 'But at least allow
me to accompany you to the outskirts of the town. I think it's
important I do.'

'As you please,' my father said.

He thought the courteous gesture was to make sure he
found his way out of town. It was only when he sat in the car

and started the engine, which did not start, and pressed the clutch that he noticed his foot almost went straight through the floor, which was paper thin with rust and corrosion. He realised that maybe the owner meant well after all. The car suddenly coughed to life after a few more attempts at turning the key and simultaneous frantic clutch pumps, a technique that the past owner obligingly demonstrated to my alarmed father. They set off, and made it to the outskirts of the town without a glitch, and two hours later my father arrived back in Auchi. He was the proud new owner of a cream Volkswagen Rio, number plate MBA 7796, vintage unknown, but a strong candidate for a museum piece even back then. That day was to mark the beginning of our endless misery. The car was to prove the bane of our existence for the rest of our stay in Nigeria.

In hindsight, we never really understood how the old clunker made the one-hundred-kilometre journey from Benin City to Auchi. The secret probably was that my father never took his foot off the gas and arrived in Auchi in one uninter-rupted homerun. Truth be told, he had never driven a vehicle all by himself before and would have been in a nervous trance bordering on recklessness. Be that what it may, from that day onwards, an effort of more than three kilometres at a time proved to be too much for the temperamental Rio.

Our inaugural three-kilometre trip to the New Quarters to show our new acquisition to our friends ended as a one-way journey. The automobile refused to start at the end of our visit and no amount of pumping the clutch brought it back to life. We were shamefully driven home by our friend who had a much more reliable car, a tiny Volkswagen Beetle. That was the day we discovered that all our friends had more reliable cars than ours, no matter what make, colour or vintage. The next morning, after a good night's rest at the New Quarters, the Rio started without a hitch, to my father's great relief. It was, however, to be very short-lived. It quickly became painfully evident that even by Nigerian standards, which were relatively low, this vehicle was not road worthy. As a general rule, it rarely started. When it did, we never knew if we would reach our destination, no matter how close it was. Often, we never made it, and we would stop on the side of the potholed road while my anguished father would go through the age-old motions of opening the bonnet to have a blank look at the engine inside. His knowledge of cars had not increased much since the purchase.

'The car is overheating again,' he would pronounce wisely. A thick black smoke would bellow from within the engine's mysterious depths, regardless of whether the bonnet was open or closed. It is of little wonder why our short and rare road trips were a source of great emotional strain for us all, and we became reluctant to drive in the family automobile even for a one-kilometre drive.

'We are going to the market to buy vegetables and fruits,' my mother would announce, as brightly as possible on our weekly shopping day. We had dragged the day as much as possible, and there was nothing to eat in the house anymore.

'Oh no, not again. Mum, you know the car will not even start. Do we really have to? Can't dad try to start it first at least?' we would beg.

'No girls, you know we can't strain the car too much. We will start it only when we are all dressed and ready to go. Now, hurry up and get ready.'

One day, quite predictably, we came to our usual involuntary stop at the side of the road, just a few hundred metres after leaving the house. We discovered, much to our collective delight, that we were standing right next to an outdoor mechanic shack. Or rather the mechanic discovered us standing in his shack, black fumes escaping from the engine. I am not sure he was as delighted as we were at this fortuitous circumstance. However, he had no other choice but to help — we were blocking his entry and exit.

'*Can I help, sa?*' he asked, a reassuring smile on his face.

We had no other choice either. We were mortified with shame and embarrassment. My father nodded his assent, mustering all the dignity the ludicrous situation allowed him. The man opened the bonnet. We momentarily lost sight of him as the usual black fumes entirely enveloped his body in a smoggy embrace. We then heard coughing, and some clanking and banging. Then the fumes slowly subsided. The man then spoke some magic words.

'*I can fix dis problem for you, sa. It will not take long.*'

He did. The magician's name was Akande. This marked the beginning of a long and lasting friendship for us all. Subsequently, we saw Akande more often and more regularly than we did any of our other acquaintances. In fact, he became like family.

That first time, we managed to get to our destination and back without a hiccup. That was a major achievement, as it was a whooping seven-kilometre round trip. It was the first time we arrived somewhere, and what's more, came back home. As we approached our house, my father must have felt like Ben Hur on the final lap of the chariot race. No one showed surprise when after this effort, the cantankerous Brazilian Rio did not start for a few days. We understood the power of miracles, and we were grateful for just that one. When my father did get it to ignite eventually, he took it straight to Akande's corrugated garage shack to be resurrected again.

With time, my family developed an efficient drill where each of us had an important part to play. My father sat behind the wheel, we ladies pushed, and gravity did the rest. By some lucky coincidence, Akande's outdoor garage was situated about seven hundred metres downhill from us in a straight line. When he saw our car rolling down silently towards him, engine dead, my mother, sister, and I breathless in the back, my father's terrified face behind the wheel (he never knew when the brakes would stop working), Akande would always have a most welcoming smile on his face. He always made it seem that the sight of four, ashen faced crazy white people, driving a dead car downhill and straight into his garage was the most natural thing on earth to witness.

With huge enthusiasm he would then unscrew everything that could possibly be unscrewed in the engine. He would throw the various parts into the hot sand and would give them a very thorough wash using petrol, which, together with a few rusty screwdrivers, and a hammer, were the only tools he had at his disposal. Akande would then screw everything back together faultlessly. Once restored, the car would consent to start and we would throttle off, enveloped in a strong petrol smell. Till now the smell of petrol reminds me of those times. This system seemed to work for us and for Akande, and we owe it to him that the three-thousand-dollar investment was not money entirely thrown in the bin. If nothing else, we at least managed to keep a pretence of owning a car, and thanks to us, Akande became a rich man, while we became much poorer.

Chapter 5

THE BOYS QUARTERS AND OUR ROYAL HOUSE HELP

'The... what, sorry?'

In due African time, and after we forgot we had asked for it in the first instance, we moved into another house in the Old Quarters which was more suitable for our needs. A Nigerian family happily moved to the termite infested house we vacated, and probably still live there till today. Our new spacious bungalow was surrounded by a vast expanse of barren land, at the end of which there was a small square cement structure.

'What is that small building over there?' asked my father, deducing it to be some sort of a chicken house, but wanting to be perfectly sure.

'*Na dat bee de boys' quarters, sabi?*' came the enthusiastic reply from the Nigerian lady in charge of our living arrangements. By then we knew *sabi* meant *you know* in pidgin English.

'The... what, sorry?' asked my father, baffled.

'*Na dis bee boy's quarters na sa. A whole family can nicely fit live der. You can have a house boy or even two house boys to help you around your new house. Dis be good solid boys' quarters. I goh find one for you.*'

'One what?'

'*Na a houseboy sa! A houseboy! You need a propa houseboy and his family to help you manage your new big house. Your wife no fitam do all dat work, she no fitam. Sabi? Dis house too big, too biiiig for Madam to clean am. Now, it so happily happens sa, dat dis my cousin is looking for a job, he just come from our village last week, no be so. He is a good man, my cousin. He got a nice new wife. He got a boy. Dat boy, he can be your new houseboy, sabi?*'

Notwithstanding the fact that we had no intention of hiring servants, the idea being as abhorrent as the long abolished African slave trade in Europe, we were mesmerised by the idea that a whole Nigerian family could theoretically fit in that tiny cement space. The place was no bigger than a chicken coop. We decided to ignore the structure altogether, since we had no use for it.

The enterprising Nigerian lady on the other hand was determined not to let such a fortuitous opportunity pass by. What we had misunderstood to be small talk on her side, something about a husband, a wife, and a son to come and live in our chicken coop, later transpired to have been a one-sided job interview and hiring, all in one magisterial coup. The only thing amiss was the employer's, in this case my parent's, under-standing of the entire process. Also missing was the employee. This did not seem to deter the stout Nigerian woman in the slightest of ways.

What followed was lethal in its simplicity. One day, we discovered to our surprise that the chicken house looked inhab-ited. There was a dirty plastic chair on the ground in front of the door. Attached by a short string to one of the legs of the chair stood a dejected chicken, dolefully pecking the barren soil within its very limited radius. An old wooden mortar and pestle stood in the doorway. There was a shuffling activity within the walls of the structure. Our startled family came to the undeni-able conclusion that we had squatters living on our land.

'Dad, who can that be?'

'Well, whoever that is, I'm sure we will soon find out,' my dad said.

We had learned by then that it would have been bad Nigerian manners on our part if we precipitated events and pried into other people's private lives uninvited — even if they were illegally squatting on our land. In the evening, our squat-ters indeed decided it was time to give us a friendly house call. An elderly Nigerian man, smartly dressed in a suit and an alhaji hat, knocked on our door and announced that his name was Jusaja — and that he had just moved into our boys' quarters. He then announced that he was our new 'house help' and that he and his son would be reporting to work tomorrow. He then very politely bid us good night and left for his new abode.

A bit late in the proceedings, my parents came to under-stand that as promised, the Nigerian lady had hired us *house help'* in the form of her *'cousin from the village.'* It was already dark outside, so my parents diplomatically decided that early the next day, they would very politely tell Jusaja that we were in no need of house help, or two house helps, or houseboys, or whatever the term was. We were perfectly fine on our own.

Early the next morning, as announced, Jusaja and his son knocked at our door. We clustered at the entry, curious as to how the events would evolve. We had never had to hire or fire servants before. We never dreamed of having servants in our lives! My father opened the door melodramatically, ready with his rehearsed speech. He was reduced to silence by the sight in front of him.

In front of our door stood father and son. One was holding a rusty old bucket, filled with holes the size of golf balls, the other a dirty mop that had seen better days. Their clothes were clean but threadbare, politely implying they were professional workers in uniform with lofty standards and unique skill sets. Both had wide smiles on their faces, which seemed to promise so many good things to come. They were irresistibly candid and looked genuinely happy to be there for us. We were still unsure as to what *house boys* were meant to be doing for us, but my parents' resolution to send them back was suddenly all but forgotten.

'Good morning sa. This is my son Sunday. We goh mop the floors first. Excuse us please, sa.'

Squeezing themselves through the doorway past my dumbstruck father and us, Jusaja and Sunday entered our house and began to work. That day was to prove the beginning of a symbiotic relationship between our two families.

We quickly learned that Jusaja used the house help story as a cover-up. After that first day, he almost immediately divested himself of all housework duties. In fact, we discovered he had a servant boy cleaning his house for him! The lowly task of mopping our floors was handed down to Sunday.

To his credit, Sunday, who in all appearances had never mopped a floor in his life, devoted himself to self-improvement with great enthusiasm. He dipped the stringy mop in the rusty bucket filled only with water and smeared it energetically all over the house, leaving dirt streaks everywhere. He would then dip the mop repeatedly in the increasingly opaque, pitch-black water and smear more black streaks in every corner of the house.

The fact was, water in Auchi was scarce. It came to our tank whenever it suited the water delivery man — sometimes once a week, sometimes once a month, and sometimes not at all. Sunday was demonstrating excellent water-sustainable practices. He only consented to throw the water out when it turned solid.

Meanwhile, his father only saw ironing as an honourable enough task for his elevated status as the head of house help. Our spare room quite naturally became his office and to a lesser extent, the ironing room. There, he presided in full glory, not necessarily when there was ironing to be done, but when it suited him to do so. Never phased by his irregular and somewhat chaotic work schedule, the worthy Jusaja was just as capable of spending a whole hour busily ironing one pair of trousers, as ironing a whole heap of clothes in the same amount of time — if by chance he happened to accidentally coincide his office hours with my mother's washing schedule.

Jusaja's main occupation, as we were soon to discover, was to be some sort of a chief. This eminent activity meant he spent much of his time dressed in rich and colourful traditional clothes, enthroned in an elaborately worn-out armchair, which stood in the middle of his courtyard. Colourfully dressed subjects would pay court to him, while he benevolently smiled at them, chasing away flies with a fly whip made of white zebu hair. There was often a goat roasting on the inventive firepit which adorned his front yard. The scrawny chicken was long gone, replaced by an impressive flock of fat chickens, neatly contained in a small, fenced area. Straight rows of cassava plants were already popping their heads through the freshly ploughed vegetable patch.

Drawn by the loud music and colourful crowds, Edyta and I would often visit during such parties. We were always welcomed with hoots of pleasure by the richly dressed Nigerians paying court to our sovereign neighbour. In retrospect, I guess we increased Jusaja's illustrious status in society because of the colour of our skin, as expatriates were a rarity in Auchi. Improbably, our chicken coop had become Jusaja's imperial home, and my sister and I seemed to have become his subjects.

Aside from helping us around the house, Sunday soon became a good friend to me and my sister. He was about fifteen, so he possessed a whole lot of adolescent know-how. He showed us a great deal of useful African life skills and taught us pidgin English — Nigeria's unofficial *lingua franca*. He also taught us, amongst other useful accomplishments, how to roast raw cashew nuts still ensconced in their thick grey shells. The process was quite simple. Sunday would first generously sprinkle the cashew nuts in their shells with kerosene and then spectacularly set them on fire. With time and experience, we mastered the art of identifying the precise moment in which to throw sand on the combusting lot, which would instantly extinguish the incinerating nuts. The trick was to not let the cashew nuts get burnt inside. We then removed the tasty nuts from the charcoal shells, and ate them. They tasted like nothing I had ever had, probably because they were heavily infused with the burnt kerosene smell. We would eat them up, sharing equally amongst the three of us, burning our fingers as we picked them straight from the charcoaled pile.

In hindsight, and as an adult, I must admit it may have been a bit of a risky operation. It involved children, kerosene, matches, and fire, in a dry bush area without adult supervision. What's more, the toxins contained in the cashew nut shells became highly toxic when burned, which we were blissfully unaware of at the time. The fact that all we ever achieved during these covert operations was to produce a heap of delicious, combusted nuts, was a testament to Sunday's decidedly evolved bush skills, and proof that none of us were allergic to nut toxins.

Occasionally, Sunday brought us birds in a cage that he had constructed himself with innate African ingenuity, using sticks, recycled rusted nails and odd pieces of twine or wire. He proudly showed us the winged prisoners, poking them with a stick to demonstrate their superior skills. That action would indeed coerce the poor birds into a flurry of panicked wing flaps and aggrieved chirps, much to Sunday's satisfaction. Edyta and I fussed with pleasure, pretending to admire the petrified birds from between their prison bars. Gratified that he had made us happy — it obviously did not take much to make two silly white girls happy — Sunday then kindly left the birds for us to play with.

As soon as his back was turned, we opened the little door of the cage and released the hapless jailbirds. We later showed Sunday the empty cage with surprised shrugs, feigning huge disappointment. After a few such 'escapes,' Sunday grew bored and stopped poaching birds for our benefit, as we were obviously too immature to be able to keep birds in a cage for over a day. Instead, he brought us two puppies. There was no more feigning happiness, as we both cooed over them, enraptured by their snowlike softness and big watery eyes. Not surprisingly, our happiness was short-lived. It lasted about fifteen minutes, until my parents saw them. They were both determined we should have no pets whatsoever while in Africa. Our life was complicated enough as it was, they said.

Chapter 6

MY PRIMATE SISTER

Chi-Chi

About a year after we had arrived in Nigeria, we visited some of our German friends who lived in a highly secure, locked-up, posh compound, compliments of the rich oil company they were working for. As our Rio could not make the round trip of nine kilometres, we hitched a ride there with our friends, in a minuscule but reliable Volkswagen Beetle, an extremely popular car for Nigeria in the eighties. Its only drawback was its size. How we even managed between the seven of us, four adults and three children, to fit in that space is a baffling thought. The successful entry of everyone required a well-choreographed manoeuvre and meticulous precision as to where to place one's limbs.

By an unspoken consensus, being the smallest, I was always relegated to sit in the miniature internal boot at the back. Although I had the luxury of all that confined space to myself, as opposed to the unsightly mass of entangled limbs of everyone in the remaining space of the car, it was still a claustrophobic experience and required contortionist flexibility to perform successfully.

That day, we were having tasty, barbequed sausages flown in on a special weekly order by Lufthansa Airlines. The plane's other cargo consisted of cartons of excellent — according to my parents — German beer. Germans back in *Mutterland* certainly knew how to take care of their nationals living a hard life in the tropics. Keeping them well-fed and in a state of uninterrupted alcoholic anaesthesia was part of the hardship package offered by compassionate *Deutschland* for those brave enough to go and work in Nigeria.

Suddenly, there was a commotion by the gate, and we saw a large group of children holding something up, visibly wanting to attract our attention. The uniformed security guards of the compound tried their best to chase the noisy group away, but they refused to go, insisting to see the *oga*, the owner of the place.

The *oga*, a powerfully built German man by the remarkably Teutonic name of Helmutt, had already gulped down a few strong, chilled German beers, and as a result, happened to be in a generously agreeable mood. He decided to go in person to investigate. He set out to the place of commotion in a somewhat shaky stroll, watched curiously by about twenty people present at the barbeque.

It was almost dark, so it was difficult to see what happened once he reached the faraway gate, however, we did not have to wait too long for the outcome. Helmutt walked back, zigzagging, and muttering something in German under his blitzed breath. He held a frantically screeching baby monkey in his hand. It was obviously only a few weeks old, as it was so small and fit easily in his palm. It had almost no hair on its bluish skin and was bleeding profusely from a cut above the eye.

'*Scheisse...*,' muttered the confounded German. '*Scheisse!*' he repeated and looked dejectedly at the furless ball in his hand.

The baby monkey was in an awfully bad state, clearly close to death from fear and exposure. In all its misery and desperation, it was still emitting piercing shrieks with a last pathetic effort to somehow scare us all away. Then it went silent. Helmutt saw he was in trouble, if only by looking at the furious face of his very sober wife, Ingrid. His gaze fell on us, as we stared at the monkey, transfixed with pity. Interpreting that as a 'yes, please,' he tossed the monkey at me and without stopping to see if I intercepted the bundle, ran straight to the fridge to get himself another fortifying German beer.

With the monkey in my hand, my sister and I ran to the sanctuary of the kitchen where we knew we would find John, our trustworthy, all-knowing Nigerian friend. It seemed the only natural thing to do, as the adults at the party had too much beer to think clearly. John was the German family's cook. He often gave Edyta and I tasty titbits between meals when we went to visit. He always let us sit in the spacious kitchen to watch him cook, while we listened to his stories — of which he had a lot of to share. Like many of his kin, John was a natural in the kitchen, and cooked effortlessly with minimal utensils and no fuss. He conjured tasty three course meals for twenty people at a moment's notice, without ever losing his calm or reading a recipe.

To John's credit, our dramatic kitchen entry did not faze him one bit. He looked at the dead monkey in my hand, saw our tear-stricken faces, and smiled tolerantly. Monkeys were a familiar sight for Nigerians. In fact, they were tasty bushmeat in their eyes, commonly sold on the side of the road amongst other delicacies, such as bush rats, jumbo snails, lizards, snakes, and pangolins, which were all neatly displayed on makeshift wooden tables, in rows from biggest to smallest. Some of the animals were dead, some still alive to keep the meat fresh.

Obviously, John did not see what all the fuss was about. We knew from his stories that he came from a long and respectful farming lineage which had been waging an unrelenting war on all primate species encroaching on their crops for many generations. To John, it was just another monkey. Dead or alive, there were so many more out there in the bush to be eaten or chased away from precious crops. However, seeing that we seemed to care a lot, he remarked good-naturedly.

'The monkey is not dead. Look at its tummy. It is moving. Look, it is breathing. This monkey is just asleep. It is very tired.'

We looked more closely at the tiny bluish hairless tummy, and saw it move almost imperceptibly up and down. John gave us a tea towel to wrap the little monkey in and we carried it back outside.

Despite their strong anti-pet resolutions, my parents knew that the monkey would die if we did not try to save it. That day we drove back home with the tiny monkey asleep on our laps. We loved it so much already and took turns holding it. We cared for it day and night, giving it powdered milk and mashed bananas, carrying it with us wherever we went, wrapped in a small warm towel like a tiny baby. We could think of nothing else to do to help it live. Whether it was accidental, or we did all the right things, the little monkey grew stronger by the day, and it survived. It was a girl, and we called her Chi-Chi. Much later we discovered it was a Tantalus monkey, an Old World monkey whose habitat ranges from Central to Western Africa.

As Chi-Chi grew, she began to show signs of acute monkey shrewdness. We fed her a rich diet of mashed bananas mixed with milk, oranges, mangoes, pawpaw, and other fruits, trying to replicate her natural wild diet as best we could. Chi-Chi did not mind this at all at the beginning, but as she grew in strength and size, she began to complement the strict dietary regime. Nothing was off limits and supplements included cookies, lollies, chewing gum, juice, bread, flour, sugar, and anything else she could raid from our kitchen, table, or pantry. She had an uncanny wit for mischief and quickly jumped from out of our reach when we discovered her in various locations around the kitchen, hurriedly stuffing her side cheeks with chewing gums and lollies still in their wrappers.

'Mum, Chi-Chi stole our chewing gum again! She is eating them! She has ten in her mouth! Oh no, that is all we had! Naughty Chi-Chi!'

We would scramble and chase her, but she always escaped us effortlessly. Sitting up high on top of doors or curtains, she watched us calmly as we furiously tried to chase her down.

With glints of intense satisfaction in her eyes, she methodically chewed the loot accumulated on her ransacking plunder, taking deliberate pleasure at slowly polishing off our favourite lollies bit by small bit, all the while looking us straight in the eyes. She would then spit the wrappers at us with unnerving aim.

When she was not busy swinging on chairs, doors, curtains, and tables, or raiding our food, Chi-Chi was the most endearing and affectionate little creature a young girl could dream of. She clung on to my mother, my sister or me with total abandon, and hitched rides on our shoulders, legs, arms, and occasionally head when we would take her for long walks in the surrounding bush. When she felt she needed to explore something on her own, she jumped off and ran through the grass and climbed high into trees with amazing agility. She foraged on leaves, flowers, seeds, insects and fruits, picking her way in the rich African nature smorgasbord with innate instinct.

The only person in the household to whom Chi-Chi did not grow lovingly attached was my father. My father, on the other hand, had to contend with a human-like, impertinent, tantrum-throwing, looting monkey in his house on a daily basis. In retrospect, I do not think it was an easy endeavour for him. Even more so, when Chi-Chi developed strong female family-like bonds with me, my sister, and our mother, similar to how she would have formed connections in the wild had she been with her female relatives. She showed her strong affection for us by lovingly grooming our hair, skin, and clothes, smacking her lips in contentment whenever she thought she found lice or a piece of the offending object. We tried to reciprocate her grooming, but quickly discovered that what she loved most was being tickled under the armpits, hands raised high up in the air for maximum effect. So, she groomed, and we tickled.

My father of course did not like this close female business one bit, and he immediately went into damage control. In a relatively short space of time, he managed to instil a high degree of fear in Chi-Chi, very much like an alpha male in a wild monkey group, although I highly doubt that was his glorified aim. Whenever Chi-Chi heard my father's car in the driveway, she would drop everything she was doing and fling herself onto me for safety. She would hug me tightly and make little plaintive vocalisations, which we had by then identified as 'the big ugly ape is back.' I tried to hide her under my clothes to spare her the agonies of abject terror she experienced at the sheer sight of my father. He obviously enjoyed the ego-boosting anxiety he was causing, and unable to resist the exhilarating feeling of dominance, he upped the ante a notch. He began to insist that Chi-Chi give him her hand in greeting when he came from work. This ape versus primate war was quite obviously giving my father a lot of satisfaction; Chi-Chi, on the other hand, could not get past the fact that my father was just a big, ugly scary ape to be avoided at all costs.

Chi-Chi showed total submission and a great fear of my father, but she certainly did not make my mother's life easy. My mother had by then discovered her strong passion for gardening. In a matter of a few months, she had transformed our barren land around the bungalow into a miniature botanical heaven. Our car was often loaded with prickly specimens of cacti succulents, and multi-coloured shrubbery, which my mother could not stop herself from collecting. We were resigned to the inevitable certitude that each of our successful car trips would end up in an impromptu botanical collecting expedition.

'Stop right now!' my mother would scream upon seeing a shrub, bush, flower, or succulent, which apparently, we still did not possess in our garden.

'Don't be silly! You know I can't stop the car, it will not start again!'

'I will only be a minute. Look at this beautiful plant... look at these lovely purple leaves sprinkled with greens and reds... I believe I have not seen this one before. Has anyone seen my scissors, I'm sure I left them here somewhere. Never mind, I will just break it off.'

My mother would run out of the car while it was still in motion, get the specimen in seconds and be back before the car began to stall. My father kept it going at turtle speed while we all nervously waited for my mother to return to the car, a happy smile on her face. A few hundred metres down the road the botanical sample collection would continue. At every destination, she would critically inspect friends' and their neighbour's gardens in search of even more cuttings for ours.

While we were at school and my father at work, my mother spent all her free time in the garden. Through natural inclination, this also became Chi-Chi's favourite hangout. In the beginning, Chi-Chi and my mum leisurely spent their days in the garden enjoying the fresh air and each other's company. It was a symbiotic relationship, full of joy and serenity. The utopia lasted only until Chi-Chi caught on to the fact that my mother loved plants. My mother simultaneously caught on to the fact that Chi-Chi loved garden mischief. And thus, the Garden War began. It brought a lot of monkey joy to Chi-Chi and a horrendous amount of grief to my mum.

On the first day of the war, Chi-Chi started the day in a deceptively downbeat mood. She unostentatiously followed my mother around the garden, peacefully catching insects, and eating seeds, grass, and leaves. My mother did not know this at the time, but all the while Chi-Chi was carefully registering her every move, mentally creating a detailed strategic assault map in her shrewd primate brain. Every plant my mother touched, planted, re-potted, watered or looked at was carefully memorised by Chi-Chi. Then, at the end of that hard day's work when my mother had her back turned, Chi-Chi unexpectedly sprang into action with devastating accuracy and deathly skill. She ate, nibbled, broke, plucked, and trampled every plant my mother had touched or even meditatively looked at. Every single botanical specimen was meticulously destroyed with obvious intent and devilish pleasure in less than a few seconds.

When my mother turned around to a heartbreaking path of destruction, she started to run in a vain attempt to catch Chi-Chi and strangle her. Chi-Chi, satisfied at finally having all that attention to herself, joyfully scrammed away, taking out the few remaining plants on the way, just to keep my mother super interested in the exciting chase. From then on, the cruel game would go on daily. Instead of looking calm and serene after a restful day in her garden, my mother looked furious, dishevelled, and strained. At the end of the day, our triumphant little primate sister sat high up on the curtain rod, safely from the murderous glances my mother threw her, and that is usually where we found her when we came back from school in the afternoons.

Despite all her malice, we loved Chi-Chi, and she loved us back in return. Unfortunately, when it came time to leave Nigeria three years later, we did not know what would become of Chi-Chi. Letting her go free in the bush was not an option, as she had always been a tame monkey and would not survive on her own. Our only solution was to leave her with a lady who already had another pet monkey, another sub-species of a vervet. The separation was as heart-wrenching for us as it was for Chi-Chi. She squealed and looked terrified as she was driven away to her new home, and my sister and I cried bitterly for months afterwards.

Chi-Chi escaped on the third day. She was seen in the bush nearby by a few local people and then we lost track of her. Many years later we were still heartbroken with grief, regret, anguish, and pain at having lost our little primate sister.

We left Nigeria in 1983. I was eleven years old. Little did I know that I would be back there again in ten years to celebrate my twenty-first birthday. My family and I lived in Switzerland for five years, and then moved to Australia, where three years later I met Harry. I was seventeen, and studying my first year of psychology. I was a dark-haired, fun-loving girl. Harry was a twenty-eight-year-old man, who had just finished his engineering degree at Kansas State University, USA. Our paths crossed at Yasmine's — my best friend — eighteenth birthday party. True to the fashion of the day, I wore long, black suede Pretty Woman boots, a black skimpy mini dress barely covering my rear, lots of silver jewellery and red lipstick.

We were all sitting inside, listening to music, and enjoying good food when the spectacular roar of a motorbike engine came straight toward us, and drowned all conversations. It stopped in front of Yasmine's house and seconds later Harry made a grand entry.

He was wearing coral pink shorts embellished with fluorescent green crocodiles, a dazzling yellow t-shirt, a red bike jacket filled with logos, and black leather gloves. To complete this astounding apparel, he wore his electric blue helmet with the darkened screen still unopened. How he made it all the way to the door was a mystery, as it was pitch black outside. When he did finally remove his helmet, after having satisfied himself that everyone noted his dramatic entry, his hair cascaded down his shoulders. It was longer and thicker than mine.

Harry looked around the room and his eyes fell on my legs. They travelled up, met my eyes, and stayed there. He was instantly smitten — he told me afterwards — and made a beeline straight towards me. Without much of an introduction, Harry flopped next to me on the sofa, and launched himself into a long monologue about his love of motorbikes, and his fast-speed racing in the Adelaide Hills; the most dangerous corners the region had to offer. I listened politely without interrupting, although I cared little for motorbikes. As a matter of fact, I disliked them immensely, with a passion verging on phobia.

'So, would you like to come for a ride with me in the hills one day?' he finally asked, when his exhaustive topic winded down to a natural finale, precipitated largely by my mute, disapproving stare.

'We would go amazingly fast. Have you ever driven over 200kph? It is a phenomenal feeling, I will show you!' he said enthusiastically, misunderstanding my horrified silence as enchanted approval.

I stared down at him, still not saying anything. It was difficult to find words to express my feelings. Then suddenly, I found the one word which summed it all up neatly.

'Idiot. You are an idiot,' I informed him, and left his company.

For months afterwards, Harry tried to arrange a date with me, and for months I rebutted all his attempts. But eventually, despite my better judgement, I agreed to go to dinner with him, and then to the opera. We began dating, and less than a year later, Harry suddenly declared that he was leaving for Nigeria because of a job opportunity. I was unprepared and totally taken by surprise by this sudden announcement, as we had not discussed it at all. Harry left for Nigeria shortly afterwards. We thought that would be the end of our short-lived relationship. How wrong we were.

I continued my studies for the next two years, during which time we exchanged mountains of letters, and Harry called for hours whenever he could get himself near a working phone. As soon as I finished my studies, three days after my graduation, I hopped on a plane to join him. My parents were aghast at my decision, and rightly so. I told them reassuringly that it would only be for one year. That did not seem to reassure them at all, as they knew that every day spent in Nigeria was a risky one, and one year seemed like a lot of risky days to survive.

They were right, of course.

Above
Our first house at the
Old Quarters.

Left
Auchi Hill Top
Hotel, where we
unexpectedly stayed
for a few months.

Left
We were amazed by
the size of the termite
mounds in the bush
behind our house.

Below
Our proud
family in front of
a newly acquired car,
a Volkswagen Rio.

Above
We often took walks on the vast Auchi Polytechnic grounds and visited different departments.

Below
My father surrounded by fellow expatriate colleagues during a graduation ceremony.

Left
My father never missed
an opportunity to
photograph the new car.

Below
Our 'new' house at the
Old Quarters.

Above
After a few months, my mother turned the barren land into
a lush garden.

Below
View from our living room. The zebu, a local variety of cows, often
grazed in the front yard of our first house.

Above
We loved walking on the vast grounds of the Old Quarters surrounded by bush and farmlands.

Below
Edyta standing in front of The Nigerian Observer street sign in Auchi.

Above
Street in Auchi.

Below
My sister and myself at Auchi Polytechnic School in front of our classroom windows.

Above left
My mother never tired of walks on the Polytechnic.

Above right
During the daily morning assembly.

Below
I am holding Chi-Chi.

Above
A daily stroll with Chi-Chi which can be seen in front of us in the grass.

Left
Chi-Chi and Edyta. Chi-Chi chose our shoulders as a safe and elevated vantage point on our exploratory walks. She always nibbled on grass, seeds, or flowers. Here, she is nibbling on a grass stalk.

Above left
The Big Ugly Ape and nonplussed Chi-Chi.

Above right
Garden Wars with my mother.

Below
Chi-Chi loved to eat the juicy red flowers of the Flame Tree.

Chi-Chi's favourite pastime. She loved to be ticked under her arms and would spend considerable amounts of time in this leisurely pose.

Chi-Chi and I investigating the inside of a giant pod.

Above and Below
Visibly absent from these photographs is our illustrious Volkswagen Rio. Thanks to the kindness of our numerous friends in Auchi, all owners of the indestructible German Volkswagen Beetle, we were able to visit wonderful and unique places around Auchi. I often had to squeeze in the very tiny rear luggage compartment.

The Beetle, the undisputed King of the Roads in 1980 Auchi.
Despite its diminutive name and size, it handled like an
all-terrain 4WD Land Cruiser of today.

Chapter 7

THE AFRICAN FACTOR

'Don't worry darling, everything will be all right'.

I stepped down from the plane, all by myself, back on Nigerian soil in 1993. I was instantly enveloped by waves of nostalgia in the form of humid, rancid, raw African air, chilling in its reassuring familiarity. It was not long before the equally chilling childhood memories came of the rat race that was inevitably about to follow the plane exit. Indeed, while I stopped for a few seconds to inhale the familiar scents of the past, the homecoming Nigerians rushed past me in a mass plane exodus. Taking a deep breath, which did absolutely nothing to boost my fast-evaporating courage, I let the crowd propel me forward.

Before long, I was back on firm African soil at the arrival doors of the airport, where the human momentum had predictably deposited me. It seemed to me that Nigerians were still, after all these years, in a huge hurry to get back to their homeland. A few other expats close to me stood motionless, totally disoriented, and pale, with their eyes popping out of their sockets. *Imbeciles! First timers!* I thought unkindly, feeling absolutely no pity for them. I felt like a homecoming local myself, elated that I knew the drill and my way around.

My fellow Nigerian passengers were already laying an aggressive siege at the first passport checkpoint, in a pandemonium of chaos, violence, and wild insubordination. I stood at the very end of the yelling crowd, together with the 'first timers' whom I had so quickly dismissed as imbeciles just moments ago. More passengers kept running in from different arriving flights, all cutting in front of us.

As I despairingly watched all hell break loose at the passport checkpoint windows, I noticed a Nigerian lady in uniform. She was laboriously making her way through the thick crowd as if looking for someone. When she arrived in front of me, she stopped and had a long careful look at the scrunched-up bit of paper she was holding in her hand.

'Are you Magdalena?' She showed me the paper. What I took for a piece of paper was a crumpled-up photograph of me, holding Harry's pet python Monti. It was his favourite photo of me, or possibly the snake, I never really found out. He took the shot just before he left for Nigeria, leaving the snake in my care.

'Yes, that is my name. That's me,' I added unnecessarily, pointing to the photo in disbelief. Clearly, Harry had chivalrously organised some help for me.

'Give me your passport and follow me,' commanded the lady, without bothering to explain anything else.

I did.

We went straight inside the mass of madly screaming people. The crowd quietened down when they saw us, and parted silently to let us through. I was too scared to look anyone in the face; I was in the middle of a terribly angry African crowd, muttering unhappily under their breaths. The lady slapped my passport in front of the emigration officer, who only seconds before had been besieged by hundreds of screaming Nigerians. He dully stamped it without asking any questions. The same happened at the following two checkpoints. By then, I felt like Cinderella who had miraculously just discovered that she had a magic godmother. Had I seen a pumpkin somewhere in my path, I am sure I would have tried to climb inside for the final leg of my journey.

Sadly, instead of the pumpkin, the magic ended abruptly with a petty emigration officer. I was trying to pass his counter with my luggage, escorted by a friendly pre-bribed officer who had taken over from my accidental godmother, when he imperiously stopped me. It was the last checkpoint before the doors to freedom. *Damn*, I thought. Obviously, he was mad at not being on the payroll of whoever organised this airport extraction. He menacingly tapped a dirty ruler on the metal table in front of him. Words were unnecessary. In international airport language, it meant '*put your luggage on this table, and I will do my best to find something in there that you didn't even know you had.*' I put the suitcase on the table obediently, without making eye contact.

'*What y be dat?*' he asked imperiously.

'A suitcase,' I said, trying to sound politely helpful. I understood his incredulity. It was hot pink in colour, the latest fashion of the day, which at the time of purchase in faraway Australia seemed like a great idea. Now, in Africa, I was having second thoughts as it stood out like a sore thumb in the sea of black luggage everyone else had.

'*Open am!*'

I did hastily, my hands shaking while I fumbled with the miniature keys of the padlock.

'*What y be dat?*' he asked again furiously, this time looking straight into the open luggage. His perplexity, if possible, had grown a notch higher.

'Clothes...' I answered truthfully.

'Clothes,' soothingly acquiesced the friendly emigration officer, after peeking into the suitcase himself to assert what was inside. There was nothing else to be said, as there were *only* clothes there — my entire wardrobe to be precise. We all stood there for an awkwardly long time staring at the soaring mountains of attire cascading out. I had a lot of difficulty fitting them inside its restrictive confines and now, regaining its lost freedom, the garb was escaping and seemingly growing in volume.

The officer stood still, mesmerised. Understandably, he had never seen such a fascinating spectacle before. A white lace bra slipped down the counter and was about to fall off onto the dirty floor. I instinctively caught it mid-flight, and stood to attention, bra in hand, trying to look inconspicuous and polite. The officer finally woke up from his stupor.

'Close yor suitcase and go. Now now!' he barked from between his clenched teeth.

I tried. Frantically and desperately, I tried to close the overflowing suitcase. At home, I had spent hours rolling the clothes into tiny bundles before laboriously stuffing them in every nook and cranny available. Now it seemed like an impossible feat to repeat, and certainly not under the incensed stare of the emigration officer, ogling my every move with scorn.

The kind officer escorting me lunged his whole-body mass into the tangled mess of garments, in a desperate effort to help me. Between two frenzied push-ups from atop the valise, he looked at me with panicked eyes.

'Madam, we must quickly get out of here before he changes his mind!' he muttered under his breath, as he desperately pushed down the escaping clothes. I simultaneously jerked the reluctant zip in a few millimetre thrusts at a time. Hurriedly picking up the odd jeans and t-shirts which had fallen off during this highly synchronised operation, we made a hurried exit towards the salvation of the airport departure gates. As soon as I stepped outside, I was ushered by my escorting officer into a huge, black, four-wheel drive which conveniently happened to be just sweeping past; it barely slowed down as I was unceremoniously pushed in.

'Hi, baby. Did you have a nice flight?' asked Harry without turning his head. He was sitting in the passenger seat and carefully scrutinising the dark surroundings.

'Welcome to Nigeria, Magdalena! I am Paul, Harry's friend. He spoke a lot about you, glad you are here!' beamed the driver. He looked back to throw me a glance before we took off at high velocity, the momentum of which sucked me back into my seat. I hurriedly fumbled for the seat belts.

'Oh... hello... nice to meet you, Paul. Thank you for picking me up. Yes, the flight was great. It's lovely to be back. Um, Harry, I am not sure you realise, but we left my luggage on the kerb back at the airport gates. It's still there actually...' I added, bewildered, as I glanced back through the window. That was indeed a surprise as all around, hawkers, beggars, con artists, and a mob of other opportunistic locals swarmed the pavement in search of anything to spirit away, and there was a small, homely crowd gathering around my hot pink suitcase already.

'Don't worry darling,' Harry waved his hand dismissively. 'My driver will pick it up. He is following us a few cars behind.'

'Well, what if he doesn't get there in time? And how will he know it is my luggage?' The question was redundant. *My* luggage was the only luggage left unattended on the street amongst the hundreds of professional street muggers.

'Will he get my passport too?' I asked hopefully. In my highly orchestrated exit from the airport, I had not had the time to get it back.

'What passport?' asked Harry, taken aback.

'My passport! A kind immigration officer was helping and took it from me at the airport. He said he knew you.'

The car screeched to a stop as Paul hit the brakes. Harry jumped out of the car, dragging me uncourteously from my back seat.

'Which officer was that? Can you see him? Show me!'

We ran back towards the airport gate. By pure luck, I spotted the man casually strolling back to his post, my passport still in his hand.

'That's him, that's my passport!'

Harry sprinted towards the man, patted him on the back, thanked him profusely for his help with immigration, and kindly asked for my passport back. Apparently, the kind man had forgotten he was still holding it. Both chortled at the amusing situation, and after patting each other on the back several times for good measure, parted with big happy smiles on their faces, calling themselves '*broda*' as they waved warm goodbyes.

'So, you knew the guy, didn't you?' I asked as we paced back to the car. It had been unceremoniously blocking the airport traffic, amongst a deafening cacophony of honking and beeping from a growing line of furious drivers.

'Never saw the guy in my life,' Harry said carelessly once we were back in the car. 'You will quickly get used to the way people speak to each other here. You will be calling everyone sister before you know it. It is so much easier. It makes much more sense and creates a nice feeling of friendship right from the beginning.'

I looked outside the windows trying to catch my first glimpse of Lagos after ten years. I was spared the sights of the slums, dirt, poverty, beggars, and utter misery because it was pitch black, and there were still no streetlights, as per my childhood memories. But this was where the similarities stopped. We were driving in a soundly insulated bulletproof car in a convoy. Two of our drivers had caught up with us somewhere along the road and were now escorting us. Then suddenly, we almost collided with another car overtaking us at high speed. I thought I heard popping sounds.

'Was that gunfire, that sound like popping popcorn?' I asked suspiciously.

'Don't worry darling, everything will be all right,' Harry said nervously, without taking his eyes off the road.

'This is Nigeria Magdalena, nothing to worry about,' Paul gave me a comforting wink when our eyes met in the rear-view window. He turned a corner sharply and we sped off into the night in our three-car convoy.

Months later, I was delighted to hear our friend, Gustav's, airport story. No one navigates through the pitfalls of Murtala Mohammed Airport in Nigeria without some emotional scarring, or at the very least, a delightful tale to share over many therapeutic drinks once it is all over. I was therefore hugely entertained by Gustav's airport adventures.

Unfortunately, his job necessitated numerous visits to Nigerian soil throughout the years. Being a serious law-abiding German citizen, Gustav was outraged at the complacency of local expatriates in their passive acceptance of the deep-rooted corruption regime. After years of sliding dollar notes to officialdom at every checkpoint desk at the airport, for no reason other than to get on through to the next checkpoint desk, which allowed him to get through to the next checkpoint desk and so forth, Gustav decided it was time for a change, and he took matters into his own hands.

'My passport is valid for the next five years, and it has lots of empty pages left. I have a valid visa to stay in Nigeria for three months, and I paid extra for it to be extendable, although I am only staying for a few days. I am staying at the Sheraton Hotel; this is the exact address, Room 135. I have had yellow fever vaccinations renewed a month ago, and I am vaccinated for typhoid, tuberculosis, polio, hepatitis A and B, cholera, rabies, meningitis, measles, mumps and rubella, chickenpox, shingles, pneumonia, and influenza. This is my up-to-date yellow vaccination booklet, stamped with all the vaccines and the dates.'

Having thus covered all the possible difficulties learned from past visits to Nigerian soil, (he was once asked for his room number at the Sheraton as a trick question, almost refused entry because he only had 'four pages left in his passport', and he witnessed a local homecoming Nigerian being extorted $75 for a visa to enter his own country), our friend pompously handed his passport and yellow vaccination booklet to the emigration officer. There was no bribe money inside.

The emigration officer took his sweet time leafing through the passport several times, yawning. He did not stop once to verify the visa or the validity of the passport. Having found nothing of interest inside, he lazily threw it back at Gustav.

'You have no visa to enter Nigeria. You may not come further. Next please.'

When Gustav recovered his speech, many stunned seconds later, he grabbed his passport, feverishly found the valid visa page, and waved the page in front of the officer.

'What do you call this then? This is a visa valid for three months, I just got it a week ago, look at it! It is right here, in front of your eyes!'

The officer obligingly took the passport from Gustav's shaking hands. He slowly tore off the page with the Nigerian visa, put it in his mouth, slowly chewed and swallowed it.

'Visa? What visa?' he then asked, surprised.

Gustav never left the airport. He went back to Germany on the next available plane. When he arrived back, months later, he had a big stack of ten-dollar notes in his pocket and fifty dollars in his passport, as bribe custom demanded.

Chapter 8

DAZHUMA THE GARDENER AND SIDI THE NIGHT SECURITY

'What noise sa...?'

When I woke up on my first morning in Nigeria, it was late. Harry had already left for work, and my brain was still a bit hazy after last night's events. I slowly took stock of my new surroundings. All I remembered from the night before was entering a double-storey house, which looked neat and was in some sort of a suburban Lagosian neighbourhood. Total darkness covered the finer details of the location. The room I was in was bathed in a pleasant semi-darkness. I got out of bed, drew the curtains, and looked at the outside world through the plantation shutter windowpanes. I noted they were ominously secured with sturdy wrought iron grids.

Looking around the street, I discovered that I was in one of many similar-looking houses. Some were nicely kept, and others were in various stages of decrepitude. They all lined a long and sinuous dry earth street, riddled with the customary potholes, which as a matter of national pride embellish all roads in Nigeria. Small children dressed in clothes of similar hues as the surrounding dirt played games in small groups, oblivious to the world around them, as children all over the world do. Stray dogs of complicated pedigrees too long to fit in a book, ribcages sticking out from near starvation, dejectedly patrolled the gutters, barely dragging their feet. Bony chickens of various tones pecked at the bare earth with acquired dexterity verging on desperation. The more energetic and optimistically minded birds dug the earth vigorously with their claws, producing occasional miniature clouds of red dust.

Directly opposite my window on the other side of the dirt road, a black goat stood on its hind legs. It was stretching its neck to impossible lengths, trying to reach the only remaining leaves, high up on a bush. Next to her, a spotted brown baby goat, incapable of the same feat, bleated sadly and resignedly immersed itself in the consumption of a dirty newspaper lying in the gutter. Totally unconcerned for her offspring, the mother goat contentedly chewed on her juicy leaves obtained from the top of the bush.

A big billboard down the road attracted my attention. It was a rectangular piece of rusted scrap metal, nailed to the remnants of a dead tree. It bore the message 'DON'T URINATE HERE. BY ORDER,' crudely painted in red. What the overall signage lacked in creativity it made up for in boldness. It stood out on the street as the most eye-catching feature, visible from far away. A man in a three-piece suit, leather briefcase tucked securely under his arm, his golden-rimmed glasses sparkling radiantly in the morning sun, stood directly below it, urinating. None of the passers-by seemed perturbed by this scene as they slowly trekked to attend to their daily occupations.

I looked out my window. I was in a securely locked compound surrounded by a tall white wall. Pieces of broken glass of different shapes and colours decorated the top of the wall in an effective, yet cheap African anti-burglar system. The big metal gates which opened as if by magic to let us through last night, now stood securely locked with a giant padlock and chain. Next to the gates, pleasurably drinking tea poured from a tiny blue teapot on a little makeshift fire burner, sat three slim African men. Their skin colour was lighter than the urban Nigerians, and their features were much more delicate. From what I gathered, their job was to open and close the gates whenever a car left or arrived at the compound. I remembered that they waved me a shy welcome as we arrived from the airport in the early hours of the morning.

When I opened the windowpanes, the loud cacophony of heavy traffic from the nearby main street, and the polluted air mixed with the humid African aromas, gave me an instant headache. I quickly shut the shutters. The friendly hum of the air conditioner drowned the outside noises once again. I looked outside. There were now two shaggy-looking individuals urinating in unison below the 'DON'T URINATE HERE. BY ORDER' sign. There was something strangely reassuring about the predictability of that place. I gathered it was the public toilet.

Suddenly, the doorbell rang, and I hurried downstairs. Stepping outside, I found myself in a big porch enclosure surrounded by black, heavy-duty wrought iron gates, the door of which was padlocked.

'Good morning,' I smiled tentatively at the Nigerian man standing behind them, politely waiting for me to start the conversation.

'*Na, good morning, madam!*' answered the man. He was in his forties, quite tall, and sported a scary-looking handlebar moustache that was dramatically curled. I had never seen such a moustache on a Nigerian man before.

'How can I help you?' I asked, instantly gratified, and flattered to be called 'madam.' I was barely twenty years old. No one had ever called me that before. My parents referred to me mostly as an immature child. My older sister referred to me as stupid at best. My friends called me by my name, which over the years was growing repetitive and boring. I was ripe and ready for a positive change in my identity status.

'*Masta said I should come and ask if you dey need somting!*' answered the walrus-looking man.

'*Masta?*' I asked astonished.

'*Na Masta Harry. He dey ask if you gonna need me. He already at work. I am Masta driver. Welcome to Nigeria Madam. My name be Cosmos.*'

'Oh! *Cosmos*. Thank you. You are the driver. Master Harry is asking if I need something. Well, to begin with, you can tell him that I need the keys to this house to be able to get out.'

Cosmos seemed to appreciate my predicament as he slowly

looked up and down the enclosure I was locked in, like an animal in a zoo. He shook the iron door with the locked padlock, which rattled loudly with no further outcome. Cosmos seemed genuinely surprised at the failure of his attempt.

'*Na, where be de key?*' he said.

'That's the problem. I do not have the key,' I explained patiently. 'You can also tell *Masta* Harry to call me,' I added, relishing in the use of the vernacular. I missed pidgin English and plunged naturally straight back into it.

'*Masta said he will call you when Nepa comes back. No Nepa for now.*'

I had forgotten that. The National Electric Power Authority governed the use of electricity in Nigeria. Otherwise known as the Never Expect Power Always. Power supply in Nigeria had always been intermittent at best as I remembered from my Auchi days. It was perfectly normal to not have power for a few days in this country.

'Don't we have a generator?' I asked.

'*Yes, you do, madam. You share your generator with your neighbour, sabi? Na, Mr Karam. It's on his side of de house.*'

I stared at him blankly.

'*He be at work now,*' he added helpfully when he saw my empty look.

'So... you are saying I will have no electricity until he comes back from work?' I asked incredulously, as reality slowly sank in.

'*Maybe Nepa goh com back before, madam?*' offered Cosmos doubtfully.

'Never mind. Is there a back door to this house somewhere?'

'*Yes, madam. For de kitchen!*' announced Cosmos happily. He seemed to realise that it was the first good news he had delivered me that morning.

'Why don't you meet me there then? Maybe you can help me with a few things.'

'*Yes, madam.*'

I found my way to the kitchen and saw the stovetop. That happy sight immediately reminded me that I had not yet had my indispensable cup of morning coffee. No wonder things did not seem right. Invigorated by the thought of its strong familiar aroma, I opened a cupboard, found the Nescafe and the cups, saw the matches next to the stove, turned the knob, lit the match, and waited for the hiss and the flame on the burner. Nothing happened. I tried another knob. And another. Nothing. Deathly silence.

'*Dey be no gas Madam,*' explained Cosmos, who was watching from the kitchen door, having navigated his way around the outside of the house to find me frenetically fumbling with the gas knobs.

'So, I see Cosmos... and when will they put it back on?' I said, trying to remain calm and dignified.

'*Who Madam?*'

'Whoever is responsible for the gas, of course!' I was quickly losing patience and sanity. No phone. No electricity. No gas. No morning coffee. There was a limit to what I could take. How was I meant to remember the name of the gas company responsible for supplying us with gas under such circumstances?

Cosmos was staring at me, blinking nervously.

'*I goh fetch gas bottle, Madam, don't worry. Masta only buys small ones. Dey cheap. Dey no good, dey don't last. This one finished too quickly. Maybe I will fetch two big ones. One spare!*' Cosmos added cheerfully, seeing my growing consternation.

It dawned on me that gas for the kitchen was always bought in gas bottles in Nigeria. There was no national company supplying it. My coffee would have to wait. Indefinitely. Or maybe I could just eat it dry with a spoon? In the state I was in, it seemed like an excellent idea.

'Yes, get two big ones. The biggest ones you can find. Um... and Cosmos?'

'*Yes, madam?*'

'I don't have any money on me...'

'*No problem, Madam, I goh see Masta at work and get money from him and goh buy de biggest gas bottles.*'

'Sure. I'm sure you know best what to do...' I was staring at the aromatic Nescafe granules. They smelled so good. Cosmos was already in his element, getting into the car and driving off on his first errand, leaving me alone to eat my coffee in peace. I felt a sense of strange calmness, as I let a bit of African sanity impregnate my whole being. After all, I thought, who was the smart genius who said that coffee should be consumed in a liquid form?

Anyone living in Africa employed house girls, houseboys, drivers, gardeners, nannies, cooks, *meghadis,* and a plethora of other loosely employed house staff. They were all attached to the household, sometimes in mysterious ways, and life in the tropics without them would be impossible. This was true, not only of the expatriate population, but was the culturally accepted way of life amongst all echelons of African society. The only differences between the various employers with domestic help were how they treated their staff, how much they paid them, and how many staff they had at their disposal.

The house staff themselves strictly conformed to an unwritten but unquestionable hierarchy of serfdom. No house girl or houseboy would ever consent 'working' in the garden. That was the gardener's job and in the eyes of the orderly ranked staff, the 'outside help' were ranked much lower than the domestic help. Similarly, a gardener had no business in the house, as he was an 'outside help,' and under no circumstances would ever be allowed to enter the house by the domestic staff.

Our gardener was a young boy of about sixteen. His name was Dazhuma, and he worked for the previous occupants of the house. It was he who told me that before leaving, the previous lady uprooted every single plant in what used to be a beautiful garden filled with rose bushes, camellias, frangipanis, and tropical ornamental plants. That explained the gloominess of our empty garden beds. After hearing the disheartening story, I renounced any gardening and concentrated instead on interior decorating, which left our 'gardener' Dazhuma with effectively nothing to do.

In the first few days, he industriously dug a few odd holes here and there in the bare ground around the house, without much conviction or premeditation as to how to subsequently fill them. He was justifiably apprehensive and knew he needed to make a good impression. Each time I looked outside the window I saw him digging a hole and dramatically wiping the sweat off his forehead. I was impressed.

Having promptly appraised me as an inexperienced and forgiving boss, Dazhuma quickly abandoned any other semblance of garden work. He pleasurably reverted to the time-honoured African way of letting the days and life pass by, with minimal exertion of body or soul. Thereafter, Dazhuma spent most of his time at work cosily sleeping on a well-shaded wooden bench in a quiet corner of the garden, away from prying eyes.

However, that leisurely workstyle proved to have its drawbacks, as he was regularly awakened by the furious honking and beeping of cars — either mine or our numerous guests trying to get into our securely locked compound. It was becoming quite evident that our 'security guards,' the *meghadis*, often abandoned their posts, sometimes all three at a time. They left for indefinite periods during the day, without the slightest explanation as to their whereabouts or expected arrival time back. That left only sleeping Dazhuma to open the gates, which proved to be a more important job than I first suspected.

'Idyyyoooot! He no fit for work!' Cosmos would fume, after yet another prolonged wait for Dazhuma to finally wake up from his slumber.

'Madam, I goh need to be paid more,' Dazhuma informed me one day in aggrieved tones. He was dejectedly rubbing his sleepy eyes after having once again been rudely awakened from his midday snooze by Cosmos' furious honks.

'Why Dazhuma, what is the matter?' I asked, taken aback.

'Well, if I goh open the gates, dat is more work. I noh be security. I be gardener. If madam want me to be gardener and security, I need to be paid more mohney!'

I could not argue with his logic, although as far as I could tell, Dazhuma's gardening duties were virtually nonexistent. But the archaic servant hierarchy code was making itself known, and I could not ignore it. It was a sensitive subject, and I knew it had to be resolved to everyone's satisfaction. It was as forceful as the Union Movement back home and one had to tread carefully.

'You really need to speak to the *meghadis,* Harry,' I told him later that evening. 'Otherwise, we will have an upheaval out there. You know how Cosmos hates the *meghadis* when they purposefully make him wait outside the gates, because he is higher placed than them, being the driver. And the *meghadis* hate Dazhuma and ignore him because, being the gardener, he has the lowest status of them all. And yet he must open the gates when they leave their posts for no reason. They will not speak between themselves since they all think it's below their status to engage each other in conversation.'

'What do you want me to tell them?' said Harry. 'You know the *meghadis* barely speak English, and I don't even think *they* understand their job very well.'

'So, why on earth are they camping in front of our gate drinking tea all day? All three of them! And why are we paying them a salary if we can't even communicate with them?'

'Everyone here employs *meghadis,* you know that! They are more reliable than the Yorubas or the Igbos and they don't need to speak English to open the gates, do they?' Harry said. Obviously, he had been in the country longer than I and understood its simple African logic much better than I did.

The 'gate people' or *meghadis*, otherwise grandly referred to as security in the Nigerian workforce, are a distinct North

African Islamic ethnic group called the Hausa Fulanis. These ancient nomadic herding people are a mixture of Arabs, Egyptians, Berbers, North and West Africans. They have light skin, fine features, and sometimes even blue eyes, and speak a dialect known as Hausa. Nonaggressive by nature, they spend their days drinking hot tea, perpetually brewed in miniature glazed enamel teapots, on mini makeshift gas burners set up next to the gates they are supposedly minding. The men are tall and thin, and usually dress in blue long shirts, with long cuts on either side, covering pants tight at the bottom, but loose around the waist. The Hausa like to keep to themselves and are exceptionally soft-spoken, almost to the point of extreme shyness.

I never understood why, out of the hundreds of tribes Nigeria had to offer, the position with the most risks involved, due to high incidences of armed house robberies, was traditionally appointed only to those gentle people. They would often run away at the slightest sign of trouble, which unfortunately for us, usually meant they would leave the gates wide open for the attacking armed robbers.

That evening, our three *meghadis* were sternly spoken to by a resigned Harry. He resorted to an entertaining linguistic verbal exertion of Arabic, French and English, enriched with an abundance *of Inchallas,* and an international body language pantomime that exhibited a lot of frantic hand waving and knee bending. The *meghadis* were told in no uncertain terms that at least one of them was to stay on duty at the gate if the other two had someplace to go. I watched, mesmerised, as the Hausas gaped and smiled, hugely honoured by the impromptu charade performed by their boss for their divertissement. One of them at least, named Sidi, seemed to understand what Harry was trying to put across, as he nodded his head vigorously throughout the ludicrous performance.

'*Yessa,*' he said reassuringly, after the entertaining spectacle.

'So, do you think they understood what you were trying to say? I for one didn't...' I said as we walked back to the house.

'*Inchalla,*' Harry said gloomily.

Loosely translated, *Inchalla* means 'by the grace of God.' It is widely used by Muslims throughout the world in every situation under the sun. Depending upon the circumstances, it can be equally interpreted as an optimistic or a fatalistic approach to life and is an absolute acceptance of faith in God's will. It had the added benefit that, being subjected to God's direct divine intervention, whatever happened was never anyone's fault. It was God's will.

From then on, much to our surprise, we saw a drastic improvement in our *meghadis* work ethics, and Dazhuma was relieved of his superfluous gate duties. He was saddened by his lost additional income opportunity. Sidi stayed with us throughout the remainder of our stay in Africa, progressing to the honourable title of our Head of Security. His heroism in dubious situations, however, was never prodigious.

'*Sidiiiiiii!*'

It was midnight, and Harry was standing in his pyjamas bellowing at the top of his voice. We had just jumped out of bed, woken by an astonishing sound coming from below our windows. It was a rhythmic metallic banging, as if someone were hitting a hammer onto a huge gong, the loud sound echoing in increasing sound waves in the quiet nocturnal breeze. As we listened, petrified, the sound became even more stupefying as it gradually intercepted with startling rattling and clanking of heavy metallic chains, loud enough to wake up the dead.

'*Sidiiiiiiiiii!*' Harry bellowed again at the top of his voice from our balcony. The noise stopped. The sudden silence must have woken Sidi.

'*Sa?*', came the sleepy reply from the darkness below.

'What is that ungodly noise from down there?!' fumed Harry.

'*What noise sa...?*'

'The big noise Sidi, from outside!'

'*I hear nohting sa,*' Sidi replied in a sleepy, soothing tone.

'There was a noise, a *biiiiiiiig* noise, right below this window! If I hear it again, I'm coming out with my rifle! You cannot sleep while on duty Sidi, you are my night security, for goodness' sake! An atomic bomb would not wake you up! You make sure that noise does not happen again, you understand Sidi?'

'*Yessa!*' replied Sidi.

That was a blatant lie. Sidi barely spoke English. Before we had time to close our eyes again, the terrifying noise erupted again with renewed vigour, sending us flying to the window once more. This time, Sidi also heard it, having had no time to fall asleep. True to his words, Harry flew out with his hunting rifle onto the balcony.

'Sidi...' whispered Harry in hushed tones.

'*Yessa?*' Sidi whispered shakily from below.

'*You hear am?*'

'*Yessa, I hear am!*'

'*What y be dat?*'

'*I don't know sa. Y dey come from outside...*' offered Sidi.

'I know y dey come from outside Sidi! I have ears! Now, go check what it is! *Na quick quick!'*, Harry said as he tactically retreated behind the thick bedroom curtains.

Suddenly the noise stopped again, right in front of our house. We all froze, stopped breathing, and listened intently in the night air.

'Who be that?' Sidi whispered into the darkness, addressing himself at the gates.

'Na me!' answered a booming voice from outside our gates.

'Who are you?' said Harry, coming back onto the balcony, reassured that a human voice was behind all the unearthly clanking and pounding. He aimed his rifle into the darkness, ready to shoot at whoever woke him from his slumber. The rifle was an antique used in the Biafra war in the 1960s, and judging by the crudeness of the specimen, it was never used with big precision. It looked more like a stick than a rifle, but Harry had purchased it strictly for its primitive appeal. In his rage, Harry had forgotten all of that, and the important detail that the rifle had no ammo in it.

'I be de night street security, sa!' came the baffling reply from the darkness.

'What?'

'Night street security sa. I be hired by all the people on de street as your night security, sa!'

'Then why on earth are you making this horrible noise?' said Harry.

'Dis is so all the people on dis very street know I am not sleeping and doing my new job properly. Nah I don't want my employers to dey tink I dey sleep at night, so every hour I dey use my gong and

I dey rattle my chains to let everyone know I no dey sleep!' said the proud voice from down below.

He banged his gong loudly to demonstrate his professional competence in waking the whole street to let everyone know he was not sleeping on duty. We all jumped instinctively and covered our ears. I heard Harry exhale loudly, trying to calm himself down.

'Well,' he said in a subdued tone, 'I do not know who employed you or why, but I live on this street, and you cannot possibly think that waking everyone up with your big gong *just* to let us know *you* are *not* sleeping is going to make us happy. It is night and *we* all need *silence* to *sleep.* You stop that noise right now or I will shoot at you.'

'Ah goh tell police you want to shoot me for doing my job,' came the plaintive answer from below.

'Well, I will tell the police that you were making such a racket that I thought you were an armed robber breaking into my house, and I shot you!' Harry shouted, waving his non-functional antique rifle to emphasise his point.

The night clatter continued for a few more weeks, but the gong and the rattling quietened down around our house, only to continue with renewed vigour further down the road. Then it stopped altogether. We presumed that the night security man was invited to seek employment elsewhere by the sleep-deprived street inhabitants. Arguably, he may have been shot by one of our neighbours down the road. We never found out as we never asked.

One evening we were invited by Robert, our very hospitable Lebanese friend, to come for dinner, as he dropped in to see us for afternoon coffee. As often happened in Nigeria, things did not go to plan. In the evening we had no phone, no electricity, and no diesel for the generator, which was not an unusual occurrence at all. However, as luck would have it, we also had no driver nor car, as we had sent Cosmos to drop someone off. Not surprisingly, he got stuck in traffic.

As the evening advanced, we felt increasingly agitated as we could not inform Robert that we had no way of getting to his house. At 8.30, as Cosmos had still not arrived, Harry decided to send our maid, Viki, on foot with a message to Robert, asking him to send us his driver.

'So, have you sent her to Robert?' I asked Harry when he returned to the living room, illuminating his way with a torch.

'No, I have sent Sidi instead. He happened to be outside, and I could not find Viki.'

'Did you give him a written note?' I said, slightly alarmed by this turn of events.

'No, of course not. Do you see me carrying a notepad and pen with me? I told him to go and tell Robert that we need a car.'

'In what language did you tell him that? You know no one really understands what he says when he does speak...'

'Don't worry darling, it is a simple message. I'm sure Robert will understand. Do not complicate things by overthinking. It will be all right, relax, and let's just wait for Robert's car to come and pick us up, shall we?'

We did not have to wait too long. Within less than ten minutes, we heard the sickening sound of a car flying at high speed, which seemed directly aimed at our house. Seconds later we heard a harrowing screech of metal scraping metal as the car rammed through our compound gates, which the petrified *meghadis* had no time to fully open. The black four-wheel drive came to a spectacular screeching halt in front of our door, thick smoke emanating from its assaulted exhaust pipe. Robert and four Lebanese friends, all close neighbours, jumped out operation SEAL style, dressed in black, rifles at the ready, belts of ammunition covering half of their bodies, only the whites of their eyes shining in the darkness.

'Where are they?' they screamed, aiming the rifles at the house.

'Who?' shouted Harry. He had come running from the house at the sound of the commotion, his torch shakily illuminating the remarkable scene in front of him.

'The armed robbers! Where are they?'

'What are you talking about? What armed robbers? There are no armed robbers here!' Harry carefully moved the butt of a friend's rifle, which had been painfully lodged in his chest in the confusion. The four-armed men continued to look for the looming danger frantically, ignoring Harry's protests.

'Sidi said there were armed robbers here!' shouted Robert.

'What do you mean? What did he say?'

Robert finally lowered his rifle. He scratched his head thoughtfully.

'Well, if I remember right, the words I *did* actually understand amongst other incomprehensible sounds were '*Masta Harry car quick quick now now...*' It sounded like you needed a car quickly to get away from armed robbers attacking your house,' said Robert, angrily unloading his rifle.'

Unlike Harry's, it was not an antique piece but an authentic deadly weapon.

'You should seriously consider employing someone who actually speaks at least one comprehensible language,' he added scornfully. 'One has enough dramas in this place without false alarms!'

Chapter 9

THE UNIVERSE, CONQUERORS, AND THE QUEEN

Cosmos, Julius, Napoleon, and Victoria

Climbing up in the domestic help hierarchy, after the gardener and the security, there were the indispensable drivers. Expatriates avoided driving their cars at all costs, as traffic in Lagos was notoriously chaotic, dangerous, and unpredictable.

Cosmos was hired by Harry when he first arrived in Nigeria. It was apparent that he was immensely proud to call himself '*Masta's driver.*' Harry told me in secret that he hired Cosmos because he was instantly impressed by the man's astonishing moustache. He had never seen one on a Nigerian man before, and he thought that in dangerous circumstances, Cosmos may have the capacity to scare large crowds away, just because of his scary handlebar. So, Cosmos was hired on the spot, because in Harry's eyes, he could easily double up as an efficient bodyguard. He liked to call Cosmos his 'Nigerian Samurai.'

Unfortunately, he did not bother to check Cosmos' driving skills before hiring him. As a result, the two of them initially spent a considerable amount of time bunny-hopping when for reasons unexplained, Cosmos tried to change gears without pressing the clutch. Harry listened with horror to the harrowing sounds coming from the engine when Cosmos did manage to change a few gears at a time or changed gears down instead of up. They also spent a lot of time stationery, when Cosmos could not get the car started at all.

In no time at all, Cosmos developed a highly personalised, forward lurch manoeuvre which he usually demonstrated in the worst possible circumstances — often when Harry's stunned boss was watching or was standing in his direct trajectory line. It was his signature trick. It never failed to impress the wrong way, and everyone learned to quickly scuttle away first and ask questions later. Normally, everyone was just grateful to still be alive.

Harry eventually asked Cosmos what made him think he knew how to drive a car when he applied for the position. Cosmos answered, quite hurt, that he used to drive a '*big trok.*'

'*Everyone made way for me,*' he added mournfully.

That did explain, at least in part, his flamboyant style of driving with no regard for his safety or that of his passengers.

Who needs avoidance tactics when driving a *big trok*? Truck drivers in Lagos adhered only to their own unique standards of driving, based on the assumption that everyone smaller than their truck must make way, or be driven into.

Our good friend Saul also hired a driver without bothering to check if the applicant knew how to drive. We were sitting in our beach hut one Sunday, Saul his wife Hanne, Harry, and I. One of the vendors selling African art, heard us speak in French and inquired politely in the same language if we were by any chance looking for a driver. Coincidentally, it so happened that Saul was, and the art vendor with excellent French was hired on the spot by our delighted friend.

Unbelievably, his name was Napoleon. I think the name impressed Saul even more than Cosmos' moustache impressed Harry, which would explain the haste in which he was hired. Perhaps Saul thought he could somehow imperiously conquer the notorious Lagosian traffic with a driver called Napoleon. Or maybe the lure of being driven by a "Napoleon" was irresistible.

On his first day at work, when Saul sat expectantly in the back seat ready to be royally driven around, it transpired that Napoleon did not know how to start the vehicle. Patiently, Saul explained to him that his car was a bit tricky to start, and he showed him how it was done. That mastered, Saul sat back again, waiting to be driven.

'Mais monsieur, qu'est-ce que je fais maintenant?' ('But sir, what do I do now') asked the newly hired driver.

'You drive my friend, you drive. We are going to my work. I will show you the way,' Saul said grandly.

'*Mais monsieur, je n'ai jamais conduis une voiture, comment je fais?*' ('But sir, I have never driven a car before, how is it done?').

Saul must have genuinely felt like Napoleon after the failed Russian campaign. Faulty logistics, bad planning, huge economic loss, and shocking defeat must have all flashed before his eyes. Being good-natured, Saul kept Napoleon in his employment, just to keep him company while he drove himself around. Thus, quite naturally, Saul became Napoleon's driver. Perhaps there was something in the name after all...

Thinking completely outside of the box, as he often liked to do, Harry's close friend from work, Tom, had hired his driver purely for his excellent driving skills.

Driving in Lagos, where the application of road rules or common sense was unheard of, was appallingly dangerous for expatriates. For the high adrenaline seekers who did choose to drive, there was the strong possibility of them being lynched to death for the smallest of traffic infringements by local drivers. Mob justice ruled in the country, where law enforcement was, for the most part, invisible.

That possibility was never an option with Tom's chauffeur and drives with him verged on the boring side. He expertly swerved, changed gears, accelerated, and slowed down, without the slightest inconvenience to his passengers. He was the most refined chauffeur in the whole company, and he knew it. He never spoke to anyone unless necessary, and when he did speak, it was in the most astringent of tones, considering himself superior to everyone else. Tom, his austere boss, never missed an opportunity to brag about his excellent hiring skills in having found the Nigerian Schumacher.

Tom's driver's name was Julius, yet another conqueror. Julius rarely smiled, so no one liked him. That did not matter much, because he did not like anyone either, except his boss Tom, to whom he had a strong loyal attachment, based probably on their singularly forlorn dispositions.

As Tom and Harry were close friends and both were engineers at one of the biggest foam factories in Lagos, Julius and Cosmos saw a lot of each other daily. After taking their boss to work, they then had nothing else to do but wait until evening to drive them back home.

The drive to work lasted less than five minutes. The ten hours during which they waited were not wasted. Julius and Cosmos made sure to park their cars opposite each other and spent the entire day staring each other down with growing antipathy. They only let their guards down when, in the middle of the day, and in the intense heat, their combative spirits would give way to a long invigorating midday snooze.

There were more than enough grounds for their natural animosity to develop. They belonged to two feuding ethnic tribes, which made them natural enemies, but there was more to it than that. Julius was the best driver in the company, and Cosmos was by far the worst. Julius was young, and Cosmos was in his forties. Julius was small, and Cosmos was big. Julius was stern, and Cosmos was mischievous. Julius was bright, and Cosmos not so much. That came to light in the following conversation between me and him during a long fuel shortage.

'Cosmos, is there fuel in the petrol station?

'*No problem with fooel, madam, but there is no petrohl!*'

Finally, simply by the fact that they worked for two close friends, the two drivers hated each other with a barely concealed passion.

'Your driver Cosmos beat up Julius and now Julius has a black eye!' Harry whispered in my ear as we entered Tom's car one day. Julius was staring ahead from behind the wheel, locked in an indignant silence. That at least explained why he did not greet me when I entered the car, which he occasionally consented to do if, on a rare occasion, he was not in a sulky mood.

'He is *your* driver *too* you know!' I whispered back, incensed by the implication that when things went wrong it was always somehow my fault. 'What happened?'

'Well, apparently Julius tried to verbally persuade Cosmos to park behind a big lineup of other cars at the factory, to make more space. Cosmos refused. Not sure if he just refused to take orders from Julius or whether he was genuinely concerned he would block other cars by doing so. Anyway, he refused, so Julius became more insistent and a crowd of onlookers gathered as the argument grew more heated. Finally, Cosmos took it upon himself to punch Julius in the face as they were getting nowhere with their discussion.'

'So, you are saying that *my* driver Cosmos won the fight?' I said, chuckling in the back seat.

I glanced at Julius to see if there were any signs of the fight, but he looked more rancorous than ever and kept his face purposefully turned the other way. Sitting in the passenger seat next to him was Tom, also enveloped in a wrathful icy silence, in total solidarity with his disgraced chauffeur.

'Yeah, he won... I told you he was tough and would come in handy,' Harry whispered with a mischievous wink.

None of us ever spoke of the incident again.

When hiring staff, I had a totally different strategy from Harry or Tom. I hired our house girl, Viki, a soft-spoken seventeen-year-old girl from the faraway city of Calabar, because she spoke English well, answered my questions demurely, and seemed as scared as I was at the interview. She was also very small in stature, which I thought, in direct reverse psychology to Harry's logic with Cosmos, was an advantage. As far as her skills went, I applied the exact opposite logic to Tom's proven excellent hiring technique.

'Do you know how to cook?' I sat in what I hoped looked like a professional armchair, nervous to perform my first job interview as an employer. The whole situation was ludicrous. I had never had a house girl before, nor had I ever given an interview before. Hell, I had never had an interview myself, I was fresh from my university studies.

'No, ma. But I can learn.'

Not from me, I thought depressed. My cooking experiments had been huge disasters, and I was hoping to hire someone who knew the basics at least.

'Have you ever worked before?'

'No, ma.'

'Do you know how to clean?'

'No, ma.'

'Do you know how to read and write?'

'No, ma.'

'Ok, you're hired' I said.

I was exhausted by the whole interviewing process. Viki was visibly as relieved as I was after the discouraging dialogue.

I never regretted my choice and with time, Viki became my second in command in navigating the daily household tasks. Very quickly, she learnt what was required of her, and I never had to repeat anything twice. She was a very hard-working young girl and possessed the skills of a natural leader. She thought little of commanding all the other male house staff members, including Cosmos, the cook, the gardener, and the *meghadis*, most of whom were twice or three times her size and age.

The only person who managed to brazenly escape her rigorous supervision was Dazhuma, our gardener, who was roughly her age, and as a righteous hormonal teenager would have nothing of that 'work hard and obey' ethos drilled into him. He still managed to spend his time undisturbed, hidden, and asleep in a corner of the garden.

Despite her diminutive stature, everyone else respected Viki because she had a sharp tongue and saw through everyone's lies and manipulations. This was an important skill set that helped me immensely, as hushed but intense tribal wars were rife amongst domestic staff who all hailed from different ethnic groups.

Viki herself was the only representative of the faraway Calabar people and did not give a hoot about all the other tribal groups, which made her even more fearsome to her feuding co-workers. She had no qualms in dobbing to me who stole what and when, who lied and why, who did not do their job properly and who did not listen to her when kindly asked to do something. She was a real gem, one of a kind, and she was a friend I could always rely on. Viki stayed with us until I left Nigeria for good, ten years later. We were both expecting our first babies.

Chapter 10

FIDEL — LE CHEF

'You have the right to one egg, monsieur.'

Cooking had never been my labour of love, and when I arrived in Nigeria at the age of twenty, I knew precious nothing about it. The expatriate ladies, much older and more experienced than I, not only knew how to cook, but had excellent Nigerian cooks as well. Each household specialised in signature dishes, the secrets of which only the wives and their cooks knew.

I was passable when I had a good recipe to follow, but I had not yet found a cook to relieve me of my kitchen duties. If I needed something to be done, Viki was my *sous chef* and whipped up simple dishes I had taught her if I was otherwise engaged. That system worked fine for a while, especially after Tom moved in with us while his house was being renovated. We had, by then, moved to a much bigger house, surrounded by a lovely tropical garden, with a guestroom in which he could stay.

Tom, by nature, was a modern-day Daedalus. His dogmatic quest for perfection, or the Holy Grail of Life itself, had by then become a long journey of perpetual experiments in areas that happened to take his fancy. Once fixated on a topic, it became Tom's sole purpose in life, overshadowing everything else and consuming him from within.

When he moved in with us, that area in life was food, or more precisely, how to live without it. Throughout his life, Tom adhered to about a dozen different diets, all as different and opposed to each other as chalk and cheese. They all, however, had the common aim of needing to improve his health, enhance his looks and IQ, and extend his longevity. By the time he came to stay with us, he concluded that with the proper food, he could become an irresistible, supercharged superhuman.

It was no surprise that when Tom moved in with us, Harry was enthralled at the prospect of sticking to his friend's nutritional regime. He also wished to become an irresistible, supercharged superhuman, and I was happy to let them be since it needed little effort on my part. To my great relief, I was not home to witness all that happened, as by then I was working. But on the weekends, I was able to observe how superhumans were made.

Both men began their days by gulping down a pint of freshly squeezed orange juice, which Viki would spend an hour squeezing. Breakfast consisted of a range of different vitamins. Tom had handpicked them based on their unique properties, which he claimed were the only essential nutritional requirements they needed for their morning meal.

After this wholesome meal, they went to work and after a few hours arrived home for lunch, which Viki would cook under strict instructions from Tom. Lunch was vegetarian because by then Tom had come to the enlightening conclusion that meat was unhealthy for human consumption. Garlic was strictly prohibited. Whole dishes were thrown away if there was a hint of garlic inside.

Tom and Harry's conversations during lunch usually centred around a strange occurrence. For some unfathomable reason, both friends had projectile diarrhea, strange stomach cramps, and eviscerating tummy aches. Those symptoms prevented them from doing any work, which did not seem to bother them in the slightest. On better days, they only complained of irritable stomachs and debilitating heartburn.

In the evenings, the two friends drank a pint of yoghurt, and an hour later cake. Not because it was healthy, but because Tom liked cake. They then swallowed their evening cup of vitamins. Then followed an excruciatingly long evening spent in front of the television, where the two comrades would sit till two or three in the morning, further complaining of cramps and stomach aches, as the vitamins ate their way through their empty stomach walls.

Tom was an insomniac, and based on that sleeping disorder had decided that humans only needed three hours of sleep to function optimally. Harry had no choice but to abide by the draconian nocturnal ritual imposed by his assertive friend, although he suffered from a case of severe sleeping addiction and was happiest when horizontal, eyes closed, for extended periods.

Things did not improve when Jurgen, a colleague of Harry and Tom's, arrived for a business trip from Holland. Weary of dietary sensitivities, I took care to ask Jurgen if he ate meat. I had not given up on my carnivorous way of life and would have loved a companion for my dinner delinquencies of beef or chicken, which the superhumans I was living with severely frowned upon.

'Oh, of course I eat meat, no problem with that!' said Jurgen, reassuringly patting me on the back. 'But I cannot eat pasta, bread, cheese or milk,' he added as an afterthought.

'Oh my God, what is wrong with you man?' asked Harry.

'Nothing is wrong with me,' said Jurgen offended.' I am just gluten and lactose intolerant.'

'So, what's left? What exactly can you eat?' I asked, confused. I had no idea what gluten was back then.

'Meat and vegetables!' Jurgen said cheerfully.

We spent the next few days eating at a Chinese restaurant. Everyone chose for themselves, and everyone was happy.

Before Jurgen returned to Holland, I invited a few friends for dinner making sure I covered all the dietary eccentricities of my guests. Amongst the invited was Stephen, who had never come to visit us before, being somewhat of an intellectual recluse. As we all gathered to eat the variety of different dishes which I had painstakingly prepared, I noticed Stephen's eyes travelling the length and width of the table, in a concerted effort to choose something edible from the platters. After watching him for a while, still with an empty plate in his hand,

I could stand it no longer. My hostess instinct propelled me forward, with a big inviting smile on my face.

'Can I offer you a piece of roast Stephen? I daresay it is very juicy. I marinated it overnight in wine,' I said, grabbing his plate. Stephen grabbed it back. He was pale.

'Oh, no thank you, Magdalena. I don't eat meat. I also don't drink alcohol.'

'Oh, I'm so sorry,' I said aghast by my faux pas, 'We have fish or shrimps if you would like?'

'I don't eat seafood either, I'm sorry.'

'That's perfectly all right. We have everything we need to cover all nutritional needs here!' I said reassuringly, although I was not very clear as to what diet I was catering for with him. 'Would you perhaps like some roast potatoes and carrots with salad?'

'I can't eat potatoes or carrots. They grow underground and are therefore impure. They should not be eaten according to the eastern diet I am following.'

Eastern diet? Sure. Great, I thought. *Now, why haven't I thought of that?!*

'However, I wouldn't mind the salad since I see it is only lettuce and tomato.'

'Yes indeed, and they both grow above ground!' I said, relieved.

'So, what is inside the dressing if I may ask?'

'Oh, the usual, a bit of garlic, oil, lemon, salt, and pepper. Nothing bad in there!' I enthused.

'Sorry Magdalena, I hope you don't find me to be difficult, but unfortunately, I don't eat garlic...' replied Stephen mournfully.

'Sure. No worries at all! How about some lovely rice?' I asked, trying not to show I was crestfallen.

'Are those not mushrooms in the rice?' asked the eagle-eyed Stephen.

'Indeed... but they grow above ground,' I explained.

'I regret to say, but I do not eat fungi of any sort...'

By now I had totally lost my appetite. And anyway, who called edible mushrooms fungi? This called forth memories of my childhood in Poland. Running out of choices and ideas as my panicked gaze ran over all the sumptuous dishes presented on the table, I suddenly saw that my last resort was right in front of me. Surely, that was going to pass the test.

'Look, another salad! It has only yoghurt and cucumber in it!'

'Is that not onion inside?' asked Stephen, suspiciously.

'Well, yes, there is a bit of onion...'

'Sorry, I don't eat onion...' whispered Stephen in an apologetic whisper.

Stephen ended up having a bowl of plain yoghurt for dinner. I was mortified. With time, he became one of our closest friends and whenever he invited us to his house, we feasted on delicious eastern-inspired meals prepared by him.

A year after I arrived in Nigeria, I began work as an English teacher at the Lycée Français Louis Pasteur, a French school in Lagos. I had to commute for long hours in the traffic between Ikeja, where we lived, and Lagos, which was a mere twenty minutes away, but with the usual traffic, congestion could last up to two or three hours. I had to relinquish my valiant culinary experiments in the kitchen, as I had no time to do so anymore. We needed a cook desperately, so we sent word through the Nigerian grapevine that applicants were welcome.

The first few candidates we trialled did not last more than a day or two each. Some of them did not even last an hour. We suffered a devastating economic blow to our budget when meal after meal prepared by the supposed "chefs" were either charcoaled, overboiled, raw, tasteless, swimming in litres of red greasy local palm oil, or simply unrecognisable in shape, colour, or texture. One "cook" managed to "bake" a chicken, totally covered in foil. He presented us with a ghastly-looking blanched bird, grey feathers still stuck to its leathery skin. Accompanying this dish was a single potato to be shared between the two of us. He was kindly asked to leave immediately.

Last in a lengthy line of successive chefs came a young boy by the name of Fidel. He was from Cotonou in Benin, and a native French speaker. He was recommended by a colleague working at the French School. Rumour had it that he was a renowned chef in the expatriate community, having worked for an Italian priest, a Belgian diplomat, a Lebanese family and a German man.

I arranged with my colleague to meet with this prodigy in her house, as she lived in mainland Lagos. On the appointed day, he arrived on time, which was already highly impressive by African standards, with a big confident smile illuminating his friendly face.

'So, Fidel, can I see your reference letter from your last employer, the 'German man' I believe?' I was cautiously

suspicious of all candidates by then, due to the shocking fail-
ures of the last few weeks. I could ill afford another bad choice,
as both myself and Harry were already economically drained
and strongly emancipated by the ordeal.

'*Madam,* I do not know what a reference letter is,' Fidel
answered, totally unperturbed by this slight hiccup, in impeccable French. Impressed by his linguistic prowess more
than his puzzling answer, as it was exceedingly rare to hear
non-pidgin English or French spoken by an African person,
I immediately let down my guard. I offered Fidel a few days'
trial period without further questions. I explained to my new
cook that he would have to stay at the boys' quarters at my
house. Fidel, however, had a question.

'*Madam a dit qu'elle va me prendre chez elle pour que je puisse
voir le lieu de mon travail et les constituants de la maison,*' my jaw
involuntarily dropped a few inches, '*mais est-ce que je pourrais
savoir si je pourrais m'assiéger là-bas?*'

Roughly, the translation would amount to something as
lofty as '*Madam* did mention that I could make a reconnaissance of my new place of employment and survey the constit-
uents of the house,' this is where my jaw dropped, 'but could
I inquire as to whether I could besiege myself there?'

This is where *my* impeccable French failed me. What did he
mean by '*m'assiéger*' or besiege?

'Do you mean, if you can live there for the time being?'
I asked tentatively in simple, normal French.

'*Oui madam, c'est ça!*' Fidel beamed.

'Well, of course you can!' I answered, relieved that we had
finally landed on the same page.

It was with boundless joy on his part, and great appre-hension from mine, that young Fidel 'besieged' himself in his designated boys' quarters room that very same day, as he was very keen to start work at once.

'So, Fidel, do you think you could bake us a chocolate cake?'

It was evening, and after having moved in, Fidel reported to work in the kitchen. As a precautionary measure, Harry and I had already eaten a quick pasta dish which I had prepared. I did not want to alarm our latest recruit with a stressful preparation of a big meal on his first day. Despite his assur-ances of great culinary exploits, I was still completely clueless as to what his cooking was like, and I was little inclined to take risks in waiting to find out on an empty stomach.

'*Oui madam, bien sûr. Tout de suite!*' Fidel said with great confidence.

He immediately began to open and close cupboards in a clutter of comforting savvy expertise. With huge pandemo-nium, he began to assemble pots, pans, bowls, spoons, and ingredients on the kitchen bench. I was suitably impressed.

'Well, you seem at ease in the kitchen. If you need my help, please use the phone to call me. I will be upstairs,' I said and ran away from the oppressive kitchen. I hated that place with a passion, and I was more than happy to leave it in the hands of such a capable chef. Finally, our prayers had been answered.

'You know what, I think we finally got ourselves a respect-able cook!' I announced happily to Harry when he came home from work. 'I can't wait to taste the chocolate cake. I can already smell it!'

In due time, the internal phone rang. It was Fidel asking if he could bring the cake upstairs for us to taste. I acquiesced, delighted, and we prepared our tastebuds for amazement. With pride exuding from every pore of his body, Fidel ceremoniously deposited his precious load on the table in front of us.

'*Voilà le gâteau au chocolat, madame et monsieur!*' he solemnly announced, proudly bowing.

We were both too taken aback to react at first. In front of us, lay what looked like a crudely deconstructed, thick, black pancake. Right in its centre featured a large gaping crater where the cake must have initially — and dramatically — risen and then, as dramatically, deflated. Various pieces of the brown mass lay craftily arranged around the abyss in a desperate effort to try to make it look like a circular object. It was obvious the *gâteau* came out of the baking tray in several burnt pieces. *How* it came out, only Fidel knew.

There was an embarrassed silence greeting this anticlimaxing spectacle. Seeing that Fidel was obviously waiting in a dignified pose for praise in front of us, I cleared my throat.

'So, Fidel, did you use self-rising flour to do this?' I asked calmly. I could not bring myself to call the creation the '*gâteau au chocolat,*' as baptised by Fidel.

'*No, madam.*'

'Ok, did you use the baking powder then?' I probed further.

'*No, madam!*' came the reply.

I gave up the guessing game as I ran out of options for what could be used in a chocolate cake.

'So, what did you use?' I asked, my curiosity aroused.

'I used yeast, *madam!*'

'Yeast?!'

I was unprepared for this response. When I came out of shock, a solid thirty seconds later, all I could do was laugh hysterically, but seeing that Fidel looked offended, I immediately stopped.

'Ok, Fidel, how about we skip baked desserts from now on? What is your plan for lunch tomorrow?' I asked, as brightly as I could.

'I have planned shrimps in red sauce, madam,' came the sulky reply. It was obvious I had hurt Fidel in his pride. There was nothing else to do but wait till the next day to see what lunch would look like. Before throwing away the deconstructed cake, I could not resist the temptation to taste a small piece. It had the texture of a cement brick, and my assaulted taste buds told me that Fidel did not bother to put any sugar in it.

For lunch the next day, the shrivelled shrimps arrived in a bowl of unpalatable-looking red soup, cosily lidded by a thick layer of red grease. Harry and I tasted it with sinking hearts, our appetites already killed at the disagreeable sight of the dish. The blubbering surface layer was palm oil, a staple in Nigerian diets, but not so much part of ours as it was too rich for our taste. The sauce was inedible and tasted even worse than it looked. We sat in front of our bowls, dejectedly picking at the downsized rock-hard shrimps.

'Fidel is asking if he should bring dessert,' the alarming message was relayed by Viki over the internal phone. We were too resigned to decline, and we could not hurt Fidel's feelings again.

'Sure, let him bring it.'

Nothing could be worse than the lunch we could not eat.

We thought wrong.

Dessert was served in bowls with a white blob of something at the bottom. Laying gloomily on top of the white substance was what looked like thick banana slices.

'Well, at least we can have bananas for lunch. That should keep us going until I prepare us something to eat,' I smiled optimistically, impaling the banana on my fork with feigned enthusiasm. Harry waited, fixing me with studious anticipation.

'What are you looking at, you can eat too. These are bananas for God's sake!' I snapped, my patience running low. I bit into the banana and spat it out immediately, choking with shock.

'For crying out loud, these are raw plantains, not bananas! How does he not know that plantains are not eaten raw? These are African fruits, for goodness' sake!' I was trying to spit the remaining bits out of my mouth before the unpleasant tingling feeling kicked in. Harry chortled dispassionately.

'Well, you hired him, good luck firing him,' he said, exasperated as he left the table, hungry.

Although by then, I too had come to the sad conclusion that Fidel was no more a cook than I an astronaut, I could not bring myself to show him the door, as he had just comfortably 'besieged' himself at his new quarters. I magnanimously decided to give him a few more days of trial, and I offered him as much help as I could in the process. But it seemed that no matter what Fidel did, he did it all wrong.

To his credit, Fidel himself seemed to be resilient to my criticism after each successive attempt at cooking a meal. He enthusiastically went on to bake '*des biscuits*' which all had different hues and shapes. It was obvious that they were forcibly removed from an unoiled baking tray, as the edges were ominously sticking out at various distressed angles. They were hard as rocks, strangely similar in appearance to lava rocks. I binned them as soon as Fidel turned his back.

His enthusiasm undiminished, and eager to show off his prowess, Fidel went on to conjure a cement-like '*mousse à l'orange*' which followed the same itinerary, stopping only for a short transit in front of me on the table.

Hoping that perhaps his main strength lay in meat dishes, I asked him to make a meal with meat. I was presented with brown cubes of unidentified protein, accompanied by an impressive mound of wilted French fries. When asked why they were wilted, soft and cold, Fidel zealously explained that he had prepared them in the morning, to be ready for the late afternoon when '*madam*' came back from work.

Resigned, I spent the next twenty minutes slowly chewing a single cube of meat, which had the consistency of a rubber shoe sole, and arguably tasted much worse. For some strange reason, the meat cubes were served with a red sauce on the side. It later transpired that in his ardour, Fidel became confused, as the red sauce was meant to supplement the vegetarian dish for Harry.

When Harry came home from work later in the evening, he was served raw stuffed cabbage leaves with half-boiled rice, without the red sauce. I had unashamedly used the sauce to the last drop for drenching my wilted French fries, in the desperate hope that they would go down my gullet faster and smoother.

It was then that I finally decided I needed to halt Fidel's freelancing and provide him with more structure. I presented him with my favourite thick French recipe book and invited him to choose a few recipes that he would like to cook. I asked him to make me a shopping list so that I could help him buy the necessary ingredients. Fidel carefully analysed the cookbook, staying up till late at night in the kitchen immersed in reading. In the morning, he presented me with a six-page shopping list. I read it, intrigued, and realised that half of the items were already in the kitchen pantry, while the other half were unobtainable in Nigeria. My patience ran thin.

'Fidel, most of the things on the list we have already. Admittedly, we may have run out of Maggi cubes, because you seem to use them even in desserts, it would seem. As far as canned chickpeas and beans are concerned, I have already explained to you numerous times that we have an extensive selection of dried peas, chickpeas and beans, and we prepare them by soaking them the night before even if the recipe calls for tinned ones.'

'Oui, madam.'

'And items like fresh raspberries, cherries, peaches, fresh mushrooms and oysters are not readily available in Nigeria, so you will have to skip those recipes.'

'Oui, madam.'

'I am going to buy a few extra ingredients from your list, and we will see what you can come up with.'

'Oui, madam.'

After I came home from work, laden with shopping bags, I asked Fidel, 'so, what are you going to cook for tomorrow?'

'Tomato soup, *madam!*'

'Fidel, you have been feeding us tomato soups, tomato sauces and tomato desserts every day now for six days. I cannot eat another tomato dish. Here,' I said grabbing the cookbook, 'why don't you make the '*véloûte au maïs et aux haricots blancs?*'

It was impossible to render justice to the poetical French culinary terms, but loosely, this could be translated to a 'smooth velvety soup of corn and white beans.'

'Look, you've got everything you need for it,' I continued encouragingly, taking out tins of sweet corn and vegetables from my shopping bags.

'*Oui, madam.*'

In due course, the soup was brought to us. Strangely enough, it tasted alright, although one thing was puzzling. The corn was surprisingly hard, almost solid in consistency. However, having been starved of good nourishment for weeks, we gobbled it up quickly without complaints. As Fidel came to ask how we liked the soup, I could not resist the temptation of asking him about the corn.

'Fidel, did you use the corn from the can for the soup?'

'*No, madam,* I used the other one,' came the reply.

'Which other one? Can you show me?'

Eagerly, Fidel went to the kitchen. He came back holding a bag of popcorn.

'*Madam* said that I should not use cans, so I followed *madam's* instructions and used this dry corn after soaking it,' he announced proudly.

I was speechless. We had just eaten a half-boiled popcorn soup. What was worse, we enjoyed it. Later that evening,

I heard Fidel working in the kitchen although I had by then strictly forbidden him to do anything without my explicit approval first.

'Fidel, what are you doing?' I asked as I came down to the kitchen to investigate.

'A pizza, *madam!*' said Fidel, gleaming.

'Fidel, I'm not sure this is a good idea. You think you know how to do it, but you don't. Why don't you go and rest, you have had a long day.'

'*Madam*, I have done pizza many times before. Do not worry. I will bring it up when it is ready. *Madam* can go and rest.'

I went upstairs and waited, resigned. I could not stop him from trying extremely hard to keep his job. I did not have to wait long, as one more of Fidel's creations materialised in front of me.

'*Voilà madam, une pizza!*' Fidel announced, bowing proudly.

Before me stood a miniature replica of what looked like a medieval castle, shaken by a devastating earthquake. Some of its crumbling walls still valiantly stood, albeit obviously on the verge of collapse. Others had already succumbed in a crumbling heap at the bottom. In the middle of all this devastation, there was a red lake of tomato sauce sprinkled with olives and tuna.

'Fidel, what on earth is this?'

'It is a pizza, madam,' said Fidel, visibly doubting my mental well-being.

'This is not a pizza — it looks nothing like a pizza! It doesn't look, smell, or taste like a pizza. What on earth did you do to make it grow like this? Did you use yeast?'

'*No, madam,* I used baking powder' answered Fidel indignantly.

'You used what?' I squawked, my voice and mind gone.

'Baking powder, *madam...*' repeated Fidel, in a barely audible whisper.

Seeing that I was rendered numb and speechless, he decided to beat a hasty retreat, walking nimbly backwards all the way down the stairs and to the kitchen. He did not attempt any new dishes that night.

A few days later, Saul needed to crash at our house, and since we, unfortunately, had a prior engagement, we had no choice but to leave him alone. I felt extremely worried about leaving him in the care of Fidel, but Saul laughed and waved my worries away.

'I can take care of myself, and I'm sure Fidel will be able to cook something simple for me. Does he know how to fry an egg?' he asked, half-jokingly.

'Hm...well, in truth I don't think so,' I answered cautiously.

This wasn't the moment to lie. What made the situation even more mortifying was that Saul's wife was a Cordon Bleu. Her excellent cooking skills were praised and renowned among the expatriates in Lagos. People begged to be invited to their house for dinners and never left disappointed. Saul, used to excellent gourmet cuisine at home, in all probability did not fully appreciate how lucky he was.

After we had left, Saul called Fidel.

'Fidel, I'm hungry. Have you got any eggs?'

'*Oui, monsieur, il y'a des oeufs, et vous avez droit à un, puisqu'il reste sept et madam a reservé six pour demain.*' 'Yes sir, there are eggs, but madam has reserved six for tomorrow, so you only have the right to one.'

When I was leaving the house an hour before, I was under the impression that I had at least a dozen eggs in the fridge, but as it turned out, those eggs inexplicably evaporated and there were only seven left. Eggs were a staple in Nigerian diets, and I was yet unaware that I was supplying the whole household staff with my eggs.

Saul did not expect this complication but was flexible in his thinking. He was never demanding, which was a testament to his unbeatable optimistic spirit and a tremendous sense of humour. He scratched his head thoughtfully.

'That's no problem, Fidel. Have you got potatoes then?'

'*Oui monsieur, mais pour les frire j'ai besoin d'huile et je ne sais pas où madam l'a mis,*' came the stern reply. 'Yes sir, but to fry them I need oil, and I do not know where madam put it.'

I had by then realised that my oil supply had been disappearing at an alarming rate, totally out of proportion to our normal cooking usage. I had decided to keep it under lock and key in a safe place upstairs and gave only small amounts to Fidel daily.

'Listen, Fidel, use butter or even only one drop of oil for my eggs, I'm sure you can squeeze something out from that bottle. Please fry two because one will not be enough. And bring me some bread, please. I'm *very* hungry,' he emphasised, seeing the doleful look on Fidel's face. 'And do not worry, I will speak to madam about that extra egg. It is my responsibility.'

'And how were the eggs when he brought them to you?' I asked amid hoots of laughter, as Saul recounted to us his memorable evening with Fidel.

'Well... the yellow was solid, and the whites were crunchy and burnt. But by that stage, I really did not care since I was so famished that I thought they tasted delicious!'

Over the two weeks Fidel was with us, I had grown very fond of him. His enthusiasm and unerring creativity for culinary catastrophes were refreshing but we could not afford it in the long run. I had to ask him to leave. Before I did, however, I wrote him a glowing referral letter and signed it grandly with a fake name.

Chapter 11

THE CHAIN OF COMMAND

'Na, who took my tyra?'

The Army

As life in Nigeria was increasingly becoming the norm for me, I grew accustomed to the fact that NEPA, or electricity, could be gone for days and weeks on end. That would not have been too much of a problem, since we all had generators, but generators ran on diesel. Diesel, like petrol, was not an easily accessible commodity in Africa's richest petroleum nation.

Ever since copious quantities of petrol were discovered in Nigeria in 1958, most of the petrol revenue had been traditionally appropriated by greedy, corrupt government officials acting as shareholders of the country's oil exports and production. As a result, the mainstream Nigerian had yet to see the benefits of such an elitist arrangement. For reasons unexplained, petrol and diesel availability were becoming a major problem in the years I lived in Nigeria. People regularly queued for hours to get fuel. We often sent our drivers to queue for petrol in the early hours of the morning, and they would come back late in the evening without having filled up. Petrol was very scarce, and no one knew why.

As a result of the interminable petrol fiasco, the political situation was increasingly volatile and as civil unrest grew, street demonstrations became common. Big crowds of people armed with machetes, branches, sticks, bottles, and rocks, paraded the streets and barricaded the main roads. They systematically stopped any incoming cars, dragged the passengers out and meticulously beat them. That was the mob punishment for those drivers who were affluent enough to have been able to get petrol from the black market at extremely inflated prices.

When the situation on the streets became too precarious, the Nigerian Army was called in. The military would make their rumbling entry into the city in an impressive convoy of vintage war tanks. They were all from the old military junkyards of Europe and were in various stages of dilapidation. Often, the war machines expired, in a well-deserved military death on the field of the Nigerian streets, either due to excessive age or lack of petrol.

However, the few that managed to move forward, did so with such an awe-inspiring roar and grinding of tracks, that the gaping populace was momentarily distracted. They watched with delight as the conquering army crashed their way over cars and debris scattered throughout Lagos.

Occasionally, a few soldiers would jump down from the hull and set a few random cars on fire as a stern warning to all onlookers, to the accompaniment of joyous cheers from the delighted crowd. The soldiers were invariably spoilt for choice when choosing their kindling for the job at hand, as there were hundreds of cars stranded along the road, abandoned where their owners had left them, having used the last drop of fuel.

In retaliation to the army's warning tactic, the ingenious Nigerian populace immediately set more cars alight, to show the military that they could fight too — in the same way, or even better. As the crisis deepened, their favourite *modus operandi* was to stop those few drivers who managed to get petrol, drag them out of their vehicles, beat them, and to up the ante a notch, burn their cars in the middle of the road. Just to emphasise the point, and in growing waves of enthusiasm, they then helped themselves to more cars sitting on the sides of the road and incinerated those too, amidst great howls of happiness, singing, dancing, hand clapping and back-patting. There seemed nothing more befitting than a huge car bonfire in the middle of a sweltering day to kick-start the great African party spirit. Everyone, except the army and the police, was invited and welcomed during those celebratory splurges.

Not to be outdone by the civilians, the army retaliated with even more sporadic car incinerations, and with the help of corrupt and fundamentally inept police officers, rounded up innocent bystanders to lock them in jail. Sometimes, some brave reporter would take a few sneaky pics of the events from under cover and send them to the media. Very few people were that brave, as possessing a camera and attempting to film the army was considered a serious offence, punishable by shooting or an indefinite prison sentence — which practically implied the same thing.

This game could go on for weeks and months, and when my parents did manage to call me — on the rare occasions the telephone lines were working — they were most concerned for our safety. They saw horrific reports on CNN, and they had more information about Nigeria's descent into increasing social unrest than I did. I did not always have access to CNN, as the satellite was often down. I had not realised that I was living in such a volatile place and that we made it onto the news coverage quite regularly. I had learned to navigate the problems by becoming ignorant of them. By then I was sane in a totally Nigerian way. I often filmed the army tanks, the burning vehicles, and the crowds of people as I was driving through the streets with Cosmos, and although I took precautions and filmed from under cover, I was risking my life to do so.

I once saw a car burning, with flames reaching ten metres into the sky. It caused no major disruption, and cars swerved expertly around it without slowing down. I had seen sights like this too many times before to care much about it. It was an established practice to show solidarity with the demonstrators and to be safe from being attacked on the road, by sticking a green branch through the car window. Knowing there would be unrest, Cosmos had put half a tree on the roof of our car. Cosmos took no chances, and so that's how we often travelled.

The Police

When petrol was available, accidents were the norm. I spent long hours on the road with Cosmos, commuting to work. Inevitably, we witnessed dozens of near misses and minor accidents, and found them quite entertaining, as they broke the monotony of the drive. We watched delightedly, as drivers involved in a small collision rushed out of their vehicles in a combative mood. Belligerently, they attempted to resolve the issue between themselves by blaming each other, in a screaming match of obscenities. That only drastically escalated matters and before long, the drivers would smack and whack each other.

The exciting situation always attracted an enthusiastic crowd of curious onlookers, who watched the growing hostilities between the different stakeholders with spellbound fascination. They loudly encouraged the combatants, if they perceived a lack of commitment on their part, and boosted their morale by offering theoretical defensive/offensive strategies, just to keep them in an antagonistic spirit for a while longer.

We were once stuck right in front of an accident that had predictably progressed into the fighting stage. The two drivers were unconvincingly tearing at each other's clothes. They were enthusiastically encouraged to commence at least slapping each other by the anticipating crowd. Suddenly, a lone police officer was spotted by a few spectators. He was dragged out from the growing crowd, much against his will, and forcibly pushed into the battleground by four sturdy Nigerians.

The crowd of captivated onlookers gasped with ecstasy. It was exceedingly rare for the police to get involved in accidents. There was nothing they could do anyway, as they were under-resourced, understaffed, corrupted, tired, and honestly, not interested. There was a sudden hush, and an expectant silence fell as everyone waited for the law to speak.

The police officer stood there for a while, surmising his chances of running away while there was still time, with his life and honour intact. Sensing his moral dilemma, the crowd began to form a tighter ring around the scene. Seeing he had to get involved in one way or another, the hapless police officer began the tortuous investigation process.

'*Na, who be the owner of dis car?*' he asked with authority, pointing to what looked like the obvious victim of the two, as his rear was smashed.

'*Na me!*' answered the aggrieved owner, obviously relieved that justice was perhaps miraculously on his side.

'*Open de boot!*' ordered the police officer theatrically. The crowd looked on in captivated silence.

'*De boot, why should I open de boot? Na, you listen to me offica, I just had an assident and dis animal almost killed me!*' wailed the owner, pointing an accusing finger at the driver of the other vehicle, who stood nearby in prudent silence.

'*Open dat boot I said, or I will arrest you!*' bellowed the now incensed police officer.

Clearly, some of the aggressive energy of the crowd seemed to have possessed him now. The woeful driver of vehicle number one opened his boot.

'*Na, where be de extinguisha?*' asked the police officer.

'*De extinguisha?*' said the astonished driver.

'*Na the extinguisha I ask! You be deaf?! Show me your extin-guisha! And hurry up! I don't have time to stand here all day!*'

As most cars in Nigeria were old relics dumped into Africa by Western countries, the extinguisher was a bit of a luxury item to ask for. The crowd gasped in delighted horror. Most did not even know what an extinguisher was.

The anguished driver began a futile search for an extin-guisher in his boot, throwing a profusion of items onto the ground in his zeal. Suddenly, much to his astonishment, he found one. It was all rusted and visibly way past its expiry date, but still, it was undoubtedly an extinguisher. He waved it triumphantly in the air for everyone to see. The crowd hooted with glee and clapped their hands. They were on his side now.

If the police officer was surprised, he did not show it. He knew he had to regain ground quickly before the mob turned on him.

'*Na, where be your spare tyra?*' he hissed threateningly, once the crowd quietened down.

'*Na my spare tyra...?*' said the dumbfounded driver.

It was clear as day to everyone that the boot had no spare tyre since he had just emptied it completely while searching for the extinguisher. However, the driver refused to be outdone by such a small irrelevant technicality. Showing the immense quick-wittedness of all street-savvy Nigerians, without a second's hesitation he turned to the unsuspecting congregation.

'*Na, who took my spare tyra?! Who be de one?!*' he bellowed, taking a threatening step forward.

The rabble gasped in ecstatic terror and took a few steps back, astounded by this reversal of events. From innocent bystanders on a scene of an accident, they had all suddenly become opportunistic criminals and suspects at a robbery scene. The subdued assemblage instantly lost interest in the car crash and everyone walked away, perfectly satisfied with their lot.

The police officer also moved away with dignity, satisfied with the fortuitous outcome. He had lost nothing of his authority nor dignity. The fact that he had not addressed the actual cause of the accident, was of no consequence. The owners of the vehicles evaporated into thin air, happy with having escaped with so little collateral damage.

NEPA, FIFA and the Secret Police

Everyone in Nigeria relied on generators to keep their households functioning. Generator sales were always a profitable venture in Nigeria, although, as with everything in the country, it was also cloaked with concealed perils as Jonas, Harry's director, was to discover.

It was anybody's guess as to how and why Nigeria won the hosting of the 1999 FIFA U-20 World Cup. For a country notoriously plagued with perpetual petrol shortages, unreliable and long-term electricity outages, inoperable phone lines, "dependable" traffic jams, and no infrastructure to speak of, it was undoubtedly a decision strongly influenced by corruption. Nigeria, thus far, had never been a tourist destination for the alert globe trotter, and undoubtedly, the government thought it needed a good publicity stunt to boost global exposure. What could be better than an international football championship, watched by millions of viewers worldwide?

Be it what it may, expats and Nigerian citizens alike were all delighted when, upon receiving news that FIFA was coming to town, NEPA released a one-and-only statement in their long and illustriously unsuccessful career. They solemnly announced that during the entirety of FIFA's duration, which would last two weeks, NEPA would not interrupt power day or night, and Lagos would enjoy a continuous power supply so that '*Nigerians will be able to enjoy all the football matches as they happen live on their TV screens.*'

The Nigerians were delighted. Being a soccer-loving nation, the FIFA event, and the unprecedented NEPA announcement, went straight to their hearts and minds. Exhilarated, they rushed in droves to purchase television sets, which till then, they considered totally obsolete due to the national rampant power outages. When FIFA started, they were ready to watch the exciting matches on their newly purchased and sparkling TV screens.

All went well, until the fateful Saudi Arabia v Mexico late-night match, played at the Liberty Stadium in the nearby Ibadan. A Mexican player had just collapsed in a heap due to a leg injury. The medical stretcher team were seen advancing at full speed towards the pained player, who was contorting in pain on the field when suddenly our TV screens went black. It looked like someone in the NEPA headquarters in Ibadan had missed the memo about *uninterrupted* power during FIFA and decided to switch off electricity during the international live coverage of the match.

The world spent the next twenty minutes looking at their dark screens while listening to the frantic Western commentator, who was trying to understand live what could well be the cause of the blackout. Finally, we saw the football field again, once more illuminated.

Like in a paused Netflix movie, we saw the stretcher team — they had frozen where the darkness hit them. When the lights came back on, they picked up their empty stretcher and ran with renewed vigour to the aggrieved player, who was still contorting on the ground. Upon reaching him, the medical team plucked him vigorously off the field. In the fervour of trying to make up for lost time, the team lifted the stretcher unevenly, overturned it and promptly discharged the distressed player headfirst back onto the ground, in front of a horrified global audience watching the unfolding situation live.

The unfortunate Mexican player stopped nursing his painful leg and clutched his head instead. As the camera action slowly zoomed in on him, he went back to holding his lacerated foot, then he went back to holding his aching head. He went back and forth in the same manner until the medical team, after a quick consultation, unceremoniously picked him up again, and carried him away for treatment.

The match went on after that, unhindered by power shortages. We never found out what happened to the injured player. We did however manage to gather a bit of information about the electricity and what happened behind the scenes that day.

The second the outage occurred, a special Nigerian military commando team, reinforced by a Special Secret Police Force — all armed to their teeth — were immediately dispatched to find the culprit of the embarrassing blackout. He was easily found. Within minutes, the director of NEPA in Ibadan was transported from the warmth of his sitting room, where he was found in front of the incriminating black TV screen, to a cold prison cell. No questions were asked from either party. The poor man was not to blame. It quickly transpired that the power for the match was not supplied by NEPA but by generators, a highly judicious decision made by some pessimistic FIFA organiser, who could only be applauded for their foresight. The generators were, in turn, supplied by Harry's boss, Jonas, who had just opened a new generator business on the side, with big profits from FIFA in mind.

He received an infuriated phone call from the Secret Service Police from Ibadan when they eventually thought to start asking questions rather than arresting people. Jonas nervously promised he would fix the problem. He called his team in Ibadan and told them to immediately amend the situation, or else they would all rot in jail forever, him included. Every second of delay increased the gravity of the matter.

The circumstances proved to be a bit more complicated once it transpired that Jonas and his generators were not to blame for the calamitous blackout either. His team of terrified workers traced the problem not to the generators, which were in perfect order, but to a burnt fuse that operated all the stadium lights. They fixed the problem, and the situation was immediately resolved. As soon as they had finished, Jonas' team were scooped up by the Secret Police team, who had been standing behind them with guns to their heads. Shortly afterwards, they joined the hapless NEPA director in his dirty prison cell.

It took lots of patient diplomatic explanations before everyone was released from prison after a few days — with a stern warning. Everyone involved thanked their lucky stars that it ended up so well. Jonas continued his lucrative generator business unperturbed.

Spain won the 1999 FIFA World Youth Championship, Japan was the runner-up, and the third place was secured by Mali.

ARMED ROBBERS AND
THE MARKET

'Jesus Christ Cosmos, stop the car...'

In 2019, the US Department of State Travel Advisory rated Nigeria at Level 3, indicating travellers should reconsider travel to the country due to crime, terrorism, civil unrest, kidnapping and piracy.

When I first arrived in Nigeria with my parents in 1980, armed robbery — which was destined to become a widely spread national phenomenon in the 21st Century — was in its infancy. The pioneer of armed robbers, leading the way in ruthless killings and cold-blooded murders, was — at least for the robbers themselves — the celebrated and awe-inspiring 'Doctor' Ishola Oyenusi. He reigned supreme until September 1971, when after several spectacular getaways from the army and police, he was finally caught and arrested.

His death by police execution was witnessed by 30,000 Nigerians, who all came to see how the Doctor would miraculously survive the ordeal. He famously claimed that he drank magic juju potions daily, which made him indestructible or invisible at will, a statement that the superstitious nation believed down to the very last second. If the 30,000-strong crowd came to witness his magic invincibility or invisibility, they were all crudely disappointed, as presumably, was the magician himself. The bullets very visibly penetrated his mortal body and killed him instantly in full view of a shocked audience.

The 1980s saw the rise of another super-armed robber, Lawrence Anini, hailing from Edo State, and born a hundred kilometres from Auchi — where we lived at the very time of his criminal activity. Anini operated ruthlessly, alternating his crime between car snatching, bus attacks, bank robberies and acts of terror. His gang was most likely responsible for the car robberies on the stretch of the Benin City — Auchi highway, which we first travelled on, back in 1980.

When I went back to Nigeria in 1993, armed robbery had impregnated the Lagosian lifestyle. Dozens of gangs operated ruthlessly on the streets in well-organised groups, armed with the latest guns and bulletproof cars. They had links with the police and the army, while government agencies shared their intel for a part of the crime profits. The armed robbers were perpetually drugged, drunk or both, and were dangerous and unpredictable. Met with the slightest resistance, they shot to kill without hesitation.

Such an armed gang also attacked the factory where Harry was working. They suddenly appeared, Ninja-like, nimbly jumping over the three-metre-high perimeter wall via an over-hanging tree. They were easily recognisable by their interesting attire, compromising an arsenal of weapons worn as personal body coats. They met no resistance as they quickly made their way straight to the main building, furiously shooting into the air to announce their unscheduled arrival. The factory floor emptied of all people within seconds.

The white collars working in the head office were in a bit of a quandary. Their only escape route was the very path the armed robbers were in the process of using. The fortunate few who fit under desks, piled on top of each other in milliseconds, all sharing the limited sanctuary space without the slightest protest. The remaining few hid their heads under chairs, limbs protruding at different angles.

The company's main secretary, a voluminous lady by the name of Bisi, headed straight to the tiny staff toilet cubicle adjacent to her office. So did a tiny man, the company's accountant. Unfortunate timing meant the terrorised man scrambled onto the safety of the toilet seat seconds before Bisi sat on top of him in agonised panic. The duo spent a good twenty minutes in this intimate position, the man in convulsions of angst trying not to suffocate under the unexpected weight crushing him down, and poor terrified Bisi shaking uncontrollably atop the unfortunate man.

Meanwhile, Tom heard the shots and took it upon himself to protect the company's money with his own life. In an astounding manoeuvre, reminiscent of the best Jackie Chan movie, he lunged out of his own office, pushed everyone out of the way, somersaulted over fallen chairs and cowering people, barged headfirst into his director's office where the safe was, and swiftly barricaded the door with a heavy set of drawers.

Bruce the director was watching his every move, dumbfounded. When seconds later the armed robbers arrived in front of the director's door, they stopped and politely tried to open it. Much to their collective surprise, they could not. On the other side, in frantic and panicked whispers, Bruce the director had talked sense into the supercharged and heroic Tom. He clarified to him that the company was fully insured and that he did not care about the money in the safe, but he did care about his life, dearly. He then curtly instructed Tom to open the door so that the robbers could help themselves to whatever they wished from the safe, which he had courteously unlocked when he heard the first gunshots. He also put the coffee machine on, as an extra gesture of goodwill, was ready to wave them a cheery goodbye and extend his dignified benevolence by bequeathing them his car as a speedy bonus getaway if they so wished.

As crestfallen Tom was trying to open the door from his side, the armed robbers, after a hushed emergency consultation between themselves, tried once more to open it from the other side. Somehow, neither side could unlock the door. By then, infuriated, the robbers shot at the handle, jamming it even further. Tom and Bruce were frantically trying to pull it open, but still, the door would not budge.

'*Open de door!*' shouted the infuriated armed robbers, kicking it furiously. They were not used to the slightest resistance in the course of their work schedule, and this hold-up was clearly confusing them. They were also drugged and in no patient mood.

'One moment, one moment, we are trying!' answered the flustered Bruce, sweat pouring down his agonised face, as he desperately tugged at the jammed handle.

The frustrated robbers took stock of their situation and retreated to gain better momentum to force the door open. This is when they noticed a motionless, pint-sized man, who all this time had been courteously sitting in a chair in the waiting room, clutching a bag to his chest. Everyone else was protruding from under chairs. The sight of the man atop his chair aroused the gang's curiosity. They approached him slowly.

'*Open am!*' one of them instructed, touching the man's bag with the butt of his shotgun for extra clarity.

The man did. He was a prosperous regular customer who had gone to buy his usual few truckloads of mattresses from the company. The bag was full of money for the purchase, amounting to about twenty thousand dollars. Without any superfluous words, the money sack exchanged hands. The armed robbers left, leaving the mesmerised customer still sitting motionless on the waiting room chair. The armed robbery was over. The man was fully refunded for his generous donation to the thieves by a relieved Bruce, when an hour later, the door was unscrewed from its hinges, and he and Tom finally managed to get out.

Another favourite pastime of the armed robbers was car snatching. They unscrupulously attacked even armed convoys, often in bright daylight. Their preferred time of the day, however, was at night-time, when they could easily ambush under the cover of darkness. It was becoming increasingly risky to be driving on the streets after dark. With time, when the situation got out of hand, Harry thought that it would be safer to purchase a four-wheel drive. The company agreed to buy one for us, strictly for security reasons. We felt much safer in it, if only because of its considerable height, which meant we could see a long distance ahead of us.

Fred, a friend of ours working for the same company, looked at our newly acquired four-wheel drive with envy for two years before the company finally relented and bought him one too. By then, the armed robbers had come to the unanimous decision that they also had a strong preference for newly purchased four-wheel drives, and began a relentless campaign of carjackings.

With time, as the situation deteriorated even further, Harry and I chose to drive our old, rusted KIA sedan, with the reassuring knowledge that we were much safer in it. Fred had no such inhibitions and flashed about in his brand-new 4WD which he acquired just before Christmas. A week into his proud ownership, on Christmas Eve, Fred was quite illogically on his way to the NEPA headquarters at night. Apparently, all his wires at home had spectacularly burnt in one mighty explosion, and as a result, he had no electricity. Luck would have it that his generator was also out of order.

What he was trying to achieve at that time of night at the NEPA headquarters, a place that was notoriously inefficient even during working hours, we were never to find out. A case of temporary insanity would be my closest guess. We all knew that the Christmas period compounded the danger of being out at night tenfold, as the bandits indulgently gifted themselves free 4WDs, meticulously handpicked from the few passing cars on the road.

Fred was spotted by the prowling carjackers very shortly after leaving his home. We later found out that they had just attacked a hired police escort convoy, returning from the airport with a rich lady. They had killed two policemen from the escort but could not get to the rich lady who was in the bulletproof car herself. They stole one car from the convoy, and still highly exhilarated by their adventures, spotted the insane Fred in his sparkling new 4WD, on his way to the NEPA headquarters. They gave him a spirited chase, honking and shooting in the air, signalling him to stop or else. Fred stopped immediately.

The soberest of the drunk and drugged robbers opened Fred's door violently, threw him unceremoniously onto the ground, and jumped into his freshly vacated seat, ready for a spectacular getaway. He turned the key in the ignition. The dead 'click' resonated like a bomb in Fred's dazed brain, which was processing events in excruciatingly slow motion while his life flashed before his eyes. The other robbers stopped gulping celebratory Red Johnny Walkers from their bottles, and threw their offended friend a few extra guns so that he could terminate the matter by killing Fred immediately, his ego intact.

'Na, you goh start de engine now now, or I go kill you! Start am!' roared the outraged robber, grabbing the comatose Fred still lying face flat in the dirt, and shoving him back onto the car seat next to him. His bloodshot eyes were twitching and his whole body was jittering uncontrollably. He held the butt of his semi-automatic weapon firmly poked into Fred's ribs, his fidgety fingers on the trigger, ready to shoot.

'Start am!' he bellowed louder into Fred's face, enveloping him in a cloud of alcoholic vapour. Fred woke up from his

stupefied daze and hastily released the hidden anti-burglar safety switch. The car ignited. Fred was projected out of his car for the second time, while the robbers drove off in a cloud of smoke from the revving engine. A motorcycle driver, who witnessed the crime from a safe distance under the cover of darkness, offered Fred a drive to the police station for a very elevated fee. Fred gratefully accepted the ride.

One day, Harry and I were driving Tom to the airport for one of his overseas trips. The political situation was at its worst, the streets were peppered with police, and army checkpoints appeared around every corner. We had carefully debated which driver to take. Expats and rich Nigerians dreaded the airport road, knowing they had an 80 per cent chance of being attacked. If it did not happen as they were flying out, chances were they would not escape as they came back into the country. It was a Nigerian roulette of sorts.

We decided to take Cosmos. By then Cosmos and I had acquired the reputation as an adventurous duo, strongly bordering on madness in the eyes of our less intrepid friends, as we often went to places no one else dared to go. Julius, on the other hand, was a posh Lagosian driver whose haughty attitude often got him into unnecessary trouble. One time at a police checkpoint, he refused to wind his window down to avoid offering a small bribe. The police officer in charge calmly opened his door and extracted Julius from behind the steering wheel, where he was obstinately lodged. The officer then proceeded to meticulously box the driver's nose and ears. Then he smashed his sunglasses, helped himself to Julius' wallet, pocketed the contents, and finally, to complete the ceremony, slowly tore Julius' impeccable white shirt at the collar. When the police officer had completed the ritual to his obvious satisfaction, Julius sat back behind the wheel, bloodied, bruised, dishevelled, and looking positively less cool without his chic sunnies. Without a word, he drove Tom to his destination. We all knew Julius would put us at risk in a hairy situation.

That day, Tom, Harry and I were nervously approaching the airport with Cosmos behind the wheel. We had been stopped several times already and had spent most of our bribe money. Tom was getting understandably edgy, as he was carrying a big sum of cash — like everyone leaving the country. People got killed for much less than that on the road we were on. In front of us, we saw another police checkpoint with scary-looking police officers gesturing for us to stop with their guns. They wore thick gold chains, and expensive watches and their gold-rimmed sunnies sparkled in the sunlight.

It did not look right to me; these could be the renowned armed robbers who dressed as police officers to trick people into stopping, before appropriating everything from them, cars included.

'Go Cosmos, go. *Don't stop!*' I instructed from the back seat, taking quick stock of the situation.

'*Yes madam,*' said Cosmos, clenching the wheel and putting his foot on the gas.

'*Stop Cosmos, stop!*' cried Harry in a panic. He was sitting next to me and was completely taken aback by my decision.

'*It's ok sa, we goh pass!*' said Cosmos calmly, not slowing down.

'Jesus Christ, stop the car Cosmos...' that was Tom, ashen-faced, rasping from the front seat where he had a full view of the looming police checkpoint, approaching at an alarmingly fast pace.

'Go, Cosmos. Go!' I repeated urgently. Cosmos stepped on the gas.

'Arghhhhhhhhhh...' was all I heard from Tom in the front seat.

We zoomed past the checkpoint at high velocity, not slowing down once. I saw the shocked faces of the supposed policemen as they briefly appeared by my window. We heard shots, but by then we were out of range and had skidded around a corner.

Cosmos and I laughed deliriously at our lucky escape. Harry and Tom were seething with rage and both equally aphonic with shock. We arrived safely at the airport, but Tom never asked for Cosmos' services again. He also informed Harry in all earnestness that 'Magdalena is totally crazy.' Harry readily agreed.

Lekki Market

By expatriate standards, I did things out of the norm. My treasured hangout place was the Lekki Market. Expatriates rarely ventured to that remote location, far away from Lagos on a dangerously empty stretch of road — a perfect location for an ambush. The market itself was a joyous ramshackle place, haphazardly filled with wooden stalls, craftily laden with colourful farm produce. Right next door to it was the African Art market, my absolute favourite place in the whole of Lagos.

'Angelinaaaaaaaaa!', 'Mandelinaaaaaaa!' came the chorus from the friendly Nigerian ladies selling vegetables, as news passed from one stand to another that I had arrived. I had become a well-known and liked presence in those parts due

to my regular weekly visits. How the lovely women found out my name and morphed it into those two versions, I never found out.

'*How are you my sista? Long time no see, welcome, welcome!*' they beamed at me with pleased smiles on their sweaty faces.

'I'm fine, I'm fine! You look well today *my sista,* that yellow colour looks good on you!'

'*Na, so! Na, so my sista!*' How is your health?'

'I'm fine, *my sista!* How is yours and how is your baby?'

'*My baby dey fine, but he dey catch cold from the rain last week. It be too cold, too cold na so, my sista...*'

By then I was already caught in a friendly bear embrace by another lady from the neighbouring stand. We politely exchanged the necessary greetings, and inquiries into the health of various family members far removed, their sicknesses, the weather, and the debilitating lack of fuel. I passed on to the other ladies, and they all greeted me warmly, inviting me to their stalls and trying to lead me away from their competitive neighbours. I always made sure to buy a little from everyone to avoid any bad feelings.

The fruits, vegetables, roots, and greens were all tastefully displayed in multicoloured heaps arranged in skilfully woven grass baskets. My lady friends liked to throw a bit of everything into my bags, pleasurably dismissing my vehement, 'Oh no, I do not need cassava, I don't eat cassava...,' 'I still have onions from last time, I will not be needing any today...,' 'I really cannot buy that bunch of bananas, it is way too big...' with happy laughter and pats on the shoulder. It is of little wonder that when I finally finished my greengrocer shopping, I was out of money.

Fresh produce prices varied from week to week and closely reflected the availability of petrol. Since petrol was mostly unavailable, the prices soared accordingly. Prices were also dependent on rainfall — too much increased the price, as did too little. There was never a "good time" for those farmers. To complicate matters, crops were also persistently damaged by numerous pests, inflating the prices even further. When I asked my lady friends what pests could cause such substantial damage as to warrant such exorbitant prices, the calamitous lineup included monkeys, giant snails, caterpillars, grasshoppers, bush rats, and pangolins.

Expenditure was also strongly affected by the outcomes of political elections — every result was bad for farm produce prices. I never knew how much I needed for my shopping and carried my money in a bulging big bag filled with fifty-naira notes held together by elastic bands. The Nigerian Naira had deteriorated drastically over the years — prices were in the thousands of naira, and money was carried in suitcase-sized bags by everyone.

Unfailingly, I always went to the adjacent African Art market to pay a visit to my other friends. They were a different group of sellers altogether and came from an interesting assortment of neighbouring African countries, including Cameroon, Côte d'Ivoire, Burkina Faso, Mali, Senegal, Benin, Ghana, Gabon, and even as far away as Sierra Leone. They each had a small cubicle space in the market where they alluringly displayed their wares. I knew each one of them by name, and many had become my friends.

I loved to walk for hours along the dark and narrow

alleyways, lined with stalls filled with baskets, wooden animal carvings, leather chests, batiks, stone carving, metal sculptures, African cloths, beads, bags, pearls, carved wooden furniture and paintings. Unavoidably, I always found something without which I could not part. I was by then a great admirer of African art.

'*Take it, take it, no trouble, madam. You go pay me next time,*' encouraged the friendly alhaji from Senegal. He saw I could not put down the string of giant pearls I had just spotted in his stall, decorated entirely with hundreds of strands of multi-coloured beads and semi-precious stones. I hesitated, knowing very well I could not leave without them, but acutely aware that I had used all my money at the vegetable market.

'But I don't know when I will come next,' I said, attempting to put the pearls away in a half-hearted attempt of parsimony.

The alhaji sprang into action and firmly put the pearls in my bag. He also threw in an exquisite and expensive necklace of giant African amber beads for good measure.

'*No problem, madam, we are friends, I wait. No problem. No hurry. When you come in few weeks you go pay, Inchalla.*'

'*Inchalla*, when I come next week, I will pay you. Thank you.'

I then came across a beautifully carved wooden giraffe and the same conversation took place. Numerous reciprocal *Inchallas* later, I left the market with Cosmos lumbering close behind, barely visible from under the wares purchased solely on my good credit rating, and left in the hands of almighty *Inchalla*.

It was so refreshingly simple to invoke the will of God under such circumstances. I never defaulted on any payment and always paid up within a couple of weeks. If by chance I forgot to pay someone, after an interval of a few months they would very apologetically remind me, always with big smiles on their faces. How I preferred this system of payment to the western credit cards and hefty interest rates.

Chapter 13

EXPATRIATE LIFE

'Ah zo, Magdalena'

Living in the 12 million-strong ramshackle city of Lagos in the 90s was tough. Everyday realities included grid-locked traffic jams, reputed to be the worst in the world, extreme air and noise pollution and crumbling infrastructure. This was compounded by the lack of basic amenities such as electricity, water or phone lines. The overpopulated city consisted mostly of hundreds of dirty shanty towns, inhabited by the destitute Nigerian population.

There was indiscriminate violence at every level of society, rampant crime was the norm, social and political chaos was an everyday reality, and frightening lawlessness reigned supreme. This mobocracy may come as a surprise if one considers Nigeria to be the world's tenth most petroleum-rich country.

Oil exploration in Nigeria began as early as 1903, but tentative drilling in the wrong areas brought zero results. After the initial lack of success, the licence for exploration was obtained by D'Arcy, a British-Iranian oil company. They continued drilling in all the wrong places and returned their licence in 1923, after having found nothing. It took another thirty years of stubborn but visionary drilling in a variety of locations, resulting in a hefty bill of over 6 million dollars, before in 1958, Shell BP finally struck black gold in immense commercial quantities at Oloibiri, in the Nigerian Delta. Following that absurdly massive treasure cove, drilling licences were obtained by Chevron, Mobil, Agip, Gulf Oil and Tenneco.

Since then, Nigeria, which until the 1950s, had relied heavily on agriculture as its main export, became Africa's richest nation. In 2000, the year I left Nigeria, oil and gas exports amounted to more than 98 per cent of export earnings and roughly 80 per cent of federal government revenue. Despite all these riches, the average Nigerian, including those living in the oil-rich Niger Delta region, have still never seen a cent of the profits come their way. The major shareholders of all oil revenue in Nigeria until today are solely top government officials.

Money from petrol is the main reason Lagos is Africa's most overpopulated and extremely dynamic economic centre. The bustling city is by default West Africa's business hub and houses the region's biggest and richest banks, ports, and markets. Multinational companies in Nigeria spread across a range of different platforms, ranging from oil and gas, telecommunications, health and wellness, consumables, banking, construction and so forth.

Lagos, despite its obvious challenges, provides enormous financial opportunities for foreigners. Although tourism is non-existent, multinational companies constantly lure more expats for several-year contracts, offering lucrative packages. Those brave enough to go to Lagos were gratified with inflated salaries reflecting the hard-to-ignore hardship ranking of the country. Their salary packages included paid housing and amenities, paid drivers and staff, long holidays with paid flights for whole families, education, health insurance and free club memberships. The expatriates in Lagos lived a privileged life, fortressed in their secure compounds at all times. They rarely left the premises.

Nigerians working for international companies considered themselves lucky. Unfortunately, the lure of a better life in a big city created a deep societal vacuum. People from all over Nigeria left their farming villages by the millions and converged into the big city in search of a better existence. Only a fraction of them secured a job, but millions more kept swarming from the villages in an endless human exodus.

The resulting chronic overpopulation, which Lagos has experienced for years, has created a city of homeless, jobless, uneducated, and often sick people, young and old. They're all living under extremely poor conditions in the shanty towns of Lagos, with no other prospects for the future than a life of extreme poverty. The unnatural demographical imbalance in the unforgiving African city has created a huge divide between the extraordinarily rich and the extremely poor — the expats and the locals.

We, the privileged minority of expats, lived in segregated bubbles of society. All in our confined mansions, within our artificial islands of security. We occupied our free time, which there was much of in the evenings and on weekends, as best we could. For the more adventurous, fun consisted of frequenting the few foreign restaurants scattered throughout Lagos in hazardous and often hard to get to places. Such trips were always fraught with extreme danger, as going for dinner at night in Lagos was never a clever idea for a multitude of reasons. If one miraculously survived the food on the menu with no ill effects on the digestive system, one may not have survived the drive back home, due to crime.

One night, Harry and I took leave of our senses and went out to dinner with Saul and his wife, Hanne. To spice things up a notch, we went without our drivers. We were driving back in a two-car-convoy, keeping closely together — which was the only sensible thing we did that night — when our friend's car behind us broke down. They were instantly surrounded by a large group of menacing 'area boys', who swiftly materialised from thin air.

'*Masta, no worry we go help you... We go change your tyra...*'

These were not the words Saul wanted to hear from the big, drugged, red-eyed man, reassuringly whispering to him through his open window. Saul and Hanne were instantly enveloped in a cloud of alcohol vapour. The man expertly positioned himself in a way that his body blocked all visibility on Saul's side, while another human form simultaneously obliterated the view from Hanne's side of the vehicle.

'We don't need your help, thank you very much my *broda*... My friend is coming back to help me. My tyre is fine.' Saul knew they were in big trouble and was trying to gain time.

He had seen that we had slowed down but were unable to turn around.

'*No worries, no worries, masta... We go help you well well.... We go change your tyra...*' amiably muttered the man, vigorously billowing a stream of foul-smelling loco weed into Saul's face, not in the least concerned by his vehement refusal of assistance.

Next, Saul and Hanne heard clanking and tapping while their car shook, rattled, and suddenly journeyed into a sudden upward incline. By the time we were able to turn around and go back, the army of invisible night bandits had already pilfered their rear tyres and evaporated back into the surrounding darkness. We left the broken car and took Saul and Hanne home, considering ourselves incredibly lucky to be alive and well. The next day when Saul returned to collect the car, all that was left was the metal frame. Everything else, including the car seats, had been unscrewed and carried away. Nothing ever went to waste in Nigeria. The nation could give precious recycling lessons to the whole world.

The more nervous expats were satisfied with the tantalising thrill of loitering at the few international hotel bars in the safe daylight hours. They paid exorbitant fees to have drinks in the hotel lounges, just for the perverse pleasure of enviously looking at Western people on short business trips. They were the "normal people," out of touch with our local realities and they were a sight we all considered very exotic.

For example, we found out much to our depraved joy, that the entire British Airways crew was forbidden to leave their hotel under any circumstances, except to travel to and from the airport — which they did in a specially chartered bus with armed security. Stepping out of the hotel in Lagos was considered too hazardous for the prudent British.

On a personal level, my expatriate life differed majorly. For me, Lagos was not an intimidating place, but a city bursting with cultural diversity, filled with entrancing opportunities, friendly people, and so many things to learn about and explore. The bubble life of the other expatriates was not a choice for me. I loved driving around with Cosmos who was always happy to show me the more interesting parts of Lagos.

I guess the main attraction for me on our city travels, was the exotically ingenious way the Lagosian street vendors made, displayed, and sold their wares. All Nigerians were creative by nature, in one way or another. The country's raw materials at the disposal of the poorer masses included wood, cane, clay, and colourful textiles. From these, the most intricate items were produced by the local people. The products were either sold on the side of busy roads or, more often than not, in more inaccessible places. My idea of fun was to find those in the most inaccessible places in Lagos.

This is how I discovered the picturesque Cane Market under the very busy Ojota link bridge in Maryland, Lagos. Baskets, chairs, tables, cabinets, and lounge sets were all made under the bridge from the cane wood lying in long bunches all along the length of the market. Everything could be made under that bridge on order. I ordered our first set of furniture from there, much to Harry's distaste. All expats' wives bought their furniture from expat-owned furniture shops.

'Why on earth did you have to buy our furniture from under

a bridge?' Harry said unhappily when I proudly told him of my exploits.

Not at all deterred by such criticism, I immersed myself in the interior decorating of our house for the first year of my stay in Nigeria. I quickly discovered on which side street the big clay Abuja pots were sold, which local market sold beautiful African patterned Bakuba cloths, and where to buy locally made textiles, woven placemats, and baskets. I made friends with the Nigerian ladies selling fresh fruits and vegetables, intricately displayed on colourful stalls along the shaded streets of Victoria Island. I bought all my culinary needs from them if I did not have time to go to Lekki Market.

There was one fruit that was elusive to buy in Lagos. I did not need it often, but it was the main ingredient of Tarte Tatin, which Harry loved. It was the humble apple.

'Cosmos, we need to get apples.'

'*Ok, madam. We goh look for a big go slow.*'

The incomprehensible fact was that the whole of Lagos did not sell apples, except for one circumstantial location. The only place to buy them was from the pedlar boys selling their products in the city's traffic jams. One had to go against all logic and good judgement and look for traffic jams to get stuck in to purchase the prized items. The tricky part was that not all the traffic jams had them. Tarte Tatin remained a very rare treat for Harry.

After I had exhausted all the possible interior decorating possibilities, I grew increasingly bored at home. Watching television was not even a reliable pastime, because we often had no electricity for days, or the generator had to rest, usually during the day. It was important to have a good sleep with the AC on during the night. I was able to borrow some books, and regularly bought TIME and National Geographic, which were also sold by pedlar boys in traffic jams. They were not always the latest edition but were my way of keeping in touch with the outside world. My only other source was CNN — when the tv occasionally worked at home.

My life changed drastically when a new and modern shopping complex opened called The Plaza. It sold the latest electronic products at good prices, had a disc borrowing facility with all the old movies which I loved, and what was unheard of until then in Lagos — it had a little café on the top level which sold drinks and cappuccinos. Yes, cappuccinos! It was as exotic to us all as consuming snow from the peak of the Kilimanjaro Mountains. The best we had at home till then was granulated Nescafe. No one even had a coffee machine. Some expatriates in Lagos had never had a cappuccino in their lives. From then on, all expatriates, Harry and I included, made weekly pilgrimages to The Plaza and spent hours in the electronics shop downstairs where we borrowed discs, bought tonnes of electronic equipment, and just simply killed time in a friendly environment — since most of our friends were doing the same thing at the same place. Then we caught up with other friends in the upstairs café and sipped cappuccinos served by two genuine Italian ladies. Our cultural life had suddenly flourished, and for a few hours, we felt like we were in Rome. Our lives were never the same after The Plaza opened. We had caught up with the rest of the world.

There was not much more one could do in Lagos, so not surprisingly, home visits were the most popular form of social life, especially for bored women accompanying their husbands to work.

Tradition had it that every Saturday, extravagant luncheons were the norm, as all the wives competed against each other with lavish culinary exploits. The established protocol for such events was to have at least thirty people at the occasion. Everyone wanted to be popular in our isolated society, so invitations flourished, and every Saturday we were all invited to a luncheon at a different person's house. Due to the frequency of these gatherings, our friend group learnt to function as a highly synchronised human herd. We all knew the luncheon drill.

1. Arrive at the venue.
2. Sip on a welcome drink.
3. When invited to do so eat lots of food.
4. When invited to do so eat lots of desserts.
5. Praise everything unreservedly.
6. Never ask the hostess for the recipe, even if you genuinely would like to have it. (No one shared recipes).
7. Drink the coffee served at the end. Refusals were not accepted even if you hated coffee. (You would be forced to drink the hot liquid anyway, otherwise, the ceremony could not proceed to its natural conclusion).
8. Say quick, relieved goodbyes to everyone with the last sip of the beverage.
9. Profusely thank the hosts for the lovely Saturday afternoon.
10. Run to the door in a mass exodus and leave.

The ladies took their Saturday occasions very seriously, as each gathering was astutely used as a political move for increased prominence in the tight expatriate society. The *table d'hôte* in the dining room was used as a centre stage for a giant buffet, where an astonishing smorgasbord of dishes were laid by the hostess, anxious cooks, and a long procession of nervous house girls. Massive silver platters laden with copious rice dishes overflowed with appetising chunks of fish, chicken, and meat. Vegetable bakes basked in a variety of fragrant sauces, while sumptuous lasagne dishes, flavoursome curries, luscious gravies, exotic salads, side dishes, olives, dips, and breads competed for space in a colourful profusion of food.

When the boastful display was finally fully laid out on the table, the flustered lady of the house invited the wives for a first look and first serve. It was an important part of the protocol to present the imperious ladies with the first view of the steaming feast. This was the point of reckoning, the time when the hostess was assessed for the realisation of her culinary performance, and the potential success or failure of her progress in the social hierarchy of high achievers. As the ladies gathered around the opulent display, jealous stares crisscrossed the table at lightning speeds, as the supercilious judges took in the perfect execution laid in front of them. Novelty dishes never seen before were immediately picked out by the assiduous wives, and a line would immediately form to taste the new *plat du jour.*

While serving themselves minuscule portions of each dish — one had to be mindful of one's waistline — the ladies mentally calculated the time it took to prepare, and the cost involved. They checked if all three protein groups were represented

— there were the obligatory fish bakes, beef ragouts and chicken delicacies. Extras like seafood and goat acquired bonus points. The hostess *du jour* was additionally assessed on the presentation of each *plat.* The ladies then moved away to peck at their plates, tight-lipped and steaming jealousy, already plotting retaliatory revenge luncheons. Their compliments as to the delicious food were always very restrained.

Then came the jovial men, who after a few cold beers were hungry for hot meat and were perfectly oblivious to the silent dramas unfolding amid their wives' frigid group. They served themselves generous amounts of everything and munched, crunched, slurped, and devoured their chow, enthusiastically going back for second and third servings. Unlike their wives, they complimented the fidgety hostess on the delicious food but had no idea what precisely they had eaten if pressed for details a few hours later back at home.

'So... what did you think of that new chicken dish Claudia made today?' a suspicious wife would ask of an unsuspecting husband, wanting to assess the damage inflicted by the hostess of the day on his meek mind.

'Hm... new chicken dish, what new dish? Was there a new dish?' the bloated husband would ask, burping pleasantly, and already half asleep in front of the TV.

In between dishes being served, husbands talked of work. There was always something happening in their factories, some crisis to be averted, some problem to be resolved, news to be shared, and jokes exchanged. Their wives — all of whom except for me and Margo did not work — spent the entirety of the social visits talking about the shortcomings of their house boys, house girls, nannies, drivers, and gardeners. They hired and fired their staff at an astounding tempo and would never be satisfied with any. Sometimes they had tolerable reasons too.

'Would you believe it, I found out that my nanny works outside!' whispered Sofia dramatically during one such gathering.

All the ladies gasped in horror. Finally, something interesting to break the oppressing boredom!

'Lately, we have been noticing that she looks dreadfully tired, falls asleep all the time, and has become careless with the children. So, when we confronted her a week ago, she immediately admitted that she works nights!' continued Sofia bright-cheeked and breathless with the enormity of the news she delivered.

'I see nothing wrong with that. She probably needs the extra cash!' I said crossly. I always sided with the local staff when conversations turned against them.

'You don't understand... she works at night!' hissed Sofia a bit louder, scandalised by my comment.

'Well, when else do you want her to work?' I asked, surprised. 'During the day she works here with your children until they go to sleep at eight. She can only work at night, the poor girl. You are lucky to have her as your nanny, she seems extremely hard-working. She is probably saving for her wedding,' I continued, ignoring the horror-stricken faces of all the ladies looking at me. There was a scandalised round of throat-clearing as the ladies stared at me in horrified silence. No one spoke for a while.

'I think Sofia means that the girl works... at night... as a... as a...a... prostitute so to speak, my dear...' Fran whispered, trying to pacify Sofia who was now being consoled in a tight circle of shushing and fussing ladies, all turning their heads back at me. A house girl was urgently dispatched to the kitchen to fetch a glass of water for the perturbed lady.

'Oh... I see.... I didn't realise, of course... at night. That does make sense now, how silly of me...' I said, slightly confounded by my stupidity. I found solace in my beer which I drank thirstily under the sober stares of the angered ladies.

'So how long has she been...um, working at night for...if I may ask?' I ventured again, genuine interest taking over good manners, once the beer had fortified me sufficiently to render me insensible to my surroundings.

'That is the problem...' sniffed Sofia into her box of tissues, charitably offered by the solicitous ladies. 'She said that this has been going on for a year now, and God only knows what she did before she became our nanny! So of course, we had her tested, and she is HIV positive!' continued Sofia, pale with horror and pausing for dramatic effect between each new blood-curdling revelation.

Seeing the conversation was taking an unpleasant turn, I decided to drift off to the men's group, who after having covered all the work problems, world politics, and jokes, were discussing their driver's attributes. Jonas was speaking, looking decidedly inconsolable.

'So, I bought this beautiful tortoise on the beach the other day. It was the most amazing thing I had ever seen. I took it home and let it loose in the garden, telling the house staff not to touch it, that it was my pet. I even had a flag attached to a long stick on top of its shell, so that I knew where to find it in the garden. After a few days, the tortoise disappeared and no one knew where it went. Then the other day, as we were driving to work, my driver tells me that a few days ago he found a tortoise in my garden.' Jonas interrupted his story to fortify himself with a drink.

'And you know what the driver said? Do you know what he said?' asked Jonas of his attentive audience. No one knew what the driver said.

'He said: '*So I catch am, cook am, make very good tortoise soup and chop am!*' That is what he said! And he smacked his lips in happy memory of the delicious soup he cooked with my tortoise! My driver ate *my pet!*'

Jonas finished his tragic tale with a bereaved nod in memory of his deceased pet chelonian. The men tried awfully hard not to laugh at this tale, and all ducked inside their beer glasses for a concealed giggle and a refreshing sip.

'Listen to this. I saw my driver washing my new car the other day, so I told him to wash it on the inside too,' Patrick said, patting Jonas on the back in solidarity. 'So, he did. He opened the doors and hosed the inside! I do not know what to do now, the car is soaking wet, and it's brand new...'

'Well, listen to this,' joined in Robert, 'I met Stuart on my way to Lagos, and as we were both going in the same direction, we stopped and I hopped into Stuart's car and told my driver to follow me. After a few minutes, Stuart, who looked in the rear mirror says 'Your driver is following us,' I said, 'Yeah I know, I told him to follow us,' then Stuart tells me, 'Yeah, but he is following us on foot, running!'

The men were getting merrier with each story, with rapturous laughter following each anecdote. I am sure the staff they were talking about shared their own stories of the crazy *oyinbos* they worked for with their friends and families. After all, who attaches a red flag to a wild food source, likes their car soaking wet, and tells their drivers to run behind the car for no reason? In the clash of cultures we were living in, it was all a matter of perspective.

Once most of the food was gone, the table would be cleared and there followed a strict protocol of good manners, where enough time had to elapse before etiquette allowed desserts to be served. The time between meal and dessert was indeed a complicated algorithm of decorum. The hostess had to be careful not to serve sweets too soon after the main dishes, otherwise, she would be accused of the worst crime in good manners — the base intention of wanting to get rid of everyone too soon.

I never liked these gatherings, as they took a big chunk of time on my Saturdays. During the week I worked, so I did not have to kill boredom as the other ladies. Margo, my good German friend, shared my sentiments. I was always sure to be entertained by her during such events, as she would vent her views with a typically German wrath. Margo knew how to choose a good moment, patiently waiting until the lull of conversation died down, usually during coffee. One Saturday, she elbowed me in the ribs and whispered in my ear with her hearty German roar.

'*Ah zo Magdalena! I tell you; we have to go to ze beach togezer zis weekend because I have ziz beautiful...*' She paused dramatically, and theatrically inhaled her cigarette while making sure everyone was listening. Everyone always did when she spoke. Margo had a strong voice.

'... *I have ziz beautiful new swimming suit which I cannot wait to wear... It is vehy black and it is open till here...*' she pointed triumphantly to her navel, exhaled her cigarette to the ceiling and surveyed the gawking assembly from behind the mysterious veil of white smoke.

All the ladies, and most of the men, gasped in unison, visualising the sixty-five-year-old statuesque German blonde goddess, sporting a black swimming suit with a revealing opening reaching down to her navel.

'Oh, definitely Margo, we have to go this weekend, I can't wait to see it!' I concurred, relishing the pulverising effect the statement had created on the assembled strait-laced crowd.

Another time, Margo conspiratorially leaned over to me, and in an ear-piercing vociferous whisper commented about her immediate female neighbour, sitting a mere few inches away.

'*Ah zo, Magdalena, can you see how zat Fausi's vife is dhessed, she is so fat she should not vear sings like zis!...Can't ze woman see herself in ze mirror?!*' she added scandalised, right in front of the mortified subject of her rant.

At another gathering, she spied another victim of her Teutonic wrath.

'*Where on earth does she sink she is, zat voman over zere?!*' pointing an accusing finger at a startled lady. '*At a gahden pahty?!... Magdalena, ah zo, look at her hohible yellow dhess!... It is totally inapphophiate!*'

Everyone stood assembled for a dignified collective mass exodus after another Saturday luncheon, when Margo, who was always first in the exit line, remarked to me in thundering mournful undertones, carried in strong wavelengths to all the assembled guests.

'I don't know vot I'm doing here... It's all ze time ze same people and ze same food! I am neveh coming again, it is a total vaste of my time! I have ozeh sings to do on Saturdays, ah zo Magdalena?!' she winked at me, waiting for my indisputable support.

In polite whispers, I tried to acquiesce as discretely as I could, but Margo, a bit hard on hearing, demanded loud approval with cacophonous throat clearings and rib punches. Not surprisingly, Margo and I were firm bosom buddies despite our big age difference, and we were regarded by the other ladies of the group with great suspicion and a healthy dose of hatred.

Chapter 14

THE PERFECT HOSTESS

'Il est venu le temps des cathédrales...'

Harry and I usually entertained a different group of people due to the nature of Harry's job. His friends and colleagues from Europe and South Africa were always visiting on short business trips throughout the year. They stayed with us at the house because it was safer and easier. By doing so, they could commute with Harry throughout Lagos and use our drivers at will, which was a much safer option than using the disreputable local taxis and staying in the distant Sheraton hotel.

One such colleague became a very dear friend of ours and went by the name of Jack Fletcher. He was the image of a perfectly distinguished English gentleman as if teleported straight from the pages of a Jane Austen novel. Jack was in his late seventies when I first met him, as energetic and charming as ever. He was a gem, and I always looked forward to his visits.

One evening, during an international conference organised by Harry, I had more drinking partners than I bargained for. After a hot and strenuous day in Lagos, all the men attending the event somehow managed to converge for refreshments. Understandably, they all needed cold beers, and the perfect place for that seemed to be our house. The idea was inspired by Harry's loosely thrown 'Come over for drinks at my house before dinner,' to everyone that day. They all did.

Taken slightly by surprise by the first arrivals, but playing the perfect hostess, I served the beers cold straight from the fridge. After ten beers I had run out, but the men kept coming in a steady stream. Before long, I was surrounded by thirty very thirsty men. Throwing all etiquette into the wind, I began serving warm beer straight from the emergency storeroom crate. For those lucky few who were served warm beer first, I threw in a few ice cubes, and the men were extremely grateful for that special touch.

I ran out of ice after only five serves. The rest of the men drank their beer warm, but none complained. The impromptu gathering quickly turned into a party, and I had to send Viki to buy beer from street vendors, as demand was quickly exceeding supply.

Jack Fletcher was amongst the happy crowd of drinking men. He had brought a guest with him, Paul, a pilot from British Airways, who had ignored all rules banning him from leaving his hotel quarantine for security reasons. Paul also happened to be Jack's son-in-law and the pilot of the British Airways plane which flew them both to Lagos. After a few beers, it transpired in the general brouhaha of conversations, that Paul had officially been declared insane by his British Airways colleagues when he switched his flight. Indeed, instead of going to South America, as per his log, he swapped it to Lagos instead, so that he could pilot his father-in-law's plane. A noble gesture that only the pilots landing in Nigeria would appreciate.

Flying planes to Lagos was the worst possible punishment, on any airline, and no pilot ever did so willingly. It was common knowledge to any incoming or outgoing crew that the Murtala Muhammed Airport rarely had functioning lights due to the constant power outages. This was even more concerning as all flights into and out of Lagos happened at night. Most of the time pilots had to resort to autopilot and rely on their night vision, memory, lots of luck and random judgement when landing. One such flight of a Swissair plane ended when the pilot, unable to see in the darkness, landed his plane safely but crashed through all the unlit lamps along the runaway, before eventually coming to a spectacular stop in the airport shrubbery, amid hysterically screaming and fainting passengers. It was a cause of common hilarity amongst the expats, that the airline was later sent the bill for the 'repair of the damaged airport lamps' by the assiduous Nigerian officials, who at some point later surveyed the crash-landing route. It was never established if the airline paid for the bill, however, it did cease to exist in 2002 due to financial problems. Perhaps too many crash landings in Lagos somewhat contributed to the airline's final demise.

As the evening advanced and the warm beer, nuts and chips ran out, the crowd began to disperse, and Harry took the last stragglers in his car to drop them off at Sheraton Hotel. Jack and Paul stayed as our special guests, as did a Belgian chap of substantial posture. I did not know why he stayed; he was a total stranger to me. All I knew was what Harry managed to whisper in my ear as he was parting with our guests.

'This guy is important. He is the highest-placed person at this conference. Be nice to him!' He also managed to whisper something in the big Belgian's ear too, I noticed. Presently, as the four of us were sitting in the eerie silence of the deserted living room, picturesquely filled with empty beer bottles standing perilously on every possible vertical structure, the Belgian spoke in deep guttural tones.

'So, I hear that you are an expert on plants, Magdalena!'

I was startled both by the fact that he knew my name, while I had no idea what his was and by his bewildering statement.

'Well, perhaps that's a bit of an overstatement... I mean, I like plants...'

The Belgian grandly interrupted my hesitant acquiescence, not listening at all.

'I have two hobbies, back in Belgium, Magdalena. I build miniature model steam trains and I cultivate plants. I have a garden with an acreage of three thousand metres.'

Remembering that I was meant to be nice to the gent, I remained silent, thinking this was not the opportune moment to fully disclose my botanical incompetence, nor my total lack of knowledge of the world of miniature trains. Thankfully, the Belgian needed no encouragement and launched himself into an emotional monologue.

'I have been collecting different kinds of grasses for the last ten years, and I have been able to obtain some exceedingly rare *pocaceae* specimens, some of which are related to grasses back from the Cretacenous period. Did you know there are more than 10,000 grass species in the world? I have recently been able to get a few rare specimens of *muhlerbergia* and I am now looking for *alopecurus geniculatus,* which is often confused with *phleum pratense*, but it flowers later in the year.'

I listened, my awe growing by the second. The only grass I knew was green and cows ate it. I also did not know that grasses had Latin names. Hell, I did not even know they had English names! Grass was grass, wasn' it? I had no idea grass collecting was a hobby.

The Belgian had stopped and was now obviously waiting for some ground-breaking botanical statement from my part. It suddenly dawned on me why the Belgian had stayed — he wanted to have a serious conversation with an insightful botanist. God only knew what Harry had whispered in his ear to impress him. I racked my slightly hazy brain in a desperate effort to remember what I knew about grass. With a sinking heart, I offered a wild guess.

'Oh yes, the *phleum*... um, indeed I've heard of it. Isn't it the *green* spiky grass?' I asked in what I hoped was a scientifically scholarly tone, emphasising my extensive knowledge on the topic by stressing the *green.* The Belgian looked at me for a moment unblinking.

'The *phleum pratense* is indeed *green* in summer, but it turns bright *red* in winter,' he eventually said and looked at me suspiciously. An uncomfortable silence ensued, and none of us found anything else to say about grass.

'So, what sort of music do you like?' the Belgian asked abruptly.

'Well, everything really,' I answered, taken aback. *Was I also meant to know about music?* I thought in panic.

'Do you know the musical 'Notre Dame de Paris?'

'Do *I know* Notre Dame the Paris? I practically listen to it day and night! I know all the songs by heart,' I enthused. It was the truth. The big Belgian man brightened up instantly.

'Would you have the disc here? Could we listen to it now?'

Relieved that I could do something to please him, I raced to the CD player and put the music on full blast, in the hopes of preventing any further conversation. At the first sounds of the opening act, the Belgian who was increasingly beady-eyed after the consumption of beers, blared in a resonant baritone, miraculously drowning the music from the loudspeakers.

'*Il est venu le temps des cathédrales*
Le monde est entré
Dans un nouveau millénaire
L'homme a voulu monter vers les étoiles
Ecrire son histoire
Dans le verre et dans la pierre...'

The vociferous crooning had the effect of startling both Paul and Jack, who till then were both entranced in the peaceful contemplation of the empty wall in front of them, lazy smiles on their enchanted faces. They had had a few bottles of beer as well. My cat suddenly appeared in front of us, ears pricked up in alarm, listening to the astonishing cacophony of sounds. The Belgian stopped blaring, mesmerised by the unexpected sight of a feline in such surroundings.

'I have a cat!' he stated matter of fact, clamouring above the noise of the music. Rudely disturbed in his joyful contemplation of the white wall, Jack stared at the Belgian. In the deafening music, he wrongly surmised that he was being addressed by the strange Belgian chap. His impeccable English manners taking over, he replied politely yelling over the music.

'No, I'm afraid I do not have cats at present! I used to have two cats! Siamese they were, like this one...' he added, waving his shaky finger at my cat, belatedly surprised at the apparition. The Belgian took offence.

'No, not Siamese! Russian they are, Russian! And I only have one, not two!' he roared angrily above Gringoire's flamboyant rendition of '*La Fête des Fous.*' Jack gave up on trying to be polite and resumed his peaceful contemplation of the wall. When Harry arrived sometime later, offering to take them all back to Sheraton in time for dinner, the three gentlemen hesitantly stood up, all a bit shaky on their legs.

'I do hope to have the pleasure of your company at the Sheraton,' slurred Paul, lustfully in my ear. 'I am not going with them all,' he waved his hand erratically at the other two gentlemen and Harry, whose house he obviously had forgotten he was in. 'But there is this lovely small Italian restaurant at the Sheraton, where we could perhaps have a *tête à tête* dinner later in the evening. What do you say...hm... Macarena?'

Chapter 15

AFRICAN HOUSES

'Where are the crocodiles?'

Every Sunday, the accepted expatriate custom was to go to Eleko Beach. Starting from nine in the morning, embassy workers, engineers, teachers, businessmen, rich oil executives, and most other expats began converging *en masse* onto the secluded palm-fringed beach, under the hopeful impression that strength in numbers would keep them safe on that customary journey. The road to Eleko beach could be quite dangerous. The beach itself was a thirty-kilometre drive on the outskirts of Lagos, past the busy centre, past the tumultuous markets, past the slums, past Lekki Market, and into the areas where the swamps and the bush began.

The monotony of the long road was interrupted only by scarce roadside market stands, typical of the African countryside. At regular intervals on the road, a woman, often carrying her baby wrapped in a colourful scarf and tied around her waist, sat next to a creative bush kitchen. She sold freshly roasted corn, giant edible snails, roasted bushmeat, or giant fat rats, artistically crucified in makeshift stick contraptions, barbequed and ready to eat. Small bunches of bananas, mangoes or little bags of peanuts complemented the makeshift stand, all produced from the little village farms invisibly nesting behind the cover of the surrounding bush.

So it was that every Sunday we arrived at our wooden huts, picturesquely concealed amidst the kilometres of palm trees gently swaying in the wind, offering welcome shelter from the hot sun. The palm leaves rustled and murmured reassuringly as we unpacked our loaded cars, ready for a day of blissful rest, food, and drink.

A few years after my arrival in Nigeria, we decided to build our hut, as we did not want to spend our weekends sharing with big family groups. We needed privacy and quiet for our weekend getaways as a young couple. By a surprising turn of events, we had recently become husband and wife, unbeknown to anyone else. Our marriage was by no means a romantic affair. Nor was there a romantic proposal on one knee by Harry, or an engagement or wedding ring involved. There was no white dress, no flowers, no bridesmaids, no priest, no marriage vows exchanged, no guests, no reception, and no honeymoon.

It was a marriage of necessity. My visitor's visa for Nigeria was about to expire and we were faced with a dilemma. To reapply for one, I had to leave the country for three months and come back. Financially, that was an expensive affair, and one we were reluctant to take. As we were deliberating what to do, a friend of Harry's whom we confided in, said jokingly.

'Well, you could always have a Muslim wedding. It is not difficult to arrange, and it will be valid at the embassy. This way, your worries will be over for good!'

He meant it as a joke, as none of us were Muslim. However, after a few discreet enquires by Harry, who was desperate for a solution, it transpired that our faith, or rather lack of it, was not a problem. This hiccup could easily be overcome with the assistance of a zealous alhaji — easily found — who would perform the "marriage ceremony" without asking any relevant questions. The alhaji was sourced almost immediately with a few further discreet enquires. The only remaining problem was the location of the venue. It was to be a super-secret affair, with only one friend involved. That friend happened to work in a big, ugly, dirty metal factory, filled with grinding sounds, sparks, smoke and horrible smells twenty-four hours a day. Harry and his friend decided that was the ideal location for our wedding.

I did not have much to say on the matter. Time was running out and things had to happen fast. On the day, I wore a white shirt and black pants and waited for Harry to come home from work on his lunch break. We drove to the metal factory, where we apprehensively sat in the friend's office in front of the alhaji already present. He produced a piece of dirty paper from his pocket and hurriedly began to read it. The doors of the office were closed, but the grinding was deafening and the smoke suffocating, so I could not hear what he was saying. As it turned out, it did not matter, because much to my astonishment, he was speaking in Arabic. I looked at Harry, horrified. He was staring at the alhaji in shock. After that reassuring sight, I went into shock too and I do not remember much of what happened next.

The ceremony was over in five minutes. Some papers were signed, I managed to shakingly sign my name, and Harry did too. None of us said a word. Our friend was our witness, he signed the document and that was it. We were now officially husband and wife for our visa purposes. I did get a spouse visa at the embassy, so it must have been a valid document. It was so valid in fact, that when a few years later we were genuinely trying to get married in Australia, we found out that we couldn't. We were already married, as per the stamp from the Embassy on our passports. We could only have a Renewal of Vowels ceremony.

These were, however, problems in the future. As we were walking on Eleko beach one day, teasing each other about our "fake secret marriage", we fell in love with one bewitching location, surrounded by beautiful coconut palm trees arching gracefully over a clean stretch of sand, where we dreamily envisioned our prospective hut to be situated. We called a local boy to find us the person in charge of the plot. While we waited in the afternoon heat, we studied the area with growing delight and fussed over the possible architectural designs.

The arrival of the boy we sent in reconnaissance interrupted our daydream. The young lad was followed, at a much slower pace, by a cantankerous-looking man.

'*Na, dis be de chief of the village, sa!*' solemnly announced the boy.

The chief, a grumpy, old, toothless man was dressed in dirty khaki shorts and nothing else. He was in a foul temper, probably having been interrupted in his midday siesta. He looked at us, blinking slowly, while simultaneously expertly taking us in. We looked back at him with happy and expectant smiles on our radiant faces. We were young. We were in love. We were obviously first home builders. That spot was indeed idyllic, in a secluded nook away from the crowds. Making a quick mental calculation of all the real estate assets and our dazed mental state, the old man, suddenly alert, brightened up, a glimmer of ill-concealed greed in his avaricious eyes.

'*Na dis fine spot oga, you choose fine spot! No one go come and make trouble for you and for your madam here. Dis is de best spot we dey have... De best spot. You have good eye, na be so, masta, you have good eye!,*' he complimented Harry on his auspicious choice of land. This was the beginning of the parlay session, elsewhere known as the sale of the land.

'Thank you, chief, thank you. So, can we build a hut here?'

'*Sa, it no be easy. It is de best spot we have. Everyone wants dis very spot.*'

We knew for a fact that no one wanted this spot, because there were enough empty huts on the beach to suffice, and no one needed to build a new one. We were probably the first customers the old man had since the huts were built twenty years ago.

'So, how will it be chief?'

The chief scratched his sweaty head thoughtfully and kicked away a stray dog that had suddenly appeared from the shrubbery and sniffed at his bare feet. It squealed unhappily and ran back to the bushes. The chief gave a heavy-hearted sigh.

'*It be difficohlt... very difficohlt... but because you are my friend, and I want to take care of you, we go manage somehow.*'

We now knew we were approaching the decisive moment of the transaction, and we tensed in anticipation.

'You go pay me ten live goats in total and two more goats to be delivered to my village over der dis week. Dis two goats we go kill em so we can start our village party to celebrate. After de party, we go collect building materials for your new hut. When we collect de materials finish, you go deliver ten live chickens to my house, and another tirty live chickens for de village. So... where do you work, sa?' asked the chief, suddenly interested in Harry. He was evidently running out of ideas on how else to fleece us.

'I make mattresses,' said Harry, naively.

'Dat is so, dat is so!' exclaimed the chief exuberantly, clapping his hands. *'You go give me five mattresses, for me and all my wives. I got four wives,'* he added proudly.

'I see you are a big chief, my friend', Harry said obligingly.

'Now, for de mohney, sa. It will only cost one tousand dollars to build, materials and labor togeder. My boys are good boys, dey go build a beautiful hut for you and your madam, sa. It will only take a mohnt to build. Only a mohnt.'

As a disclaimer to everything he just said, the chief also added that there may be extra costs and unforeseen circumstances such as material unavailability, inclement weather, sudden sicknesses, and unexplained labour shortage, which may increase costs and delay the finishing date.

But before work would start, he stressed, two goats were to be delivered as a deposit and they would be used for a big village party signalling the beginning of the construction. That said, and without even waiting for our reply, the chief turned away and left to resume his slumber in the village.

We were a bit dumbstruck by the offer, which was costly and full of uncertainties, but nevertheless, we delivered the two goats within two weeks and waited to see if work would indeed commence. It did. A whole two months later we saw some movement on our plot. Six months later, and two thousand dollars extra on top of the one thousand already spent — due to the above-mentioned circumstances happening in progressive succession — we were finally informed that the hut was ready for our occupation.

We arrived at the beach, exhilarated at the thought of finally owning our first house together, even if it was only a palm beach hut with a thatched roof. We were overcome with emotion. As I giddily climbed the stairs, Harry held me back.

'Welcome home, my beautiful princess!' he whispered, kissing me tenderly. He ceremoniously picked me up and carried me across the threshold. We then, spectacularly, disappeared in a plume of dust as the putrefied termite-eaten wood beneath us gave way. We crashed through the floor of our new house, landing on top of each other on the cold sand under the hut.

Slightly shocked but unhurt, we climbed back to our abode through the substantial hole in the floor. This time, on all fours, we carefully tested each plank before crawling over it, in a measured undulating caterpillar motion, expanding and contracting rhythmically. We arrived safely at the table on the veranda, and relieved by our success, sat on the bench. The bench instantly gave in, and we both crash-landed on the floor with a loud heavy thump.

Our antics were carefully observed by a local boy of about seventeen who had perched himself comfortably some distance away on a palm tree stump. He ran towards us. He had a pleasant and honest face and was visibly eager to help in whichever way he could. Helping us off the floor, he was full of commiseration for our double crash landing.

'So, what is your name my friend?' asked Harry, massaging his painful backside as the boy helped him up and dusted his clothes as best he could.

'Samson, sa. I am Samson. If you need anyting, I can help you. Just let me know. Ask anyone for Samson, dey all know me for here. I goh take care of your hut for you. Chief told me I am to take care of you.'

Samson was as good as his word. He had the floor and the bench fixed in no time and was always present to greet us every Sunday, help us unpack, get the barbeque ready, and chase all the other local boys away. He would then get us fresh green coconuts and skilfully open them up with his machete on the sand in front of us. Our day at the beach would thus blissfully begin.

Over time, we became acquainted with the local fishermen who went out to sea in their handmade wooden boats in the early mornings and came back around noon with the catch of the day. We bought fresh fish from them and barbequed them too. Soon, instead of bringing our own meat, we relied only on what we could buy freshly caught. We had a regular lady fishmonger, who carried her mobile seafood shop all along the beach. The giant basket on her head was filled with fresh tiger prawns, craftily wrapped in fresh green banana leaves to keep them crisp in the heat of the day. It was a real feast to enjoy those delicious local foods. We washed them down with fresh coconuts and bottles of cool Guinness, the locally produced beer.

As years passed by, and Harry and I became increasingly intertwined in the African landscape, we also became one of the must-see Lagos attractions, thanks mostly to Harry's unrelenting wildlife-saving efforts. At any one time, walking in our half-wild garden, our guests could suddenly encounter peacocks, deer, monitor lizards, crocodiles and my personal favourites, monkeys. We kept the ten ball python snakes in a vivarium at home, together with a couple of chameleons. In another vivarium lived three dwarf crocodiles, Croc, Croco and Croca.

Matters got more complicated when we acquired a cat and two dogs, one of them a puppy Rottweiler, Harry's thoughtful birthday gift for me. In a matter of months, that gift resulted in a litter of ten black puppies, as Yuke — the Rottweiler — got better acquainted with our female dog Sheba — herself the direct result of an absurdly long list of dog breeds.

Those guests who were adventurous enough to visit us at home, arrived at our compound securely locked in their cars. They then vehemently refused to get out of their vehicle until reassured that the crocodiles, which were always free roaming under the thick cover of the green foliage of our garden, were not near their car. To make things a bit more ambiguous, no one ever knew the exact whereabouts of the crocodiles, and worst of all, how many there were in total. I lost count very quickly, as Harry bought some, and released others, while a few more disappeared into the surrounding gardens in search of food.

'Where are the crocodiles?' the apprehensive first-time visitors would demand through our gate.

'*I don't know sa... I saw one dis morning. He was under dat big tree ova der.*'

The honest but hardly reassuring answer of the nervous gateman was a standard response. As an additional piece of information, he would sometimes ominously point his jittery finger to our ancient Moreton Fig tree, standing about thirty metres high. The Fig tree was surrounded by leviathan buttress grooves emerging from all around its massive trunk in swerving grey waves. Hanging down in thick curtains, massive columns of aggressive aerial roots mingled with other vines and shrubs to create an illusion of a miniature tropical forest. The ancient tree looked like it belonged in a Jurassic Park movie, and there was certainly no way of knowing where and what hid right behind or hung down those giant waves of bark and foliage.

After the car of visitors had slowly rolled in, the apprehensive *meghadis* hastily shut the creaking gate with an ominous clank and rattle of chains. It signalled that the tour had begun and there was no escape from the terrors held within. Our *meghadis* securely remained on the other side of the gate. All our gatemen had long since decamped from the premises and lived outside, together with the armed robbers, beggars, stray dogs, passing cars and all manner of evil things. It was still preferable to sharing their quarters with hungry prehistoric reptilians.

Meanwhile, the visitors would clamour to us with honks and shouts that they had arrived. That was the signal for Viki to open the door. Once that was done, and only then, would they all agree to step out in a wild dash straight from their car to the elusive sanctuary of our house. Scenes from survival of the fittest ruled here. Men carrying bawling children overtook screaming women, without even a guilty glance, in the endeavour to save themselves and their offspring from the scary unknown. Our growing Rottweiler Yuke quickly warmed up to this amusing game. With lazy two-metre-high bounces, he joined the general stampede, barking enthusiastically. He dispensed generous saliva-dripping licks and nibbles all around, amongst increased clamouring and panicked calls from our running friends.

This was usually when our melancholic resident peacock, perched high up at a safe vantage point, rapturously joined in the amplifying racket. The bird lived resignedly on top of the boys' quarters' roof, having discovered at its own peril that this was the only sanctuary offering refuge from the looming dangers underneath. My monkeys, Alibaba and Sindbad, serenely watched the whole drama unfold, mischievously concealed in the dense foliage of the bushy bougainvillea over-hanging the main entry. They unfailingly chose the perfect moment to unexpectedly swing upside down right in the path of the oncoming mob, baring a full set of canines in welcoming howling grins, exactly like Barbosa's crazy monkey from *Pirates of the Caribbean*. I often wondered if one of the movie's crew has visited us on one occasion to later re-enact his terrifying experience onto the big screen for the entire world to see. The similarity was uncanny.

Mission thus accomplished to their obvious satisfaction, Alibaba — named because of his love of stealing food — and Sindbad — who had an adventurous streak — scampered up the bougainvillea and clamoured to be let in through the window. Once inside, they would jump on my shoulders, and we would go down to greet the guests. My apparition with two grinning monkeys on my shoulders, which just seconds ago greeted them outside, did nothing to ease their nerves. The bewildered visitors would huddle close together on the sofa, still breathing heavily from their breakneck entry. They half expected silent poison darts to whizz through the air and giant roped booby traps to ensnare them upwards.

'So.... where are the snakes? Will you show them to us? Are they loose in the house?' asked the anxious guests, with nervous anticipation. Harry led the visitors to the vivarium which was in a small room adjacent to the living room. The guests stared with delighted horror at the ten beautifully speckled pythons, curled up in a ball, hence their name. These non-venomous snakes, also called royal pythons, are native to a large part of West Africa and Harry acquired them on credit when I was away in Poland for a few months, mostly to regain my sanity. When I came back and saw the ten snakes in the house, sharing their quarters with the already cramped three dwarf crocodiles, all remains of my supposedly regained sanity evaporated instantly.

'Really?! That is what you have been doing while I was away? Buying snakes? And who is going to feed them? Don't I already have enough of a zoo to take care of? You don't even know what animals we have anymore!' I fumed.

'Of course, I am going to take care of them, darling. Don't you worry about a thing. I do not understand why you are so angry. Relax, I will take care of everything.'

This was Harry's standard response by now. I had heard the same reassuring answer when he purchased two baby deers, which it turned out, had to be bottle-fed every three hours night and day for four weeks. Harry's enthusiasm lasted exactly three hours, and then he went to sleep and lost total interest. I did not sleep for a month as I tried to keep them alive all by myself. Then came the chameleons. I never discovered what their dietary requirements were because they had the good sense to skedaddle on their first day in our household. The yellow iguana-looking lizard, of a species unknown to anyone, tried the same trick. It was unfortunately discovered mid-flight, hanging on the gate, attempting an excruciatingly slow great escape and was dully brought back to us by Sidi. I told him that next time he could just turn a blind eye to such an escape, or better yet, to help a bit. I spent the next two days catching flies on the balcony, but the reptile would have none of them. Cosmos suggested that lizards liked to eat fish, and under that pretext went fishing for the day. The resulting meagre grey catch was offered to the iguana-looking creature. It turned its head away in great disgust.

'*Dat is a very stoopid animal, madam,*' concluded Cosmos with contempt. '*Dat fish, it took me two hours to catch am. It good food... I go eat am myself,*' he decided, and took the fish home to his family.

No one had a clue as to what that creature was and what it ate. Least of all Harry, who bought it on the side of the road being sold as bushmeat. Sidi, our security man, did some deep individual thinking of his own. One evening, he triumphantly brandished a hideous rabbit-sized African snail right in front of my face. I jumped away aghast. At least thirty centimetres in length, the nauseating grey plodder shot its four moving tentacles with eyes attached to the East, South, North and West, looking for an escape route. I estimated it weighed just below a kilo. It would have easily fed a whole family of hungry French nationals. I was quite sure the sluggard would eat the diminutive lizard overnight, but I thanked Sidi for his offering, and the next day let both the lizard and the snail free in a faraway location in the bush. Hopefully, they did not get caught a second time as bushmeat.

Then came the turn of the tied-up, huge, ugly, and vile-looking primeval monitor lizard. As Harry removed it carefully from the boot of his car, it began to wiggle its two-metre body and move its tail in ominous spiralling motions, in the obvious intention of biting his hands off — a heartfelt thank-you gesture for saving its life. I hurriedly left the scene, leaving Harry surrounded by the *meghadis,* all scratching their heads in unison. They indeed had a big dilemma to resolve. To the security men, this was tasty, fresh, free bush food. To their *masta,* this was obviously another dangerous new pet. Be that what it may, it had to somehow be untied from its ropes. It was firmly packaged as bush food, ready to be roasted on a fire, fresh and alive. Putting their collective brains to work on the impending problem, they eventually released the ugly lizard by cutting the bonding ropes, keeping themselves at a safe distance by ingeniously using a knife attached to a long pole. Then everyone scattered in different directions, Harry to the safety of the house, the *meghadis* to their usual safe spot behind the iron gates, and the terrified reptilian lizard in the general direction of the fig tree. It roamed free with the crocodiles amongst the garden vegetation for a few months. We did not venture into the garden during that time. Somehow, the lizard seemed much scarier than the crocodiles. And then it mysteriously disappeared. I dared not imagine its fate.

Then came the tortoise, an owl and a dik-dik. Harry bought all the wildlife which was being sold as bush meat, to save them from a cruel fate. I was always left to take care of them all. I had a job by then, woke up before six, left home before seven, and arrived home exhausted after four in the afternoon. I was beginning to feel overwhelmed by my job, shopping, house-work, frequent house guests, and my animal rescue duties.

After my prolonged absence in Poland, I also discovered that we had acquired a new form of house pet, a type I was much more familiar with. As we were sitting downstairs with some guests, I observed with shocked horror as a rat strode noncha-lantly through the living room. It was obvious he had done it before, was very much on home turf, and did not seem to fear humans. I was stunned. So was Harry.

'You know, they usually only show themselves upstairs, in our bedrooms, but *only* at night,' announced Harry, as an expla-nation when the guests who had mercifully not seen the rat, left and we were getting ready for bed.

'What do you mean, we have rats in the house? Up here, where we sleep? Oh, my God, and you find it normal?' My rat phobia instantly set into motion, and in my panic, I jumped onto the nearest chair, too terrified to even reach the bed.

'Yes, but they don't bite darling. You have nothing to be concerned about. Don't be so nervous. *Relax.* On the bright side, I only counted eight ball pythons in the enclosure today, so two of them must be loose around the house somewhere.

Give them a few days and they will get rid of all the rats for you, my darling.'

One afternoon, just a few days later, I had the great satisfaction of seeing a massive rat trot steadily past me and straight into the bedroom where Harry was enjoying his afternoon siesta. I waited with my feet up on the sofa for a safe five-minute interval, and then I carefully walked to the bedroom door and shut it. I thought Harry would benefit from a *tête à tête* with a rat when he woke up. After all, I thought, finally relaxed, they don't bite.

The guests had the right to be overwhelmed in such an environment. Dangerous animals aside, we had also gathered enough African art to be considered respectable connoisseurs in the wider expatriate community. Our house resembled no other, with African artefacts everywhere. In the fourth year of our stay in Nigeria, we had hired an incredibly talented Nigerian sculptor, improbably blessed with the biblical name of Moses. Moses' sole occupation during his long tenure with us, was to sculpt immense wooden statues using whole teak trunks as his medium. Moses did not carry his name in vain and must have been divinely inspired in his daily toil. The resulting collection of colossal totem figures, looking down at us, lilliputian mortals, with godly contempt from every corner of the house, was not a sight for the faint-hearted. Nor were the traditional Nigerian masquerade costumes, displayed in full dance motion, which at one stage we thought interesting to have as part of our décor.

The walls of our home were adorned with imposing paintings depicting the famous Kano Durbar. Wildly running stallions, mounted by exquisitely dressed emirs in full regalia exploded in rich riots of colours, in warm hues of orange, red, yellow, blue and purple. In the middle of the expansive living room throned a behemothic square teak table, hand-made by Kaode — our personal carpenter — in strict adherence to our instructions. I once arrived home, aggrieved after visiting a new acquaintance.

'Harry, you will not believe what I saw today! Tina has a table *this* big in her living room!' I said, outraged as I tried unsuccessfully to indicate with my arms the size of the table I had just seen.

Harry was just as affronted. No one had things bigger than us. This was wrong.

'Wait,' he said. Hurriedly, he brought a measuring tape. 'So exactly, how big was that table, darling?' he asked soothingly.

I showed him, greatly exaggerating the size in the process, due to my great agitation. We measured the resulting imaginary outline and made sure to design a table dwarfing the one I had seen at Tina's. With Kaode's expert woodwork, the table was soon ready. The imposing three-metre by three-metre square table was the central piece of our living room. It was composed of four separate interlocking tables, leaving an empty square space in the middle. Imposing white stone statues from the ancient Osun Oshogbo Sacred Grove stood in that central spot, representing the different deities dear to the Yoruba culture.

I once went alone with Cosmos on the 500-kilometre round trip to Osogbo in order to bring those magnificent statues to Lagos. How we survived the journey, on despicably dangerous roads, I do not know. To complete the exotic ambience of the house, the floor was covered with a multicoloured assortment of sumptuous Moroccan carpets. African patterned cushions, made with handpicked fabric from Lekki Market and sewn by local tailors, lay scattered on the chairs and sofas. A selection of local terracotta pots stood scattered throughout the vast space. I liked to fill the pots with a variety of collected or bought plants.

One day on our way back from Lekki Market, in the middle of nowhere, I saw to my delight a gigantic stack of freshly cut, thick bamboo poles. They were beauties.

'Cosmos, didn't you see that? Stop!' I shouted, outraged as I saw Cosmos accelerate when he saw the pile.

Cosmos had learned, through long-suffering years as my driver, that I stopped anytime and anywhere to collect vegetation. I had inherited that trait from my mother. In Cosmos' eyes, it was pure madness. Harry shared his view and developed the same technique when behind the steering wheel. I had learned, by reverse psychology, that when they unexpectedly accelerated, it was in a futile effort at preventing me from seeing something of interest. They both knew precisely what sparked my creative spirit.

'*But Madam, dey no go fit for car. Look am, dey be toooooo long!*,' answered Cosmos mournfully, slowing down and reluctantly reversing the car to the pile and the seller.

'Don't be silly, of course they will fit! They are not that long! We will leave the boot open,' I said, looking at the six metre giant bamboos delightedly.

'*Madam, I tell you, dey no go fit!*,' Cosmos insisted desperately.

'Go tell him that I want the thickest and the longest. And they cannot be split on the sides. The ones at the very bottom of the pile seem perfect. Tell him to start putting them aside. I only want the thickest ones please.'

'*Yes, madam...*'

Cosmos went out of the car and morosely began the negotiations of price. He walked back suspiciously quickly, a triumphant smile splitting his face in half.

'*Madam, he says he want N 300 for each. He dey saw you and he de tink you are a stoopid tourist!*' chuckled Cosmos.

Everyone knew there was a 'stupid tourist' price and a seasoned expatriate price for everything under the sky in Nigeria. But since no lady expat had ever bought a green bamboo pole before, we were all in unchartered territory. I was a bit unsure myself as to how much to offer, as I had never bought construction material before. I looked inside my wallet. As usual, I had no money left after my shopping spree at the markets.

'Nonsense. Tell him we will give him 250 Naira.' That was the equivalent of 5 dollars. 'We will need ten. They must be the longest and the thickest. And he also needs to shorten them a bit for us because they will not fit in our car,' I said, after having surveyed the pile from close quarters. Cosmos had been right. They were quite long.

'*Madam, he no go agree, he said 300 Naira each one,*' Cosmos patiently tried to explain.

'You go tell him I offer N250 for ten of the biggest. And you will help him if he has an extra saw. We do not want to be stuck here long, there is no one on this road. It's scary. We've already been here too long. Hurry up, we need to get moving, you know it is dangerous here.'

I spent the next half an hour watching my morose driver and the happy seller sawing away bits of the bamboo so that they would not be twice the length of our car. If there were any robbers ambushed in the nearby dense bush, they must have been too mesmerised by the sight to do anything other than watch. They also would have thought twice about robbing me of ten green bamboo poles, as they would have shared Cosmos' view on their value and utility.

We arrived home late, sneezing and coughing, ornately covered in a thick layer of red harmattan dust as we travelled the fifty kilometres back with an open boot. Miraculously, we were not hindered by anyone, but we did get a lot of uncomprehending stares from the local slum's populace, and from Harry. He was speechless for once.

From then on, the bamboo poles lived triumphantly in my large terracotta vases, almost reaching the high wooden cathedral ceiling above. I accessorised them with torch ginger flowers, anthuriums, birds of paradise and my favourite tropical flowers, the spectacular pendant heliconia. My bamboo poles, which with time had dried into beautiful rich yellow hues, were the envy of my lady friends. Conveniently, this was also where Alibaba and Sindbad and sometimes a rescued bird or two, chose to perch themselves as they surveyed the bemused visitors below.

Chapter 16

INDOMITABLE YUKE

'Run Samson, now!'

If rats were not a hazard in our house, Yuke, our Rottweiler puppy, was quickly on his way to becoming one. At first, as a cuddly ball of black fur, he was everyone's friend, lolloping, slobbering, and licking everything in his path. He spent his joyful and carefree days pouncing around the house and garden. He was in a state of endless jubilant energy, always on the move, elatedly wagging his stumpy tail ready for a game or a chase, which he knew he would always win. Even at that early stage, he ran as fast as a torpedo and bounced like a ping-pong ball.

After carefully assessing his intelligence, unique skills, and direct danger level to them, the higher-thinking mammals of the house — Sindbad and Alibaba — concluded that Yuke was just a controllable, soft nitwit. He had indeed no fine skills, no detectable intelligence levels, and was of no great danger to them because he was quite uncoordinated. The only special skill he seemed to possess was that he was growing increasingly strong. He also bounced. Alibaba and Sindbad, therefore, concluded that the best way to use Yuke was to ride him like a bull — rodeo style. Up until then, Safi the Siamese cat had been used as a reluctant and uncompliant donkey, despite their best efforts to train him. A bull was an upgrade and offered a world of new and exciting possibilities.

Once the monkeys' new idea settled in, there was no stopping them. Thereafter, Alibaba and Sindbad ambushed Yuke from every conceivable angle and place. In the garden, they clutched vines in patient anticipation and then unexpectedly jumped on his back as he sniffed around in the shrubbery on his garden walks. On firm flat ground, they pulled at his tail and nimbly climbed up his backside in full gallop, before he knew what had happened to him. They also attacked from the top of curtains and bounced off furniture in the house, landing on his neck. Nothing was off limits to their agility and quick-wittedness.

The fun only began when Yuke realised, often quite belatedly, that he had monkeys on his back. The desperate efforts to dislodge them included high-velocity gallops, skyrocketing bounces, and desperate back rolls, all accompanied by the monkeys' delighted shrieks. Balls of fur flew in the air as the little primates tore whole clumps of fur off Yuke's back as they tried to stay astride.

Slowly, however, Yuke was becoming a big, strong, and formidable dog. His barrel-shaped body consisted entirely of strong lean muscle, a result of the high protein and calcium diet of fresh meat and bones he was enjoying. With his strong ribcage, he could now easily bulldozer the much smaller Sheba, which looked like a lean cocker spaniel next to him. Yuke was beginning to assert his dominance and we all felt it. His motto in life changed from wanting to play with everyone to wanting to attack.

Anything. Anytime. Anyone. But mostly Nigerians if he could have his preference. Which really meant everyone, except for me, Harry, Viki, and Cosmos. Yuke was by then astute enough to distinguish between household staff and all other members of the public. When launched, there was no way on earth I could stop him from the damage he wanted to inflict on his victim. We quickly learned that it took three extraordinarily strong and very brave people, me always included in the *mêlée*, to stop Yuke from killing someone. That is what had become of Harry's thoughtful birthday gift for me.

I still recall my consternation that day, when I came back from work, exhausted as usual, and found a puppy, hind leg shakily raised, forcefully squeezing a few more drops of precious urine onto the leg of my cherished sofa. Judging from the various-sized puddles all around the living room, he had been busy marking his territory for some time.

'Harry, what on earth is this dog doing here? Why are there puddles everywhere?'

'Surprise! It is your birthday gift darling! It is a Rottweiler. He will grow big and strong, and he will protect you. Rotties are excellent guard dogs. Happy birthday!'

'Protect me from what? You? I can take care of myself, and I do not want a dog. Who is going to take care of it and train it? Do you have any idea how much time and effort it takes to train a dog? Rotties especially?'

'I will take care of everything, darling. *Relax.* Why are you so angry? You really need to learn to relax. Look how beautiful he is. It's a boy.'

A boy Rottweiler. That is exactly what I needed to add to my already remarkably complicated life. I was struggling to cope with an immature human boyfriend, a bunch of wild animals, a job and a household always filled with guests. Incidentally, Harry lost total interest in the puppy when Yuke, just to make clear the lay of the land between the boys, unequivocally asserted his male dominance in the household. He was by then barely an adolescent, a mere 20 kilos of sheer glorious Rottie. As Harry came out of the car one day, Yuke jumped at him in a subdued friendly pounce from the back. Taken by surprise, and propelled forward into the shrubbery, Harry finished his impromptu flight through the air spread-eagled in the garden bed. Hurried rustling and shuffling in the foliage near his head pointed to the fact that his resident crocodiles must have been just as befuddled as he was by the sudden attack. When he came to his senses, Harry tried unsuccessfully to pick himself up, but with each successive attempt, Yuke danced and pranced around him and pinned him firmly back to the ground with renewed joy and boundless energy, foaming saliva dripping from his gaping mouth.

'That's it! I have had it with that stupid dog! Don't you know how to train a dog? Can't you at least teach him to not jump at people? He almost killed me just now!' Harry showed me scratches and bruises resulting from yet another joyful greeting with Yuke.

'First of all, I told you I did not want a dog, nor did I have time or capacity to train one. Secondly, I told you Rottweilers are not the smartest of breeds. He was only playing with you. How could he know you did not want to lay there in the dirt for twenty minutes while he licked you? Thirdly, can I remind you that I am only 45 kilos. That dog will be heavier than me in a few months and I will not be able to stop him, even if he wants to eat you up.'

I only spoke Polish to Yuke, and he only obeyed or understood commands in Polish, which may have played a small role in this state of affairs. Harry always made sure I was in the near vicinity when he and the dog were ever together.

Being Yuke's owner was not an easy task. One of the few Nigerians whom Yuke had to have close encounters with was his vet. I had arranged for him to come to our house, for Sheba's and Yuke's yearly injections. Things went fine until the day the vet, me and Yuke simultaneously discovered that Yuke was now stronger than both of us. As he got jabbed, he escaped from my grip, jumped on the vet, and went straight for his throat with his sharp teeth.

'Madam, please, help me...' whispered the ashen-faced vet from under Yuke. My dog was laying on top of his near kill, growling contentedly, his massive fangs slowly clamping down on his doctor's bulging jugular.

'Yuke, stop! Stop right now.' Yuke stopped growling, propped his ears, and popped his head sideways, deep concentration showing in the folds of his massive forehead. It was a good sign. He was at least trying to think.

'Let go. Now.' Yuke wagged his tail in a friendly attempt to invite me to play the killing game with him. 'Come here, Yuke.'

I got up and slowly walked away deliberately taking my time and calmly called to Yuke again. Very reluctantly, Yuke let go of the vet's throat and followed me outside of the room, stopping several times to regretfully look back. The figure of the motionless vet lay spreadeagled on my living room floor.

I locked Yuke safely away and ran back inside, fully expecting to have a dead body on my hands. The vet, however, was sufficiently alive to flee through the kitchen door as soon as I'd left the room. Despite his terror, he knew he could not move an inch before Yuke was safely locked away, so he played dead. He had good instincts.

After that little incident, I did not see him for another year. When the time came again for the yearly vaccines, I sent Cosmos to forcibly bring the vet back. He was a good and brave man, and I had profound respect for him. Unfortunately, I do not think he reciprocated my warm sentiments. When he arrived, with Yuke still securely inside the house, the vet handed me a muzzle.

'I will not come in until this is on his head, securely fastened,' he said, without a hint of a 'nice to see you again' smile.

Puzzled, I took the muzzle and went inside. By the looks of things, it was made for chihuahuas, possibly sausage dogs at best. After one attempt, I came back to the vet, sitting safely in his locked car, the muzzle still in my hand.

'Um... doctor? The muzzle is a bit too small for Yuke, it barely covers his nose,' I reported, handing it back. Sighing sadly, the vet took his muzzle back and rummaged in his well-worn leather suitcase. Finally, he handed me a dirty, but reassuringly long elastic bandage.

'Tie this around his muzzle then,' he said resignedly.

I went back inside. I looked at Yuke. Yuke looked at me. He wagged his tail expectantly. I frowned worriedly. Yuke was obviously anticipating a new exciting game involving the long appendage. I was anticipating a lot of trouble. I was 45 kilos, none of it muscle, slightly built and measured 165 cm. Yuke was a stocky 50 kilos of toned sinews and when standing up leaning on me, he was my height. His head was twice the size of mine. It was going to be a very unequal game. The round began with me slowly approaching Yuke, the long bandage in hand. Talking to him calmly, I tried to unexpectantly wrap the bandage around his massive jaws. The subterfuge did not fool him for a split second. Before I even touched him, he had already snapped at it and was playfully pulling it away, inviting me for a very uneven tug of war.

'Yuke, this is not a game. Give it back now!'

Yuke pulled harder, I yanked it back. After a hard scuffle, where I unclenched his fangs one by one repeatedly from the bandage, I finally got it back and decided to change techniques. I launched myself at the dog, landing with my body on his back, piggy-backing him. Using his delighted surprise at this new development, I tried desperately to tie the bandage around his wet nose, which was by then dribbling with excited saliva. That plan only lasted until he had enough of the game and eventually stood up, effortlessly throwing me off his back and onto the ground. He shook himself vigorously, spraying me with drools of foamy saliva, waiting for the fun game to continue.

It did. For the next twenty minutes we rolled, ran, slobbered, scuffled, drooled, bounced, chased, and played hide and seek behind every piece of furniture in the room. I then skid the total length of the room on the floor, desperately attached to Yuke's thick neck, in a resolute effort to topple him over. Eventually, I corralled him into the narrow corridor, where there was no escape. There was, however, a big clear window facing the garden, where soon everyone who was on the premises gathered to watch.

Under the captivated eyes of the vet, Cosmos, Kaode, Moses, Viki and Sidi, all pushing each other for the prime spot at the window, I rolled on the ground with overjoyed Yuke. I was once on top, once under, once on top and under again. There was no end to the game. Each time I was at the bottom I was gratified with slobber-filled wet licks. Each time I was on top I tried to tie the appendage, which now resembled a cheesecake cloth, onto Yuke's muzzle. When I finally succeeded, I was dishevelled, covered in slobber, and weeping with frustration.

Not satisfied with this outcome yet, the vet then asked me to attach Yuke to a secure structural column inside the house using a thick lead. I knew that even in the remote possibility that the thick structural column would not break, the thick leather lead may snap in seconds. I had seen leads snap on him before, without significant effort from Yuke. I was in no state to discuss alternatives. I did as I was asked. When that was done, the vet finally conceded to come inside the house. Viki held the kitchen door open for him, just in case. Shaking all over, the good vet jabbed Yuke in the backside, extending his arm to an improbable length, and standing over a meter away to have a head start, just in case. Amidst the resulting furious barks and howls from the outraged dog, the brave vet was gone in a flash. He had the presence of mind to stop mid-gallop, his professionalism taking over for a few seconds.

'Madam, I would ask you to massage the area for five minutes, and the pain will go away. I wish you a good year,' he was gone before I had time to open my mouth to thank him.

When we took Yuke to the beach hut with us for the first time, slobbering and foaming with excitement in the back seat, we were not sure what to expect, but we knew there would be casualties. He lived up to our worst fears when, as soon as we opened the door, Yuke jumped out of the boot straight onto Samson's throat. The poor boy had silently materialised from nowhere as he usually did before we had time to warn him of the danger. The resulting *mêlée* of hands, feet, paws, legs and black fur rolling in the sand attracted half the village from nearby. Harry and I eventually sat on Yuke together, grabbing him mid-flight as he was about to pounce on Samson's jugular, in a mercy kill. That gave Samson a chance to get up. He had a split second to do so.

'*Run Samson, now!*' we shouted once we managed the impossible feat of holding our raging dog secure under us.

To our great amazement and even greater puzzlement, Samson shot straight up the nearest palm tree, climbing all the way to the top. Was he planning to stay there long, hanging with both arms and legs for dear life? Together and with great difficulty, we dragged Yuke to the hut where we attached him to one of the palm tree foundation posts. We used a rope and a chain to make sure he did not run away.

He did not. Until, to our great surprise, we suddenly saw a beautiful chestnut horse elegantly galloping on the beach, mane blowing in the gentle sea breeze, his owner proudly astride, obviously greatly enjoying the exhilarating experience. Then to our horror, we saw — in slow motion due to our shock — our chestnut Rottweiler. His muscles rippled from under his glimmering pelt, as he vaulted across the sand dunes in clouds of dust, tearing past our hut, course set firmly onto the noble stallion and his exalted rider. In seconds, he had caught up with the steed and in one last stupendous bounce, Yuke leapt straight onto the horse's arse.

The startled horse reared with a terrified squeal, the owner barely hanging onto the reins. Looking behind and seeing what had attacked him, the stallion thundered away in a cloud of sand and splashing seawater, Yuke in tumultuous pursuit. By then Harry was also galloping, way behind, screaming madly for Yuke to stop. The spectacular race was enjoyed by thrilled expats, gleefully watching the unexpected Sunday morning show from their comfortable recliners.

The show ended as abruptly as it began when Yuke miscalculated. Velocity and gravity all came together in an instant when the horse's hind hoof smashed straight into Yuke's chest. Momentarily winded, Yuke stopped and sat down. Harry was still a long way back, breathlessly ambling through the sand. Suddenly, from his sitting position, Yuke saw a golden cocker spaniel setting off for a leisurely walk with his owner from a nearby hut. Without a second's thought, Yuke threw himself at the ridiculously groomed tasty morsel and proceeded methodically to shred its fur.

What saved the spaniel was not Harry's belated arrival, five long minutes later. It was the owner of the dog — an American Marine, as we later learned. He could have walked straight out of a Calvin Klein swimming trunk ad. He wore only skimpy shorts, so there was little left to the imagination. His perfectly chiselled body popped muscles from every imaginable angle. His biceps the size of monoliths barely flexing under the strain, he lifted our 50-kilo dog off his mauled dog and threw him, like an oversized Olympic disc, far into the distance. Surprised, Yuke flew through the air squealing and landed with a dull thump five metres away. This is where Harry found him, a few minutes later, where he lay, winded a second time that day.

Harry spent the next half an hour apologising to the furious animal owners. When he arrived back at the hut breathless, dragging guiltless Yuke by the collar, we decided it was time to go home, despite having just arrived. Yuke, who had had a remarkably successful day from his perspective, slept the rest of the day, dreaming about his newfound adventures. We spent that Sunday bored at home, with nothing to do.

From then on, every Sunday, Yuke did his absolute best at worsening his already shocking beach reputation, and in no time at all acquired the well-deserved notoriety of an uncontrollable and insane dog, incapable of being restrained by his lunatic owners.

Above
Our house in Lagos.

Below
In the garden surrounding our house. I am holding fallen Flame Tree flowers.

Above left and right
Our friend bought this baby gorilla on the side of the road before it died of malnutrition, exposure, and shock. He later opened a sanctuary for gorillas and saved many more. Spending a few hours with this baby gorilla was a privilege and an experience I will never forget.

Below
The dik diks suspiciously watched by Alibaba.

Left
At home with the
ball pythons.

Below
Taking a nap with
the Siamese cat,
Safi, and Sindibad.

One of the dwarf crocodiles. If not held properly around the neck, their bite could be quite painful.

Above

The upstairs of our house. The wooden furniture was designed by Harry and handcrafted by Kaode, our cabinet maker.

Below

The inseparable trio, Sindbad, Alibaba and myself. They never left my shoulders when they were babies.

Above left and right
Alibaba and I. Our resident iguana.

Below
Yuke and I when he was a puppy.

Without Viki, my life in Nigeria would have been very different. She was born in Calabar, in Southern Nigeria.

Viki was my second in command around the house and garden. All the staff members, from the meghadis to the drivers, respected her as she was astute, fearless and from a different ethnic origin to everyone else. Viki was about my age, and we developed a very strong friendship.

Cosmos, the 'Nigerian Samurai', was my driver, bodyguard and friend. We spent hours on the road, living through many hilarious, dangerous and special moments. We shared a daredevil attitude on our numerous Lagosian adventures and were nicknamed the 'Crazy duo'. We both shared an irascible sense of wicked humour which was probably what kept us safe.

My favourite hangout, the Lekki Market, on the way to the beach.
I bought beads, chairs, chests, carvings and masks from the
numerous stands along the dark alleyways. Some of the traders there
became dear friends, always offering to sell me things on credit and
never reminding me to pay up.

Above
Our Sundays at Eleko Beach were a mixture of relaxation and enjoying African art sold by passing beach vendors.

Below
Our beach hut.

Above
Typical Sunday at Eleko Beach.

Below
Beach vendors added an unforgettable touch to the whole experience.

Above
In front of our new hut with Margo and Saul.

Below left
Leather chests sold by Tuaregs.

Below right
Assimilating with the local hairstyle.

Our hut was always filled with passing vendors. We built a special meeting place for them, where they could rest in the shade. The vendors knew us by our names and quickly caught on to our weak spot, African art. Each Sunday we came laden with more artefacts purchased at the beach.

Above left and right
Grown up Yuke at the beach.

Below
Yuke as a proud father of eight puppies.

Above
Samson opening
a fresh coconut with
a machete.

Below
Fresh catch of
the day.

Above
Another happy Sunday beach day.

Below
These Tuaregs came from the sub-Saharan desert to trade with
leather goods a few times a year.

Above and left
Eleko Beach.

Chapter 17

MEGA ENGINEERING

There is pleasure in the pathless woods...

There is rapture in the lovely shores...

Two years after my arrival in Nigeria, I began working as an English teacher in the kindy section of the highly prestigious Lycée Français Louis Pasteur in Lagos. It was a coveted position, and I was surprised to have passed the interview process, as the competition was fierce. Jobs for women were rarely available in the Lagos expat world, and this one was a rarity. The position became vacant as the previous teacher had left due to a nervous breakdown. It was a detail which I later discovered when I confided in a colleague, as I was under the strong impression that I was going insane. By then it was unfortunately too late to decamp and so I stayed on for two years.

The fact that I was a young, inexperienced, and certainly not a trained teacher did not seem to be of a big inconvenience in the recruitment process, which at the time, I did find a bit strange. I put it down to the fact that I spoke French, Polish and English fluently, so I was a good linguistic candidate by any standards. During the interview, I also lied to the lovely, trusting lady, and said I loved children. I spent the next two years trying to convince myself that at the very least I did not dislike them. I succeeded in that task. I still work with children today and I do love them now.

I was thrown into the deep end of my new job almost immediately. I applied for a relief role. The *conseilleure péda-gogique* promised me that I would have a full month of training with a Year 1 teacher from France before I was given any relief classes. That was a reassuring thought, as I did not know how the French education system worked. Truth be told, I only knew how the education system worked from a student's perspective.

On my second day at the school, Florence hurt her back and came to work for a total of ten minutes, on her way to the doctor. She handed me the lesson plan for the day. The *conseilleure* then came in to ask me if I would be okay to take over the class. I was too shocked to say no. Besides, the question was purely rhetorical as there was no relief staff available. That was why I was in the process of being hired in the first place. Adrenaline and the fear of being ridiculed by a bunch of unruly seven-year-olds helped me survive that day and the following week without major mishaps. Indeed, as it turned out, Florence was bedridden for six days. I had completed a teacher's job in French, at a prestigious French School without any training for a week. After that stunt, I felt like I could do anything. When a few weeks later, the school's kindergarten English teacher job became available, I applied without any major forebodings. Despite many other candidates, I was able to secure the position. It involved teaching six classes of children between the ages of three and five. It seemed to me like a feasible thing to do, despite my total ignorance of the field of teaching. How difficult could it be to teach little children?

On the bright side, once part of the school's interior circle of teachers and their connections, my social life suddenly flourished into a rich, multicultural, fun-filled rollercoaster. Gone were the days of boring lunches and dinner parties. I was now amid the Lagos *crème de la crème* society. Diplomats, embassy workers, and heavyweights of foreign petrol companies all revolved in our growing circle of acquaintances. These francophone expatriates were the parents of the students attending the school. Every weekend, we went from one gathering to another, breakfasted with one group, lunched with another, and had dinner with a third.

My job as an English teacher at the French school was a bit of an ambiguous affair. We were in an English-speaking country, where theoretically everyone spoke English. Forcibly, English was therefore the 'foreign' language taught at the school. I was unsure of the level spoken by the kindergarten children, but on my first visit to all the classrooms, I discovered with relief, that they all spoke English. The problem was that it was pidgin English, probably picked up from Nigerian household staff. My task was set right there and then. I had to eradicate the pidgin from the classrooms. Unfortunately, I had no

English curriculum to follow and not a single book of stories to read. The previous English teacher also used nothing. No wonder they all spoke deplorably.

For the next few days, I went on rounds of shopping sprees with Cosmos, feverishly trying to locate children's storybooks in markets and the very few bookstores Lagos had to offer. To my great joy, I did source several classic Ladybird Nursery rhymes and storybooks. I also bought a cassette of children's English songs. By then, it had also occurred to me that I was brought up in Poland until I was eight, and had missed out on traditional English children's stories and songs. This job was going to be harder than I originally thought.

Thankfully, the Ladybird books were a phenomenal success. That was great news, as they were my only English resources for my tenure there. The children loved my lessons. I knew this because the teachers told me they were unusually quiet during my sessions. I did try to keep the program simple yet invigorating. Typically, I read the storybooks, asked questions about them, and discussed the stories and characters, all the while encouraging proper English sentence structures. We learnt poems and songs to support correct pronunciation and vocabulary as well.

With time, I developed a more refined curriculum based on different year levels needs. For the older children, I produced worksheets and introduced concepts like verbs, nouns, adjectives, and their proper use of them, and expanded my poetry and song repertoire with the younger age groups. I had a wonderful time at the school, but after two years of working with children, I decided I needed a change, so when the position of office manager at Mega, an alarm installation company materialised, I did not hesitate to apply.

As in a *déjà vu*, I went through the interview process with surprising ease and again came out with flying colours. The fact that I was still young, inexperienced and knew absolutely nothing about alarms did not seem to bother my new German boss, Wal, who conducted the short interview with great benevolence and even greater absent-mindedness.

My complete ignorance of what it was that an office manager did, worked significantly to my advantage, as my job very rapidly went beyond the scope of a conventional office manager's position. Whatever that job title normally entailed, I never knew, and it's safe to say I never actually found out.

My first task, funnily enough, was to define my own job description as the position of an office manager, as the role was previously non-existent. This was probably why my new German boss and I stared at each other in embarrassed silence in his office on my first day of work. Obviously, he had no clue what to do with me either.

We spent the day drinking countless cups of foul instant coffee, generously laced with locally produced canned Peak milk. We alternated in mutually preparing the beverage for each other with exceeding politeness, and an escalating feeling of desperation as to what else to do to look busy. After that excruciating day was over, I had an even more excruciating sleepless night, due to the excessive caffeine I had consumed. I was strongly determined to find something, anything to do at my new job, other than sit opposite Wal and drink instant coffee.

On the second day, summoning all my moral courage, I marched into our shared office and pushed my desk to the far corner of the room, so as not to be in Wal's direct line of vision. That achieved, and satisfied with my housekeeping, I announced that I was going to give myself a tour of the company.

'Of course, great idea, go ahead!' Wal smiled encouragingly at my first valiant effort at productive work.

Apart from Wal, a German engineer, Johan — who was always in the field on a project — and a silent European partner living overseas, I was the only expatriate person working at Mega. Summoning more courage which was evaporating fast, I ran through the corridor and abruptly opened the first door which happened to be our administration area. My rapid inspection revealed our startled accountant, Adelomo. Being the only person in the room, he was nonchalantly perched on his desk, leisurely talking on the phone in a private conversation in his home dialect. That at least explained why he was at work so early. He had personal business to discuss and what better way to do it than by occupying our only company telephone line. Although it was past nine o'clock, no one else was there, although I knew we should have a full house of clerks, secretaries, and office staff.

As Adelomo nimbly jumped off his desk, I introduced myself as the new Mega office manager. We had briefly met the previous day, but I thought a new formal introduction was much needed.

'So, Adelomo, where is everyone?'

'Who, madam?' asked Adelomo, clearing his throat, a look of genuine innocence and surprise on his face.

'Whoever is meant to be at work here. It is past 9am. We start work at 8.30, as you know,' I answered pleasantly.

'They are coming, they are coming, madam. They are probably stuck in *go slow*. You know the traffic is bad in the morning. They will be here soon.'

Adelamo was looking at me carefully, trying to see how far this obvious deceitfulness would carry him. It all depended on whether I had lived in Nigeria long enough to be receptive to such subterfuge.

'Indeed, and yet I managed to be here on time, as did you because we know about the traffic, as does every Lagosian. Could I please have the names of everyone working here?' I asked, looking around.

Judging by the empty desks and chairs, at least six people were absent. The great look of disappointment and growing unease on Adelamo's face was gratifying enough to push me to consolidate my obvious advantage. I was not a newcomer as Adelamo had hoped, and he was now fully alert.

White people in Nigeria fell into two categories — the newcomers and the locals. If they had the bad luck to fall into the first category, they were immediately picked out and treated like idiots by the local populace. To any Nigerian, they were such easy targets to detect that I suspect they had a distinctive smell to them too.

It was a secret to no one that all Nigerians exerted themselves in ingenious mental gymnastics to discover how easily they could trick those naïve *oyinbos* who had just arrived in their country. They slapped themselves on the thighs with hoots of raucous laughter, as they delightfully shared duplicity stories amongst themselves. They probably had some sort of a *stupid oyinbo scale* and measured their accomplishments accordingly. Everyday Nigerians were not devious or meant to harm the expats. They had lived in utter poverty for generations and were used to the rich having all the power, and the poor none. Quite naturally, they possessed the ingenuous skills of self-preservation. Nigerians, for which I have a heartfelt and profound admiration, were genetically programmed to effortlessly succeed even in a world of doom and gloom.

The white locals which had lived in Nigeria for several years were a distinct species of *oyinbos.* Hardened by years of unveiling the thick layers of complicated networked deceits the locals had shrouded them in, they had forcibly acquired the same skills as the Nigerians, but the other way around. They could smell a lie from a distance and knew every trick in the book of the Nigerians. Nothing fooled them. After two years in Nigeria, plus extra as a child, that was me. Adelamo tried again, hoping he was mistaken by his first judgement of me.

'But, madam, some of them are at work on the project and they will not come at all for a few days!'

'Admin people in the field on a project? You must be mistaken. And since you are obviously the only person present here now, you will take me on a tour of the company and tell me all about the people who work here, won't you?'

'Madam, I am terribly busy, I have urgent and important work to do,' answered Adelamo, outraged by my demand.

I looked at his empty desk. There was not a sign of past or present activity, not a single paper graced the empty expanse of his accountant's kingdom. I smiled.

'I am sure whatever it is you have to do urgently can wait. Now let us get going.'

'Yes, madam.'

Thus, forcibly recruited, my reluctant guide showed me the different areas of the building. It took me a few more days to grasp how the company worked and who were its workers. By that time, I was sufficiently muddled and began to perceive the labyrinth of intricate complexities associated with the three competing ethnic groups working at Mega. What I had managed to determine was that the administration staff held fort in the upper floor of the building. They consisted of Adelamo's close relatives, occupying important positions that they never gained or had worked in before. Some of them were outright ignorant as to their title or job responsibility. They were hired based on Adelamo's family connections and often did not come to work at all for days. When they did, they did nothing except sit around and use our unique phone line for private phone calls. Whether they showed up at work or not was not reflected in their payslips, which they all received regularly in full, compliments of the generous Adelamo.

On the other hand, the people working in the field with Johan, the German engineer, were hired by the site manager — who was from a different ethnic group and hired them all based on *his* family connections. Then there were the truck drivers, the security, and the lower staff, who formed another ethnic group, following the same hiring procedure. This resulted in three separate entities all trying to pilfer away as many materials and money as possible. Mutual distrust, hostility, and religious antipathies added to the multifarious nature of the workplace. The three ethnic groups consisted of the Hausa Fulanis from the north, the Christian Igbos from the south, and the urban Yorubas. I was slowly beginning to realise that I had unwittingly walked into an intense tribal war zone, which by the look of things, had been brewing underneath the surface for some time.

I was soon to uncover just how bad and widespread the theft and subsequent muddling of proof was in the first few weeks of work at Mega. Shamefully enough, it struck remarkably close to home, and both me and Harry were the implicated, injured, and guilty parties. Harry's foam company had ordered the installation of a whole new expensive alarm system, complete with sensors, water extinguishers, fans, and loudspeaker alarms. It was the first project I was involved in, and I was very keen on it progressing without a hiccup. I was therefore mortified when a few days later I received a phone call from Harry, informing me in stern tones that *my* Mega workers had appropriated eleven expensive industrial fans and had in addition pilfered parts from another eight, rendering them useless. Those fans were an awfully expensive part of our alarm system installation.

I was furious. I immediately called the police and instructed all the workers to come back from the site at once. With swift and commendable speed, the police arrived within the hour and promptly arrested six random Mega workers, although they were not even connected to the site of the theft. After they were taken away in two police cars, creating quite a stir on our usually quiet street, Adelamo strolled calmly into the office. I was in the process of vividly debriefing Wal of the deep-rooted sabotage activity within our own workforce, and congratulating myself for the quick action I took to call in the police to finally resolve the matter.

'Yes Adelamo, what is it?' I said angrily, looking at his justifiably gloomy face.

'Well, madam, the police just arrested six of our workers...' he began achingly.

'Yes, I am aware Adelamo. The whole street is aware. The crowd is still outside enjoying the spectacle of our company having to call the police on its own people. It's shameful and I know you knew all about it!' I snapped angrily at him.

Adelamo cleared his throat. He knew denying the truth was useless. He chose to ignore the accusation for now. 'Well, madam, as you know, they were working on the installation of the new fire alarm system at the foam plant...'

'I am also aware of that Adelamo! My husband is the one who informed me of the theft! It is a dishonour I shall never forget!'

'Yes madam, so as I was saying, six of our site workers were arrested and now we have no one else left to finish the job at the foam plant. As you know, ten Mega workers are working in Abuja on the Clinton project.'

We were indeed commissioned to install security cameras in the hotel where then President Clinton was going to be staying on his impending two-day Nigerian visit.

'But we have other workers!'

'Yes, madam. As you are aware, as of Tuesday we have a team of ten working on the Port Harcourt project. Yesterday, as you recall, we sent an additional team of five for the Clinton project in Abuja, and the team up in Calabar is not due for another two weeks, madam.'

'But we still have some local workers left!'

'Yes, madam, we have three Mega teams working locally on smaller projects in the embassies, but they cannot come to assist us as they are already behind schedule due to delays in the delivery of materials...'

'Delays of delivery of materials?' I interrupted, outraged at the shameless manner in which Adelamo was enumerating how reliant we were on their corrupted workforce.

'So, this being the case, madam,' continued Adelamo mournfully, 'how would you like us to finish the foam factory project? Would it not be better if we finalised it quickly to clear our name?'

'Of course, we have to finish it quickly! What do you suggest we do? Hire new people?'

'No, madam, that will take too much time and they will have to be trained anyway. It will be much easier if we get our workers back.'

'But they just got arrested for theft!'

'Yes, madam, but no charges have been laid yet. Also, they were not the workers involved in that project in the first place. It makes no difference to the police anyway. I can assure you that until we pay the police a handsome sum for an inquiry that will prove nothing, they will just sit in jail until we buy them out. The police are only interested in making money, not catching the guilty party. They have no time or human resources for that.'

'So, you're suggesting we buy them out?'

'Well, I can ask our secretary to call the police and ask for the initial price of release for each prisoner. Once we have settled on one, we can pay the sum and our workers would be free to finalise the foam project.'

I looked at Wal. He was pretending to be engrossed in writing something extremely important on his computer. He obviously did not want to get involved. I suspected he had also tried but failed to eradicate the sabotage within the company. I understood our limitations. This was not our country to change.

For the next few hours, Adelamo — delighted that he had finally gotten the better of me — shuffled to and from our office to inform us of the progress. The secretary in charge of the transaction haggled with the police for each one of our workers, like for a head of cattle. The price was of course exorbitant and unacceptable at first, which was the standard practice of any haggling exchange in Nigeria. To do otherwise would have been in bad taste. Towards the evening, at quite a cost to our company, we had our jailbirds back on payroll and ready to work the next day.

My severe reprimand and subsequent repeated disciplinary measures to avoid any such incidents to happen again had absolutely no effect. I resigned myself once again to limit the financial damage to our company to the best of my abilities. Seeing my increased vigilance, the workers swiftly adapted to this new and challenging environment and showed heightened, commendable levels of ingenuity and shrewdness with their subversive dealings. With new levels of zeal, they pilfered what they could in broad daylight and then dutifully raced to me to accuse each other of the deed.

For example, a driver and a purchase officer were sent together to the market to purchase a list of materials necessary for a new project. After the purchase, they arrived back at work and within minutes sheepishly were at my desk in quick succession.

'*Madam, I wish to inform you dat on de way from de market I noticed we are missing five items which we have just purchased at de market. It must be dat purchase offica who tieved it as der were only two of us, and I am no tief, madam!*' the driver murmured to me in melodramatic whispers, pounding himself on the chest in theatrical assurances of his blatant innocence.

'*Madam, I wish to inform you dat te driva stole five items from my purchase list. I put dem in the car after I buy dem and when we arrived back here, I noticed dat five items are missing. I came straight here to tell you, madam,*' the purchase officer devotedly confided to me minutes later, after having courteously held the door for the leaving driver who had just reported on him for that same theft.

We all knew that no number of investigations and questioning would conjure up the five items or reveal who took them. There was most likely a third party involved at the market or no sale took place at all, but money for the sale disappeared. It did not matter, as it could not be stopped.

After a few weeks of sharing my office with Wal, I grew increasingly uneasy. A lengthy line of Mega workers leisurely snaked around the corner in the long corridor, waiting to meet me with a merry 'Good morning, madam,' as I arrived at work. They were all waiting to see me with their problems and ongoing company issues. In order not to disturb Wal, the employees took to muttering long monologues of woes in front of my desk. We had long whispered conferences, and many times

I could not understand or hear what it was they were saying, as the subtle mutterings were almost inaudible. In general, the more serious the problem, the less audible the confession was. I realised that I was not doing my job properly as many things were escaping me, lost in the whispers. I decided it was time to ask for a promotion.

'Wal, I really need an office for myself. This is becoming unacceptable. We are disturbing you daily with the procession of employees and I am sure you can't get any work done with the constant hum of conversations at my desk,' I said after a Yoruba worker whispered to me in pidgin English and I could not make out a word of what he was mumbling. Steadily increasing the volume, we ended up having a full-blown loud conversation, as I tried to understand the issue, while a bemused Wal looked on from his desk.

'Oh, no Magdalena, that is completely unnecessary. You are not disturbing me at all, don't worry.'

'But Wal, I need a desk where I can sit and do my work undisturbed. I have too much to do and too many people to see. Surely, an office just for myself would facilitate your work and mine,' I insisted, surprised that I was refused what seemed like a perfectly natural request.

'What's wrong with sharing the office with me? And you cannot have an office because there are no spare rooms for one,' announced Wal with finality, visibly relieved and delighted to have improvised such a great excuse to end the conversation.

'But there is the room at the end of the corridor? It is empty and we do not use it. That is all I need Wal. It makes no sense not to use it!'

'That room, as you know, is used for storage of our demo packs and alarms. It is filled with important expensive equipment,' said, Wal dolefully. He obviously resented the hurtful idea that I clearly did not want to work opposite him.

'I will think about it...' he sighed.

It took a few more days of my visible unhappiness for Wal to finally relent.

'Fine... you can use that as your office, but nothing from there can be removed,' he announced one morning.

Wasting no time, I ran across the corridor to take stock of the room. I was elated. It was my first office ever, and I was determined to make the most of it. I ran around the company and commandeered an office chair from a bewildered secretary and asked the admin workers to bring me a spare desk. I did not feel brave enough to take the desk I was presently using from in front of the still-sulking Wal. I spent the next two days beautifying my space with the equipment I had available. I had one wall completely covered with a stupendous assortment of fire alarms, sirens, fire extinguishers, door handles, cameras, monitors and control boxes. It looked impressive and very much like a high-tech security control room. My desk sat opposite a beautiful wide window, occupying half the wall. It looked out to the biggest house on the street. The house stood surrounded by a lush garden of banana and palm trees, providing a welcome sight of greenery in an otherwise bare urban neighbourhood.

After a few days, Wal walked over to my new kingdom driven by curiosity and in need of a good friendly talk. From the door, he gaped at the wall filled with demo models of every conceivable alarm item we offered to install.

'Now that equipment is finally displayed nicely, we can show it off advantageously to our clients,' I chirped, happy to highlight the new showroom/office space.

'Indeed... You know, we have twenty boxes of new monitors arriving here tomorrow, and they will have to be kept here. I hope you have the space?'

I looked around the room. Every corner and all the space had already been used by some sort of device or other. I smiled, undeterred.

'Of course, we can put everything in here. Heaps of space!'

When the monitors arrived the next day, they were stacked in my office one on top of another, creating instant carton skyscrapers. I carefully picked my way through the narrow spaces between them to arrive at my desk, and swore under my breath at the injustice. But I was determined more than ever to fight for my little corner of paradise. I had earned the space, and nothing was going to drive me out of there.

'Magdalena? Are you there?' Wal asked sometime later as he stood at the door, which I could not see. His voice was muffled by all the insulating layers of cartons surrounding us. I mustered all the professionalism I could before I answered crisply from behind my desk.

'Yes, I am right here. How can I help you Wal?'

'Oh, you *are* there! I just came to see if the monitors had arrived, which I can see they clearly have...' I could hear Wal picking his way slowly amongst the towers of boxes, murmuring something I could not hear.

'Yes, they have indeed, as you can see for yourself,' I said, amiably, once he finally emerged triumphantly in front of me.

I gestured him towards the closest standing cartons.

'Please, have a seat!' I said grandly.

'Oh, thank you, thank you indeed...'

Wal looked around searching for something more appropriate to sit on. Finding nothing, he perched himself snugly on one of the cartons, trying to look dignified.

'Perhaps we could find you a couple of visitor's chairs so that our clients will have something a bit more appropriate to sit on...' he began.

'I would not mind at all. But I am not sure I would be able to fit anything more here. It is a full house as you can see.'

'Well, the monitors are leaving for Abuja in a couple of days so you will have your space back.'

I was relieved. 'Well, in that case, two visitor's chairs would be good to have', I agreed.

As soon as the cartons left for Abuja, two chairs were brought in and ceremoniously placed in front of my desk. It was a sweet gesture of goodwill from Wal, which I fully appreciated. I was ready to fulfil my role as a respectful office manager.

My first employee of the day, an unusually early bird, arrived just after 8.30 am and ensconced himself comfortably in one of the newly installed chairs. Luxuriantly revelling in the moment, and still half asleep, he crossed his legs, scratched his head, and was visibly inclined to yawn but changed his mind midway, seeing my disapproving face. Instead, he smiled at me with a wide and happy grin. I smiled back expectantly.

'Good morning, Femi, how are you?'

'*I de fine, madam, I de fine. How are you?*'

'I am fine, thank you.'

'And how is your hosband?'

'He is also doing fine, thank you.'

'And how is your moda?'

'She is also fine.'

'And your foda is in good health I hope?'

'Yes, my family are all fine, thank you Femi. So, how can I help you? Is there a problem? Why are you not at work?' I asked patiently. I should have first asked about the health of his mother, father, sisters and brothers, grandmas, and grandpas and if they were deceased, I would normally have to offer my deepest commiserations and sympathies, even though the event could have been years in the past. But I was not falling into the trap of wasting an hour on chit-chat.

'Well, madam, I cannot work, you see, because I de sick.'

'You are, are you? You look perfectly in good health to me!' I countered.

'I wish to inform madam dat I cannot work because what I have may be contagious to my other fellow workers, na so,' Femi said, solemnly.

'And what is it that you have if I may ask?' I asked mockingly. I opened my computer.

'I've got STD, madam.'

'And what is this STD?' I said, by then entirely distracted as I tried to open my emails on an internet line which, as usual, was not working.

'It stands for Sexually Transmitted Disease, madam,' replied Femi languidly, positioning himself even more comfortably in my new chair and lazily scratching his groin area. I looked up sharply, suddenly alert.

'Of course, it is... I was not thinking.'

The horrified look on my face would have been extremely rewarding to witness. Femi looked at me with a huge grin, waiting.

'And what do you expect me to do about it?' I finally asked after I had composed myself enough. I had never been confronted with such a problem before. All I knew in my growing panic was that I wanted him out of my office instantly.

'I don't know, madam...' Femi was obviously enjoying his moment of glory.

'Well, I will tell you what to do. First, you are going to remove yourself from my new chair right this second. Secondly, you are going to march off to Dr. Lida across the street and get yourself examined by her. Thirdly, if you catch another STD, you do not have to come through my office to inform me of the matter, but instead, take yourself straight to a doctor. Now, I do not want to see you at work for at least two weeks and bring a medical certificate stating that you are totally cured when you do. And please, go wash your hands for God's sake!' Femi had reluctantly removed himself from the chair at the beginning of my rant, and the smile on his face was totally gone by the time I had finished.

'Yes, madam. Good day, madam...' he said as he slowly left my office.

I was still shaking at the audacity of the man when Wal arrived in my office with two cups of steaming coffee.

'Good morning, Magdalena, I thought we might discuss the advertisement issue before things get too busy today. I saw the marketing man was here yesterday, has he finally come up with something? We paid him over two months ago! These chairs look good by the way.'

Before I could do or say anything, Wal had contentedly sat on the very chair that the diseased Femi had just vacated. I could only watch speechlessly, horrified, my mind blank from dread. I knew nothing of how STDs were transmitted other than the obvious ways, and I had planned to thoroughly disinfect the chair as soon as Femi left.

'Is something the matter?' said Wal, looking at my horrified face.

'No, no everything is fine! Yes, these chairs have proven to be... extremely useful so far. Yes, I did want to discuss the advertisement with you today, in fact.'

I got up, fumbled behind some display monitors, and presented Wal with the actual-sized printed copy of a proposal for a poster advertisement. It was a one-and-a-half-metre high by a two-metre-wide panel. On it was a picture of a wet-haired, voluptuous goddess, flirtatiously taking a steaming, and apparently arousing shower. Below it, the advertisement read:

'There is pleasure in the pathless woods.
There is rupture on the lovely shores.
There is a society where none intrudes.
There is Mega Engineering Limited...
Security Systems, Fire Extinguisher/Alarm and Electrical
Installation.'

The rainbow-coloured font was intricate, and the letter size increased with each line, as did the brightness of the rainbow-coloured hues of the text.

'So... what did you tell him when you read this breathtaking piece of, um, rainbow art?'

'Well,' I said, hiccupping with laughter. 'I told him that I was displeased with the proposition. I told him to stick to a simple black font with the same sized letters, to change his syrupy poem about the paths and wilderness to a serious slogan suitable for an alarm company, and I instructed him to bring me at least three proposals next time, to save time. The man was positively crestfallen. He thought he had an undisputable masterpiece there!'

'To say... we have paid the man... thousands of dollars for *this*.' stammered Wal unbelievingly.

One day, Wal stormed into my office, visibly perturbed.

'Magdalena, we have a big problem!'

'What is the matter now?' I asked. We had big problems daily.

'Well, one of our representatives is locked up in prison in Port Harcourt!'

'What on earth did he do to end up in prison?'

'Well, it would seem that it is not what he did but what *I did*. A typical case of 'Don't shoot the messenger' which went terribly wrong, if you know what I mean...'

'Actually, I have no idea what you mean Wal. Would you like to enlighten me?'

'Well, I had sent him with a quote for the government-commissioned project for the installation and servicing of the new electrical scoreboard for the international stadium in Port Harcourt...'

'I see nothing wrong with that. It's perfectly legal as far as I am aware.'

'Well, apparently, when the officials read the quote, they locked our representative in jail, and the Sport Commissioner in charge of the case called me to say the price was exorbitant and that they would hold him prisoner until we lower our price!'

'Wal, for goodness' sake, how much did you quote him?' I asked, laughing.

'Not a lot, I can promise you that!'

'Well, in that case, there is nothing else left to do than to lower the price, as kindly requested by the government representative,' I giggled.

'But this is illegal and unjust!'

'I daresay, the more you wait on the matter, the more you will have to reduce your quote. Remember how time was on our side when we had to bail out our workers from the police station? I would assume the same rule applies here...'

'All right, all right, I will do it. But that's not the way we do things in Germany!'

Chapter 18

ZANZIBAR

'Where are the dolphins...?'

Having spent many years in West Africa, Harry and I decided it was time for an extended holiday in the renowned East African safari regions of Tanzania. Zanzibar became part of our itinerary when we looked at the map and delightedly surmised that it was practically within swimming distance off the coast of Tanzania. In fact, after having dreamily looked at some more magical photos of Zanzibar, with a backdrop of a translucent, turquoise Indian Ocean, fringed only by endless kilometres of deserted sandy beaches, we concluded that the picturesque island was the only befitting place to say goodbye to the past and welcome the 21st century. It was December 1999.

We landed at Abeid Amani Karume, Zanzibar's main airport, at the same time as the other international planes, all filled with dozens of sweaty passengers from across the globe. A colourful, thorn green banner with the reassuring words, 'Welcome to Zanzibar' and a dilapidated air traffic control tower greeted us as we arrived at a stop on firm ground. We waited in the long queue for our visas to be stamped, resigned to the heat, flies, humidity, and general chaos. We were used to it, we lived in African time. We happened to be right behind an American couple. We could not help but overhear the ear-splitting conversation between the man and the customs officer when it was their turn at the checkpoint window. Judging by the drawl, the couple must have come all the way from Texas.

'What do you mean, a hundred dollars for a visa? I was told it was fifty dollars! My travel agent said it was fifty dollars! The person before me paid fifty dollars, I saw it with my own eyes!' the enraged Texan shouted. His diminutive wife was gently tugging at his elbow in a vain effort to calm him down.

'It's a hundred dollars for Americans only. Special price. Every other nationality pays fifty dollar,' replied the Zanzibari customs officer politely, swiping the only accepted mode of payment, a VISA card.

'But I don't want a special price! I want to pay fifty dollars like everyone else!' bellowed the furious American.

'That is not possible sir. Special price only for Americans. Next please!' The man was towed away by his wife, still convulsing with rage.

As Australian citizens, we paid 50 dollars for our visa. It was not a good time to be American then.

'Masta, madam, I can help you find your luggage. What colour is it? Only for twenty dollars, I will find your luggage,' whispered

a friendly voice in our ear. We were standing hopelessly next to a mountain of luggage from all the incoming flights. They were separated into several trolleys, and it was impossible to spot ours in the pileup in front of us. We did not resist the temptation. We knew a good deal when we saw one. Twenty dollars later our complete baggage was found with its colour as the only identification clue.

As we walked out of the airport, we did not react straight away to the very amiable-looking man holding a sign high above his head. In fact, we would have missed him entirely, had we not collided with him. It was only then that we read the sign. Surprisingly, it had our names on it.

'Welcome to Zanzibar, mister and madam!' chimed the tour operator, with a friendly welcoming smile. We followed him to the minibus waiting for us nearby.

'Please come inside, make yourselves comfortable and enjoy the drive! There is not a lot of traffic in Zanzibar because there are only five main roads and not a lot of cars,' he announced with a reassuring smile.

He threw our luggage into the rear of the bus, sat down behind the steering wheel and enthusiastically turned the key in the engine. After a few aggrieved splutters and coughs, the loud engine roared to life, convulsing the vehicle, and immediately enveloping it in a thick plume of black smoke. Those were the last words we heard or said to each other until our destination. Seconds later, without warning, we were propelled forward with a jolt, jitter and clatter as we bounced through the streets of Zanzibar in a dark cloud of exhaust fumes.

We had chosen to stay at Zanzibar Sunrise at Bandas which was beautifully located on the other side of the island, along a gorgeous stretch of white coral beach. It was about 50 kilometres away, or over an hour's drive. We vibrated our way onto the main gravel road, filled with potholes, bumps and rocks, which was to take us all the way to our dream location. If we had hoped for a smooth and relaxing ride in the tropical countryside, we were in for a surprise.

Once the wind blew in the opposite direction, we were able to see past the black smoke we were travelling in, as we passed tropical forests and mangroves. We waved back to the friendly Zanzibari children tending their goats. The last stage of the journey saw us perform teeth-rattling, bone-shaking convulsions, as we zigzagged and skirted sideways from one side of the road to the other at speeds of up to 70km an hour. When we finally reached our destination, we were speechless, covered in white dust and unable to feel any part of our body other than through strange tingling.

'Welcome to Zanzibar Sunrise Hotel! I hope you have enjoyed driving on Zanzibar's famous Dancing Road,' the driver announced, opening our door for us with the biggest of smiles.

Harry struggled out of the car. He opened his mouth and spat out a cupful of dust. He looked grey from the layer of dust covering him from head to toe. After passing my tongue tentatively around my mouth, in a careful inspection to ascertain that I still had all my teeth, I spat out the same amount of dust. I gathered enough dignity to answer for us both.

'Dancing Road, you said?'

'Yes, we call the road, Dancing Road, because it makes you shake and jump and move around!'

From the Reception Area, we were taken straight to our accommodation. We had booked one of the best self-contained bungalows right on the beach, under an enchanting canopy of coconut palm trees. Before our eyes stretched an astonishing and translucent Indian Ocean, ornately bordered with spectacular white sandy dunes disappearing far away into the sunlit horizon. Beautiful shells and large pieces of coral lay scattered in the sand as far as the eyes could reach. It was heaven.

We spent the next week exploring the nearby caves, bicycling, and sun tanning in front of our bungalow. When we got hungry, we ate seafood freshly caught by Zanzibari fishermen in their little dhows, which we watched sail on the horizon in the early morning. We had lobster in red wine, in white wine, fried in butter, barbequed, swimming in garlic sauce, *à la moutarde,* garnished with aromatic European herbs, and infused with bewitching Zanzibar spices. We had lobster in every conceivable option there was on offer for breakfast, brunch, lunch, and dinner. It was cheap and fresh. At the end of the week, I could no longer look at a lobster, dead or alive.

On Christmas Day, we hired a dilapidated rusty motorbike to explore the nearby lagoon. Harry took it upon himself to gather and hunt his own seafood since according to him, it was so plentiful and easily obtainable. It was also a change from the strict lobster diet we had been on for a week.

'It's very natural darling. These things are just waiting for us to pick them up and eat them,' he said when I expressed my anger at him for destroying the beautiful marine life I was admiring.

'I beg to differ. Leave those things alone! You are not hungry, we just ate a huge lobster, why would you want to kill an innocent sea urchin just because it is there? It has done you no harm!'

'It is not about him harming me or not my darling, it is the way of life. He is at the very bottom of the food chain, and I am on the very top,' Harry said as he carefully picked his way into the coral-rich lagoon, and studiously examined the bottom of the ocean floor in search of his sea urchin appetiser. Moments later, I heard a splash.

'There, I caught one! It is gigantic! Look at the size on this one!' cried Harry in ecstasy, brandishing a purple spiked sea urchin above his head to give me a better view of his wonderful catch.

'You have hardly caught it! It is not like it was running away from you. Sea urchins do not have legs, so you have kidnapped him from his home,' I fumed, outraged at this act of desecration of a beautiful ecosystem.

'Now, let us see how good it tastes. I have never had sea urchin before...'

'Hopefully, it is poisonous, that would teach you...' I muttered under my breath, as I admired a beautiful red starfish hiding under a rock.

Harry spent a good twenty minutes swearing and raging while he tried to extricate the stubborn urchin from his spiky dome, using his newly acquired Swiss pocketknife. He eventually gave up, after he poked himself painfully with the spikes. He tossed the urchin back into the sea.

'Maybe I can try spearfishing next time...' Harry made his way towards me in big angry strides.

'*Owwwwwww! Owww! Ow!*' Help! I've been stung!' he howled, as he hopped on one leg in knee-deep water.

'By what?' I asked curiously from the security of the sandy beach.

'I don't bloody know by what! *Ow!* It hurts! Don't just stand there, come help me out of here! *Ow,* I can't walk!'

'I am not going anywhere near that water. I don't know what stung you and it could still be out there. You have to make your own way here,' I said, unsympathetically.

Harry limped as quickly as he could, slipping on the sharp algae-covered stones and cutting his feet on the pointy corals in his rushed sea exit. He threw himself onto the sand next to me with moans of pain.

'*Ow!* I can't feel my leg anymore! *Ow!* See quickly what sort of a bite this is, hurry up!'

I checked his foot carefully and unhurriedly. I knew there were no poisonous marine animals anywhere in this part of the ocean, having done my research on the subject.

'Well, my darling...'

'Yes, what is it? You must tell me, don't lie... how bad is it?'

'Stop wailing and let me talk...'

'Is it spreading? I can feel it spreading!' Harry agonised, wriggling in pain.

'Well, if you just let me explain without interrupting...'

'Go ahead, tell me the truth, I can take it.'

'It looks like you have stepped on a sea urchin... a big one judging by the size of the spike. Now the spike has broken off and it is lodged deep inside your foot... I can't get it out, it would require a lot of digging with a needle. And a lot of extra pain. I think I have read that the spikes have a toxin that gets released once the spike is broken, as a protective mechanism against predators. It is not lethal though, just very painful. How do you feel now, from the top of the food chain?'

'This is no time for jokes! Now we have to figure out how to get back home on that blasted machine. It was barely drivable under the best of circumstances and now I cannot even use my leg...'

We managed to drive the rusty bike back to the bungalow, accompanied by moans of agony and yelps of pain every time we drove over a coral or a shell, which abundantly garnished the secluded coastline. Harry spent the rest of Christmas Day trying to remove the spike from his foot, digging it out with his Swiss knife. He only succeeded at creating a deep tunnel wound without coming closer to the offending spike. In the evening, having given up, he angrily limped onto the charter bus which was to take us to the spectacular Matemwe Ruins for a star-lit Christmas dinner.

When we booked the event back in June, it seemed like a good idea at the time. It promised to be an extravagant affair. Together with a few patrons, who like us paid dearly for the experience, we would share the unique Christmas table set under the stars, served by a procession of groomed waiters responding to our every need. The surroundings were to be the magical Matemwe Ruins, right on the beach.

As I finally sat in that magnificent place, next to all those wonderful people, with the splendid banquet in front of me, I tried to eat for the both of us, and drink likewise. Harry's mood was as dark as the night surrounding us. His foot was still hurting.

Every time I took a sip of my champagne, a waiter standing right behind me gallantly poured more sparkling liquid into my glass. After valiantly trying to keep up with the balance of demand and supply, I realised that I had to stop drinking altogether, from fear of drinking a bucketful of champagne out of sheer reciprocal courtesy. As the champagne flowed, and the evening progressed, conversations built up in volume as the guests lumbered gaily through the magnificent food dishes, exquisitely spiced with aromatic Zanzibar spices. Everyone was enjoying the magic of the evening, except Harry.

'Good Lord, young man, you have not said a word all night! Where are your manners?' an elderly lady with injured indignity said, throwing a wrathful glance at Harry. She was draped in a sumptuous golden silk garment, shimmering in the moonlight. Big, grape-sized pearls dangled from her ears and a matching three-layered pearl necklace garnished her neck. Gold rings with giant semi-precious stones adorned her fingers and bracelets clattered on both hands. Her grey locks were arranged in an intricate, pineapple-shaped dome extending at least forty centimetres upwards.

Sitting next to this goddess, Harry looked like a kaleidoscopic butterfly. He was wearing his flamboyant shirt, depicting all manner of flashy birds. Pink flamingos, yellow toucans, scarlet macaws, peacocks, and birds of paradise all competed for space in the backdrop of an imaginary rainforest habitat. It was purchased in the shop of our hotel. We loved to blend in with the local people wherever we went, as a sign of respect and a sure and pleasant way of supporting the local economy.

Sensing remedial action was in order, I kicked Harry under the table, making sure I aimed at his unhurt leg and gestured for him to engage in conversation. Harry hissed and gave me a dirty look from across the table.

'I have been stung by a poisonous fish. My foot hurts, and I have been in pain all day. Sorry if I am bad company,' he said, sourly, to the old lady. He spoke at the top of his voice, whether in reverence for the lady's perceived advanced age or just to make sure that half the table heard his dramatic announcement.

'Oh my, a poisonous fish? I did not know there were any around here! No one at the travel agency told me there were poisonous fish in Zanzibar when I booked my holiday. '*Pristine idyllic beaches, and warm tropical waters,*' that's what they said!' The elegant lady was visibly upset at having been so horribly misled.

'That's because there are none. What he means is that he stepped on a sea urchin and was unable to remove the spike. His foot is a bit sore that is all. That's all really, right Harry?' I nudged him again under the table.

'Sea urchin or not it hurts like hell...'

'I heard vinegar helps with marine stings!' offered a charitable soul, listening to our conversation. In fact, all other conversations had died away as everyone tuned in to listen. Harry regained his good humour. He was in his natural element only when he was the centre stage of an event.

'Hot water should do the trick. Or was it icy water with marine stings?' offered a suntanned individual from the other side of the table. He was wearing an intricate hat made from locally grown palm leaves and had a necklace of spices and flowers around his neck.

'Perhaps if you tried to extricate it with a pair of tweezers? I just happen to have a pair in my bag with me, I am always ready for any emergency when I travel!' a female guest announced proudly, fumbling in her spacious grass and bead bag, obviously also purchased locally.

'I heard if you urinate on the sting, the pain goes away instantly...' a long-necked, turtle-like individual made this announcement and retreated into a stubborn silence of shame for having professed such a stomach-turning idea at the elegant dining table. There was suddenly an embarrassed silence as the guests, assembled around the sumptuous Christmas Eve feast, chewed the expensive food whilst simultaneously digesting the new piece of unpalatable information. Harry's voice broke the perplexed silence.

'Hmm, actually, I have heard the same thing. To hell with it, that's worth a try!'

He got up and vanished into the darkness. Soon we heard vigorous rustling coming from the nearby bushes and the unmistakable hissing sound of someone relieving themselves. The bewildered Christmas guests looked at each other in stunned silence. I gulped half a glass of my champagne, and my friendly waiter immediately filled it up again to the rim. I drank that too.

'Is this young man your husband by any chance?' asked the shimmering goddess, looking at me from across the table with the utmost disgust.

'No... no, of course not, he is only my boyfriend! Very temporary boyfriend, in fact, I assure you!' I lied. We were long married by then. Harry's arrival at the table mercifully coincided with the launching of the Christmas fireworks, and while everyone was distracted by the sights and sounds, I dragged him away from the table. We found a taxi in one of the sleepy side streets and made our way back to the hotel in icy silence.

'In case you were interested, it didn't work,' Harry reported as I was falling asleep, curled up on the couch sometime later.

A few days passed, and we excitedly went on one of Zanzibar's renowned 'Swimming with the Dolphins' tours. It promised swimming up close and personal with the dolphins amongst the waves of the beautiful Indian Ocean, in an environmentally friendly way. Not being much of a swimmer, my plan was to watch from the boat. Harry, having recovered most of his misplaced bravado after his encounter with the sea urchin, could not wait to jump in the water.

'You wait and see, I will hug the biggest dolphin of them all! Be ready with your camera when I do, I will not do it twice,' he instructed me grandly, removing his glasses, and putting his snorkelling gear on.

'Are you sure you will be okay?' I asked, worried.

Harry waved at me pompously as he positioned himself on the edge of the boat, waiting for the signal from the captain that the dolphins had been sighted.

'Dolphins to the left ladies and gentlemen!' came the awaited announcement, and everyone eagerly jumped to the left of the boat. Except for Harry. He jumped to the right. As everyone else swam in an orderly manner towards a school of peaceful dolphins, Harry was blindly swimming in the opposite direction, kicking, and splashing furiously as if pursued by a shark.

'Is this gentleman with you?' asked the concerned skipper of the boat.

'Yes, he is...'

'Madam, he is swimming in the wrong direction. The dolphins are on the other side.'

'I realise, but he is too far to hear me. I'm sure he will come around when he gets tired.'

Having reached the limit of his endurance, which was about ten metres, Harry stopped swimming and looked around. I anxiously watched him, waiting for the right moment. I knew he could see nothing from that distance, not even our boat. Without his glasses, he was blind as a bat.

'Oh Harry, *yoo-hoo*, here we are, right here to your left. *Yoo-ho! Ahoy there!*' I yelled encouragingly. Having thus reached the full extent of my naval vocabulary, I took my hat off for extra visibility and waved my hands enthusiastically.

'*Ahoy!* Here! We are *here*! *Ahoy* to your left! Look to your left! Your *other* left Harry!'

'*Maaag?* Where are you?' Harry shouted from amongst the waves. He squinted his eyes myopically and tried to decide which direction my voice was coming from.

'Right here, darling just swim back! The dolphins are on the other side.' Harry swam back, following the sound of my voice and heaved himself onto the side of the boat, spluttering, splashing, and depositing half a boatload of seawater with him.

'Where are the dolphins?' he asked between two breaths, removing his snorkels, and squinting his eyes.

'Right here, on the other side!' I pointed my finger right in front of his nose.

'Dolphins on the right' announced the skipper. The dolphins had indeed playfully made their way to the other side of the boat, with the swarm of snorkelling tourists in hot pursuit at a respectful distance.

'Where are they?'

'There,' I pointed. I tried to photograph them as they were close by and looked marvellous in the sunlit waves. I heard another splash as Harry set himself again in the perceived direction of the dolphins, which were by then peacefully swimming far away into the ocean. All the other swimmers came back, sharing their wonderful close encounters and contacts with the friendly mammals. Harry also came back to the boat after a few disheartened strokes.

'Where are the dolphins?' he asked for the third time, as he heaved himself onto the side of the boat yet again.

'They swam away man, didn't you see them? They were right here! Next to the boat! You could have touched them!' answered an ecstatic diver, as he took his goggles off and spat a mouthful of water out.

'Of course, I saw them!' answered Harry furiously, as he put his wet glasses back on. He scanned the horizon methodically in all directions, full visibility restored.

'Where are the dolphins?' he whispered in my ear as the boat full of satisfied snorkellers swam away from the area.

'You will see them once we have developed the pictures if you have not spoilt all our cameras with the saltwater you bathed them in,' I hissed back.

Our next stopover was Stone Town, Zanzibar, where we spent two nights in a hotel furnished like a lavish sultan's palace. During the day, as we walked the cobbled streets of the wonderful Stone Town, we saw firsthand the exceptional fusion of Swahili, Arab, Persian, Indian and European influences. We were entranced by the intricately carved Zanzibar wooden doors which traditionally adorned the old prosperous houses. In the evenings, as we dined, we watched the city and the passing dhows at sunset from the rooftop of our hotel, comfortably lounging on sumptuous cushions scattered on the floor.

On the second day, we sailed north six kilometres off the island of Zanzibar to visit Changuu Island, named in Swahili after the type of fish common to the area. The tiny island, only 800 metres in length and 230 metres at its widest point, had quite a history and a few name changes to go with its unconventional past. On the old maps, the island was called Kibandiko Island. In the 1860s, the first sultan of Zanzibar, Majid bin Said, gave the island to two enterprising Arabs involved in the lucrative slave trade. The Arabs used the convenient island for the detention of the more rebellious slaves, who they later shipped on to further destinations around the globe or sold them at the infamous slave market in Zanzibar's Stone Town. Following Zanzibar's inclusion in the English Protectorate in the 1890s and the subsequent ban on the slave trade, the island was bought back from the Arab owners by Zanzibar's first British Minister, Lloyd Mathews.

On our last day in Zanzibar, we finally enjoyed a most entertaining Spice Tour, which entailed visiting the spice plantations and villages scattered around the island. It was my first time seeing a cinnamon tree with its aromatic bark, which our guide promptly cut off for us to smell. I had never seen a vanilla pod growing on a vanilla tree either, and I was amazed at how big it looked hanging in long clusters straight from the branch of the tree. A vanilla pod takes nine months to mature, and each pod matures at different times. No wonder they were, and still are, so expensive.

Between each botanical specimen along the tour, Abasi, our guide, enthusiastically trampled through a thick scrubby forest of trees, shrubs, and vines planted higgledy-piggledy across the terrain. Occasionally, he abruptly stopped, making us all collide with each other as we hurriedly stampeded after him, trying to keep up with his upbeat tempo. He waited politely for us to disentangle from each other, then joyfully identified a variety of medicinal and edible plants which were growing all around us. Making full use of bush theatricals, Abasi made us smell, taste, and guess a vast variety of fruits and spices.

'What is this smell?' asked our guide. He shoved the dirt-encrusted root which he had triumphantly uprooted, straight under the nose of an unsuspecting Nordic tourist, who was busy wiping his sweaty forehead.

'Um, now, I know this smell. I have smelled it before, let me think. Yes, it's coming to me... is it possibly nutmeg?' said the hapless globetrotter, so brutally put on the spot.

'No, it is not nutmeg, this is ginger!' announced Abasi, and laughed heartily at such blatant ignorance. I laughed with him, pitying the poor individual who was under the delusion that nutmeg grew in twisted rhizomes under the ground. Everyone else kept a careful silence, not relishing to be chosen at question time in front of the next native botanical specimen.

A few strides later, our knowledgeable cicerone glibly climbed a five-metre-high tree, sheathed in a canopy of big shiny leaves. Before deftly sliding back down, he picked a branch ending with a cluster of beautiful vibrant flowers. I had never seen such flowers before. Some were pale green, some were turning pink, while others had turned a vibrant red.

Abasi gave us time to examine and admire the branch, all the while looking around our group for his next victim. He instantly saw a diminutive young woman unsuccessfully trying to hide behind someone's broad back. Abasi's eyes shone with suppressed glee, and he made his way purposefully towards her.

'Have you seen flowers like these before?' he asked bombastically, with an encouraging smile.

'No, no I haven't seen anything like this ever before,' assured the nervous lady.

'Would you like to smell it? I'm sure you know this smell very well. You must use it in your cooking,' Abasi encouragingly shoved the flowers under the lady's reluctant nostrils.

'So? What is this smell?'

'I don't know, I really can't tell. I have smelt it before... maybe it is anise?'

'No, no, no! It is not anise! Anise does not grow in Zanzibar! It is cloves! People say that the smell of cloves is so strong on our beautiful Zanzibar Island that you can smell it kilometres into the sea before you even see land. When you smell cloves at sea, you know Zanzibar is not far away,' announced Abasi, his patriotic pride shining through. He picked a bunch of grass and shoved it under my nose.

'What is this?'

'Lemon grass,' I answered instantly.

Abasi looked crestfallen and from then on disdainfully ignored me. He hurriedly trampled through more bush and tore through the shrubbery, with us in hot pursuit. We stopped in front of a vine, covered in miniature, long, green clusters of grapes. Abasi turned his back to me reproachfully.

'Who knows what this is?' he asked, looking at the audience, obviously in need of another good laugh to regain his good humour.

'Miniature grapes!' offered a brave soul from the back of the group.

'No!'

'Cardamon pods!'

'No!'

'I know! It looks exactly like unripe coriander, it has the same shape and size!'

'No, madam, it is not coriander.'

'Maybe giant poppy seeds?' asked someone who obviously had never seen an opium poppy plantation. 'Or maybe even sesame seeds?' he went on pensively. 'It is almost that shape.'

'It is neither poppy nor sesame...'

'I know! It is green chilli peppers!'

Abasi's stomach had been quivering with suppressed laughter for a while. He could not hold it in any longer and finally burst out laughing.

'No this is not green chilli peppers... but it is pepper. You all use it every day in your food. All over the world.' Abasi left us to ponder our collective mental shallowness in an exquisitely calculated silence. Then, satisfied at having almost reduced us to tears, he trampled on, us in tow. He next stopped in front of a pre-prepared pile of green coconuts and expertly shaved them with his machete. He gave us one each, to quench our thirst. He did not ask us to identify the coconuts for him.

We then moved on to the plantations to discover, with wonder, the nutmeg tree, cardamom pods, ginger, turmeric, durian fruit and the incredibly aromatic jackfruit. We dug out liquorice roots and we picked a yellow cocoa fruit attached directly to the cocoa tree trunk. Abasi opened the ripe fruit, and we stared in amazement at the beautiful beans inside, clustered in their white bed of glutinous jelly. The grand finale of the tour was when Abasi stopped in front of a tree with metre-long fluorescent green leaves shooting upwards towards the sky. He cut off a cluster of the long green fruit.

'And this, what is this fruit?' he asked.

No one said a world. We were all shamed into silence by our immense botanical ignorance about the native flora of Zanzibar. I was not going to stand out from the crowd with my suggestion, although the answer seemed simple enough.

'I am sure you have all seen this fruit before?' encouraged Abasi.

Again no one opened their mouth.

'Can anyone tell me what this fruit is?' insisted Abasi gently. The air was thick with silence. Everyone kept their head down, avoiding direct eye contact. Abasi waited for a long while for full dramatic effect.

'These, ladies and gentlemen, are a bunch of green bananas...' he finally said succinctly, with great pity in his voice. Abasi was rewarded with a lot of tips for his wonderful spice tour. Everyone wanted to compensate for their blatant bone-headedness with exaggerated monetary generosity. Abasi should have been Zanzibar's top tourist operator. He was one of a kind.

Chapter 19

TANZANIAN SAFARI

Where the trees talked

After Zanzibar, we flew to our final destination, the safari in Tanzania.

We landed at Arusha Airport, in one of the most extraordinarily significant anthropological regions on the planet. We flew aboard a single turboprop Cessna, with about twenty other passengers. The tiny airport consisted of a single diminutive building, serving as a cafeteria, customs, arrivals and departure lounge. It was refreshingly empty after the chaos of Zanzibar airport. We were relieved to discover that recovering our personal belongings was a very organised and simple procedure. All we had to do was remove our luggage from the trailer parked next to our plane. Having done so, we looked around to assess the situation.

We were already beginning to shiver in the cool breeze, and I made a mental note to commandeer the only pullover we had between the two of us. I had not thought East African nights could be so frisky, and I had packed only tropical gear. Close to where we stood was a fence, with an orderly row of drivers, each holding a sign with the respective names of visitors. We spotted our driver straight away — he was holding Harry's name the highest and upside down. Undeterred, and as if his life depended on it, Harry ran to him, lest he miss us in the slow-moving crowd of twenty-odd tourists. Harry then began to stammer in Kiswahili, which he had endeavoured to learn in Zanzibar.

'*My name is Harry... me and my wife have arrived.*'

The driver looked at him with a big welcoming smile. Seeing that the man did not understand the language, Harry used suggestive body language in an attempt to communicate, resembling a knackered ape with his hands outstretched, and knees bent.

'*I will go help... my wife... carry the luggage. It is heavy,*' he said, knees bent to emphasise.

'What are you doing?' I hissed, as I arrived with all the luggage, unaided. He was still parading ridiculously in front of the bewildered row of drivers.

'I am explaining something to our driver. He doesn't speak any English,' Harry hissed back.

With a friendly gesture, the driver invited us to follow him to his Jeep. Once he put all our luggage inside, he closed the door of the boot, wiped his hands with a sparkling clean hand-kerchief which he produced from his pocket, and extended his hand to shake ours.

'Good day madam, good day sir Harry. Welcome to Tanzania. I hope you have had a pleasant flight from Zanzibar. My name is David. I am going to be your driver for the four-day safari. Please take your seats in the car and we can start to our first destination, which is Tarangire Park situated one hundred and forty kilometres from here. The drive should not be longer than three hours.'

David's accent was Oxfordian. Harry's wasn't. His jaw dropped involuntarily by a few inches. He stared silently at the smiling man, who addressed him with such elegant locution and phraseology in the middle of a Tanzanian plain. Harry, who suffered from a profuse gift of gab — which I commonly referred to as verbal diarrhea — was speechless. A heavy, stunned silence hung in the air following David's calm announcement. If his introductory speech had a crushing effect on Harry, it did the exact opposite to me. I also had the obvious advantage of not having totally embarrassed myself by a dubious ape-like charade, complete with grunts, only moments before.

'Good day to you David, lovely to meet you. We had an exceptionally smooth flight, thank you. I am Magdalena, this is Harry as you already know. We are very much looking forward to spending the next four days visiting your beautiful country in your company,' I chirped happily and installed myself comfortably in the back seat of the Jeep. I unceremoniously propelled a dumbfounded Harry into the front.

En route through Arusha, we passed colourful market stalls, stacked artistically with tall pyramids made of fruit and vegetables. Watermelons, pineapples, pawpaw fruits, yams, tomatoes, red onions, sweet potatoes, avocados, oranges, cabbages, and carrots all passed at great speed in front of our eyes as we looked from the windows. Gradually the streets became less congested, and we left Arusha behind. We could see, far away on the horizon, the magnificent outline of Mount Kilimanjaro shrouded in a layer of clouds at the very top.

'On clear days, you can see its snowy peak from here, but it is quite rare. There are always clouds next to the mountain because of the humidity surrounding it,' David explained.

We drove on and slowly the landscape surrounding us transformed into the iconic image of the African plains everyone around the world has now become so familiar with. Vast expanses of yellowed grassland, dotted with flat domed acacia trees, stretched as far as our eyes could see. In the faraway blue haze of the horizon, the gentle outline of the Great Rift Valley escarpment stood tall, a testament to past dramatic geological forces which shaped its outline millions of years ago.

'Oh Harry, a Maasai, look!' I squealed a while later, with unconcealed delight. I saw the familiar sight of a red-clothed, lanky figure walking on the side of the road in the faraway distance. His body was undulating in the waves of heat emanating from the scorching asphalt road. I had read so much about the Maasai culture and its people that I was almost overwhelmed with emotion at seeing the real apparition coming straight towards us.

'Can you please stop next to him David? He is so beautiful! I need to take his picture,' I was adjusting the zoom on my camera, ready to snap my first photograph of a Maasai. I was frantic with excitement. David must have heard this request a thousand times before. I am sure he cringed internally when yet another camera-laden simpleton asked him to do such a blatantly inconsiderate thing.

'I can only slow down the car for you, madam. Unfortunately, the Maasai people learnt the value of money a long time ago, and they treat all tourists solely as a source of income. They charge per photograph, per camera *and* per person. They have a set price for everything. They are very clever with money,' he explained with a patient smile.

'Well, I cannot afford to photograph him then. Slowing down would be great, thank you David, and I will snap what I can as we pass him.'

As the solitary lean figure, clad in the traditional red Shuka passed our car — which David dutifully slowed down enough for me to take a photograph — I tried to register every single detail of jewellery, hairstyle, and mannerism. He was young, as his elegant and distinctly long gait indicated, even from a distance. He strode effortlessly, creating the illusion that it was the most natural thing on earth to walk a hundred kilometres, in a forty-degree semi-desert environment, wearing only a thin cloth, open strap sandals, and carrying no water. Only a short wooden club with a round head hung nonchalantly from his waist. As an extra precaution against any nasty surprises, the young man also carried the traditional walking stick, which could easily transform into a fighting weapon should the need suddenly arise. The Maasai did not hesitate to strike wild animals or enemies in their path.

As all self-respecting Maasai warriors, the young man was handsomely covered in all manner of hand, elbow, and arm bracelets, and in addition, a nice assortment of colourful necklaces cascaded from his long neck. He wore a beaded head-band around the upper part of his forehead and his enlarged earlobes sported dashing big metal plates. His elaborate hair-style consisted of a multitude of small braids forming a lovely crown on his head, while a ponytail held the remaining braids in place.

All too soon, the beautiful vision vanished into the distance as we sped away on the surface of the ancient African Rift Valley. Occasionally, we gaped at other Maasai men in the landscape, clad in their striking red Shukas, vigilantly standing guard next to their large herds of cattle, long stick in hand, like apparitions from an era long gone. The Maasai men are renowned for their love of cattle, and their even greater love of pilfering cattle from their neighbours or close friends. In fact, rifling each other's cattle is a noble and accepted part of the Maasai culture. Cattle is everything for a Maasai — and whilst it is accepted and polite to share one's wife with the occasional guest, cattle sharing is not on the Maasai's politeness agenda. Unlike in the western culture, wars for Maasai are fought for cattle, not women.

We passed small clusters of circular mud houses, built entirely by the Maasai womenfolk, surrounded by the tradi-tional thorn fence, the boma — which acted as a protective barrier against hyenas and the few remaining lions which prowled at night. The mud houses looked small and dark but had remained unchanged for centuries in their design and construction materials, so they must still serve the Maasai people well. The houses were constructed with sticks, grass, mud, cow dung and human urine. The sticks were used for the frame of the hut, both internal and external. The mud and cow dung were used to plaster the walls, making them waterproof. The straw was used on the roof. The human urine, I had no idea. Probably a binding agent? Nothing went to waste in Africa.

We hurtled along the single Rift Valley Road leading to Tarangire Park for over three hours. The sun had already set behind the horizon in a dazzling veil of purple, crimson and orange hues. We travelled in the last moments of a magical dusk on the 140-million-year-old landscape when we passed an entrance gate that appeared suddenly in the middle of nowhere.

Welcome/Karibu

Tarangire National Park

We had finally arrived. This was where my dreams suddenly became a reality. For most of my life, ever since I first arrived in Africa as a child, I had always wanted to visit the great vast expanses of the African savannah, teeming with herds of zebras, impalas, and wildebeest. I had always dreamt to see the magical place on the planet where elephants strolled nonchalantly across the horizon, where statuesque giraffes peacefully crunched the acacia leaves towering above the plains, and where lions slept lazily amongst the tall yellow grasses. I had waited so long for that moment.

I strained my eyes in the darkness in an exalted effort to catch at least a glimpse of a tail of an animal, no matter which one. A cat or a domestic dog would have easily done the trick. As would a mouse or a rat, as a matter of fact. I got something much better than that.

'Oh, my God, look Harry! Wild ducks!' I gasped in ecstasy as a flock of normal-looking ducks passed in a panicked waddle right in front of our car, forcing David to brake abruptly.

'They are normal ducks, nothing wild about them. They must have migrated here from Europe for the winter months. They probably swam in your grandmother's pond in Druzykowa a few weeks ago,' grumbled Harry unkindly, disturbed in his intense scrutiny of the darkness. He had his eyes peeled for his first sighting of a lion, the king of kings in the animal kingdom, in their natural habitat.

'Oh, look at that beautiful ostrich!' I cried moments later when I spotted the long neck and fluffy body.

'Where...?' said Harry and David simultaneously.

'Right there, on the right!' I pointed excitedly.

We all gaped as we slowly approached the bird. It stood right next to the road, motionless as a tree... which it quickly turned out to be, to David's obvious relief. His safari skills would have been put seriously into question if I had been the first to have spotted something as ostentatious as the biggest bird in the world.

'Ostriches are thought to be the direct descendants of the dinosaurs, and they have lived for more than 60 million years.' David was kind and professional enough to cover my obvious embarrassment, by making an impromptu scientific discourse about ostriches in front of my delusional tree stump.

'They possess the biggest eyes of all land animals. In fact, their eyes are bigger than their brains. They can see moving objects from three kilometres during daylight. At night they see up to fifty metres into the distance. We will be seeing a lot of them during our game drives in the next few days.'

Having so tactfully paid homage to the tree stump, the ostrich and my stupidity, David started the car again and we slowly moved on. Harry was still laughing at me when we suddenly came to an abrupt halt.

'Why are we stopping, David? What's the matter?' asked Harry, wiping away his tears of joy.

'Elephant...' whispered David.

'Elephant? Where?' we whispered back, looking around in the semi-darkness, unable to see anything.

'Right there.'

David pointed straight ahead. Indeed, there it was. Standing merely a few metres away from our car was a grey elephantine mass. It did not move or make any sound. I did not understand how I did not see it in the darkness, it was so close and yet such a part of the surroundings as to render it invisible, despite its great size. We watched the giant form in awe and total silence, holding our breath. Despite our proximity, the elephant did not look disposed to move away, so ever so slowly, David manoeuvred the car in a wide circular detour, and we continued our way. I turned around and enchanted, looked back at the first elephant I had ever seen in the wild until he disappeared in the growing darkness.

We saw our second elephant of the night when we entered the Tarangire Park camp area, and David pointed in the direction of our tent. It was the only one standing under a gigantic baobab tree. Right under it, in the shimmering silver moonlight, we saw the unmistakable shape of another elephant, and a baby elephant standing right next to it.

'Are they wild elephants?' Harry asked, aghast.

'They are wild elephants, but they are used to people. This is a very gentle young female elephant, who likes to visit the camp a lot, you have nothing to fear. She will soon move away for the night's rest. I suggest you get yourselves acquainted with your tent, you have about fifteen minutes before dinner is served in the main hall, right over there. I will see you tomorrow at 6.30 am for our first game drive.'

David bid us a warm goodnight and disappeared. Much to my disappointment, the friendly mummy elephant and her baby did move away as soon as they saw us carefully edging towards them in the peaceful night, filled only with a spirited chorus of crickets. We quickly transferred our belongings to our tent and raced to the dining hall. The evening air was crisp, and a chilly breeze was blowing from the nearby Tarangire River. I was grateful for Harry's sweater.

Dinner was served on the terrace of the Lodge, beautifully situated on a gentle hill overlooking the Tarangire River. The full moon illuminated the silvery estuary of the river. Tarangire Park is situated in the Manyara Region in Tanzania, between the Maasai Steppes to the southeast and the lakes of the Great Rift Valley to the northwest. It covers a whopping 2,850 square kilometres of swamps, granite ridges, acacia woodlands, grasslands, savannahs, scrub plains, and lagoons. Apart from its stunning diversity of African animals, Tarangire Park is also famous for its colossal ancient baobabs scattered profusely on the grasslands. The Tarangire River, snaking its way along the plains of the park throughout its entire length, is the most important water source for thousands of animals in the surrounding areas. During the dry months from June to November, the animals — which temporarily migrate to the adjacent Maasai Steppes and Lake Manyara region — return in enormous numbers to Tarangire Park and its river. About 250,000 animals enter the park in search of water, the highest concentration of animals in the country.

Apart from the elephants, large herds of zebra and wildebeest abound in the region. Giraffe, impala, dik dik, eland, cape buffalo, Thompson's gazelle, greater and lesser kudu, are all hoofed animals that congregate symbiotically in the ribbons of forests and vast savannah plains of the park. The canopies of trees lining the river offer a welcome sanctuary for the primates, mostly vervet monkeys and olive baboons. Where there is an abundance of food, there is no shortage of other optimistically minded predators, ready to stalk and pounce on their unsuspecting prey. Tree-climbing lions are a unique feature of the park, as are leopards and spotted hyenas.

With the delightful prospect of seeing the animal haven the next day, we finished our dinner quickly and strolled back to our tent to get a good night's sleep, before the early morning started. Harry, who walked a few steps behind me, muttered something under his breath.

'What are you saying?' I asked impatiently, interrupted in my wondrous contemplation of the millions of stars blanketing the velvety African sky. I had just spotted the Southern Cross and was mesmerised by how much bigger it looked than in Nigeria. I remembered seeing it for the first time when we first arrived in Africa with my parents, all those years ago, and in another lifetime.

'I am not feeling that well,' Harry said. 'I have a bad headache, and I am nauseous. In fact, I think I will throw up...'

Harry held his breath and veered straight into a nearby bush. He stood there half-bent, ready to vomit, grumbling about too much food, freezing weather and big wild elephants lurking everywhere.

'Why don't you just stop complaining and let us just go to sleep? You are tired. Here, take my hand and let us walk slowly together,' I said soothingly.

Visibly disenchanted at not having regurgitated his dinner in the bush, Harry followed me reluctantly towards the tent under the colossal baobab. A welcoming hurricane lantern, lit by invisible hands while we were dining, illuminated the entry of our tent. It was intricately decorated by a multicoloured moving patchwork of gigantic moths, and all manner of buzzing bugs, wildly flying in circles around its hypnotising light.

'Great! That's all I needed. Bugs!' Harry said. 'Thousands of them. I hate bugs! They drive me insane. Make sure you open the tent very slowly, do not let a single one of them in or I will not sleep all night.' Harry waved his hands frantically in a vain effort to shoo the insects away.

I carefully opened the tent flap just enough to let us both in and zipped it back immediately. I found the light switch in the darkness and turned it on. As we looked around us in the sudden glare of the light, Harry gave out an anguished squeal, paralysed with fear. We were surrounded by what looked like the totality of Tarangire Park's bug population, flying, buzzing, colliding, and clearly having a wild midnight bash in our honour. The flying congregation of winged cockroaches, moths, beetles, termites, and crickets converged in elated wild masses around the light, burning, buzzing, free-falling, frying their wings and committing mass suicide just for the privilege of going close to the source for a millisecond. But even at the speed they were going, it was obvious they would never be able to self-exterminate, as the more of them fell, the more bugs appeared from thin air, crawling desperately through all the gaps in the tent.

'Oh my God...' Harry stood amidst it all, unable to move. I switched the light back off again.

'What are you doing? Switch it back on again, I need to see where they all are...!'

'Why do you need to see them? They will settle without the light, and they will fly out or go to sleep and do whatever bugs do at night,' I answered, trying to find my way to my camp bed in total darkness, hands outstretched in the unfamiliar surroundings. I touched something soft. That was followed by a yelp and something heavy crashed onto the ground.

'Something just touched me! Something big just touched me!' Harry whisper-screamed. 'Where the hell is my pocket torch? Where is my bag? Switch back the light...'

'It was me, silly! Can you just find your bed and lie down before you hurt yourself?'

I switched the light on, ignored the buzzing insects, and set about brushing my teeth, showering, and preparing my three cameras for the safari drive in the morning. My preparations were accompanied by quick rhythmical thumps coming from everywhere in the tent, as Harry took it upon himself to exterminate all the bugs by squashing them with his shoe. When I came out of the shower, the floor was black with the bodies of dozens of silk moths, green bug beetles, giant oleander hawk moths, and other unidentified bugs. Thousands of insects were still circulating around the party light in a hypnotic trance. Harry was holding a shoe in each hand, a crazed look on his face.

'Another one bites the dust...' Harry muttered between his teeth after another successful squash with the shoe. 'Just a few more, I am almost done. Just *one* more...there, *another* one bites the dust. One more, just one more...'

The rhythmical thumps were slowing down as Harry was overwhelmed with exhaustion, sickness, and shock. He was shivering and sweating as he systematically squashed the bugs, which, if anything, had only grown in numbers and variety. It occurred to me, belatedly, that Harry presented all the symptoms of cerebral malaria. I searched my medicine bag frantically, spilling its contents on the bed.

'Here, swallow these tablets.' I said, taking Nivaquine tablets out of the box, trying to ignore the pangs of guilt at not having recognised the symptoms earlier. It did not matter much at this stage what sort of malaria the tablets covered. As far as I could remember, cerebral malaria did not have a good diagnosis. If untreated, it was fatal.

Without asking what the tablets were for, Harry wolfed them down and sat on the bed, momentarily defeated in his futile bug war. However, a worrying thought began to creep into his mind as he sat there strangely motionless. I saw him slowly reach inside his pocket and take out his beloved Swiss pocketknife. He opened it carefully, testing the sharpness with his finger. I watched his every move with great concern.

'Is the knife for the bugs?' I asked, to break the uneasy silence.

'No... it's for the lions!' he said sombrely. I shivered all over. I did not think he would survive the night. He was obviously delirious. The night was filled with the most entrancing African sounds I could have ever imagined. A warthog kept snorting and dug right under our window throughout the night. On the baobab tree above us, birds shrieked harmoniously, while millions of crickets chirped a bewitching lullaby. Once in a while, a solitary owl's haunting cry pierced the captivating evening orchestra. Harry lay awake all night, tightly clutching his pocketknife. I stayed awake all night, listening to the enchanting sounds and watching him with great concern.

In the morning, despite a sleepless night, I was full of enthusiasm and ready for the morning drive. Harry, on the other hand, looked positively grey. At least I did not have to shake him awake as usual. His eyes were wide open as I pointed the torch in his direction when the alarm rang at 5.30 am. Relieved that he was still alive, I helped him get up and ready for the drive.

We made our way slowly in the cold, misty, grey morning to the guest lodge, which to my delight already smelled deliciously of freshly brewed coffee, toast, and fried sausages. I went straight to the buffet and helped myself to everything that was on offer. I came back to our table, carrying two copious plates of ham, cheese, eggs, tomatoes, fried beans, an omelette, and an enormous cup of steaming coffee with milk.

'Why don't you have some breakfast? Those eggs are delicious!' I said and ignored Harry's crestfallen face at the sight of my enormous breakfast. I figured if he had survived the night, he was going to be all right. He was not delirious anymore and even looked a bit more energetic than the night before. I had downgraded my initial diagnosis of fatal cerebral malaria to a case of fleeting indigestion.

'I can't swallow a thing. I do not understand how you can work up such an appetite at five o'clock in the morning...'

'It's almost six, Harry, and I am positively starving. We will be driving around for hours. Better to have something in your stomach. Eat up,' I said in between delicious mouthfuls.

'I will pass, thank you. I will have a few sips of strong tea, that is exactly what I need right now.'

'Suit yourself. Swallow the Nivaquine tablets with your tea. You can't stop taking them now since you took the first dose, although honestly, I do not think you have malaria. It is not a good idea to have meds on an empty stomach, by the way. It is pretty strong stuff.'

'Don't worry about my stomach, I will survive,' Harry muttered, swallowing the meds.

After breakfast, we found David next to our Jeep. Impeccably dressed, fresh as a daisy after an incredible night's sleep, he greeted us with a warm welcoming smile.

'Jumbo Harry and Magdalena!'

'Good morning, David! Jumbo!' I greeted him enthusiastically, climbing into the front seat. Harry grumbled and grimaced as he slid into the back.

'I hope you had a restful night. Welcome to your first safari drive in Tarangire Park! It is going to be a fine cloudless day and there are reports of lots of animals on the move. Please feel free to ask me any questions about animals, plants, or birds and if you wish me to stop to photograph anything please let me know, I will be happy to do so at your request. We have an entire day ahead of us, so we are in no rush, and I suggest we take our time to enjoy and watch the game at a relaxed pace.'

'I totally agree David. We are here to watch the animals away from everyone else, so if there are any places away from popular tourist spots, please take us there and let us stay off the beaten track. We are here for the animals, the birds and nature, not people. We want to take everything in slowly.'

There was another ominous grumble from the back seat, which we both ignored. David smiled at me, started the car and we were off to our first safari. We hurtled along for a while, turned off the beaten track onto a small road, and David stopped in front of a gargantuan hollowed-out baobab.

'We do not often show this baobab to tourists, but I thought you may want to have a look. This particular baobab tree, you see, which is about five hundred years old, is called the Poacher's Hide and the story behind it is sad and still very recent.'

David waited until I snapped a few photographs before continuing.

'Up until a few years ago, the inside of this hollowed-out baobab served poachers as a hiding place. They even installed wooden steps on the outside of the trunk, which you can still see now, which served them to climb up the tree and scout the surroundings for their next prey. They could, of course, also see the patrolling rangers from a distance and would hastily retreat inside the tree which would hide them from view in the middle of their poaching territory.'

'That is terrible! What a sad use for such a majestic tree. So, what happened to them?'

'They were caught one day when rangers spotted them in the process of dragging an entire wildebeest inside. On inspection, the rangers discovered, to their shock, that the poachers could dry a few big game animals like zebra, bison, and wildebeest at a time inside. The poachers were imprisoned of course, and this baobab serves as a reminder of that day.'

As we sat there watching the magnificent tree which had been used for such macabre purposes, a herd of about twenty elephants came into view, carefully walking amongst the shady woodlands of the swampy savannah grass. Awestruck, I watched as they slowly walked towards our parked car, obviously not concerned by our presence. Fortunately, David did not look concerned either. He only lowered his voice when he explained further.

'As you know, during the dry season, hundreds of elephants come into the park in search of water from the Tarangire River, and the park is considered to have the highest concentration of elephants in the world. Herds of about 300 individuals are commonly seen here, the last place left in Africa with such large family groups. This is a small family in comparison.'

The animals were obviously intent on going towards the exact baobab we were observing, and within moments, a few of the bigger females were close enough to help themselves to small chunks of its stringy bark. The grey giants were so close that we could see every wrinkle on their bodies, but whilst they fumbled and searched around for the juicy pieces of trunk, their eyes were keenly observing us. We ogled each other with equal amounts of curiosity. Three insignificant sweaty humans, in a rumbling mechanised contraption, so out of place on the ancient land, versus the majestic gentle grey giants, living monoliths of the savannah, which had trodden the place for millenniums.

Having satisfied their curiosity about us, they moved their long agile trunks in graceful arches, stripping the bark from the baobab and crunching it methodically between their strong molars. I looked at Harry to see if he was enjoying the special moment as much as I was. He was holding his stomach and was white as a sheet. He was not even looking in the elephant's direction.

'I told you it was a bad idea to have meds on an empty stomach,' I hissed and threw a packet of tea biscuits at him. I had rifled them from the breakfast buffet, expecting exactly this to happen.

'Oh, my stomach...it hurts.'

'Eat your biscuits, you are hungry and weak. You will feel better when you have more energy.'

We let the elephants have their fill and when they slowly moved away David, explained that the baobab tree was in fact very sponge-like and accumulated litres of water in its bark. The elephants munch on the baobab tree's bark to quench their thirst as one of many adaptations to the arid environment they live in. Remembering about water and thirst, I looked at Harry and seeing that he had finished his biscuits, handed him a water bottle. He drank greedily.

'I'm cold...' he announced when he had finished, shivering in the morning freshness.

We were driving through a magnificent forest of baobab trees, each with a spectacular, barrel-shaped cylindrical trunk covered by wildly growing branches all pointing to the sky, characteristically devoid of any leaves that time of year. The tall acacias growing next to those pillars of nature looked ridiculously small and fragile. I was busy photographing and filming the beautiful scenery surrounding us. David was quiet, sensing that words were superfluous. That was the time Harry chose to ask his first question.

'So, at what time is the plane from Arusha back to Zanzibar?' he said in a pained voice.

David froze, as did I. I glared at Harry with silent reproach. He looked down, and carefully examined the tips of his shoes. I knew that David was prepared to answer any question under the sun, ranging in diversity like:

1. When will we see a lion?
2. How long do elephants live?
3. Are there any cheetahs in the park?
4. When will we see a lion?
5. Will we see a rhinoceros?
6. What is the scientific name of that small grey bird, sitting two kilometres away on that branch on the tree to the left?
7. Why haven't we seen a lion yet?

He had an extensive answer to all those questions, and he sure knew all the favourite spots for the lions. He was, therefore, taken slightly aback when asked about the plane timetable in Arusha in three days.

'Er... I think it is sometime around three o'clock,' David mumbled, his impeccable manners momentarily shattered.

I am sure that none of his previous guests, after having paid thousands of dollars for a personalised three-day safari, had produced that question before. We drove on in silence and saw our first glimpse of zebra, peacefully grazing on yellow savannah grass in a big monochromatic herd. They all stopped grazing, looked up and flicked their tails nervously as we stopped to watch them. The click of my camera as I snapped away was the only sound around us, except for the buzzing of flies around our ears. Those same flies sat in swarms on the zebras and went inside their eyes and noses, doing what flies do best — making a big nuisance of themselves. The oppressed zebras twitched and stomped their legs incessantly, in futile attempts to dislodge the pests from their bodies.

Having had at least five minutes to digest the last information, Harry spoke again, looking dejectedly through his window, in the opposite direction to the fly-molested zebra herd.

'And how long exactly will it take to travel from Lake Manyara to Arusha?'

David, taken aback again, took some time to compose himself before answering politely, but curtly.

'About two hours.'

I decided it was time to interfere. 'David, those elephants over there seem to be a big family. Do you know how many elephants come to the park in the dry season?'

David breathed a sigh of relief — back to a familiar subject.

'We estimate between 5,000 to 10,000 come through the park during those months. Tarangire Park has the biggest concentration of elephants in the world. They come here for the water from the Tarangire River, which provides them with water to drink, but also enough vegetation to eat. Elephants also are partial to water and mud baths, and love to frolic in water on hot days.'

'And at what time do we have to leave from Lake Manyara Lodge on Friday in order to get to Arusha Airport before the flight? We need to get there a few hours earlier. I am sick,' announced Harry dolefully, as he held his stomach — he looked positively green.

David was too shocked to answer.

'I am nauseous, I do not feel well. I am coming down with a headache as well...' Harry whispered grievously to me when he saw the look of undisguised outrage I gave him from the front seat.

'These are the effects of the malaria medication you have swallowed. It is strong stuff and has loads of quinine. Stop complaining and try to enjoy the animals. Here, swallow these Panadol tablets for the headache.'

Satisfied that he could gobble up more tablets, Harry swallowed his pills and was silent for a while. We continued our journey and before long, David pointed to a family of four giraffes eating acacia leaves on nearby trees.

'Oh, giraffes! How tall they are! How beautiful! I need to take some photos David, could you please stop here for a while so that we can enjoy them?' I asked, thrilled to the bone at the unique photo opportunity. The iconic sight of the slender, gentle giraffes towering over the horizon, grazing on the leaves of the thorn tree of the African savannah was breathtaking. David obligingly switched the engine off, and we were once again surrounded by the ethereal sounds of the African bush. Unperturbed by our presence, the giraffes continued to nibble delicately at the acacia leaves, their long blue tongues picking their way carefully amongst the thorny branches.

'How on earth do they not hurt their tongues and lips on those gigantic thorns David? The pain would be excruciating!' I whispered.

'Well, a single giraffe can eat up to 30 kilograms of acacia leaves and branches a day. The tongue, which you can see is blue in colour, is about 45 centimetres in length and is highly prehensile. It allows the giraffes to comfortably negotiate their way amongst the biggest of thorns. Of course, if the giraffes had it their way, at such rate, all the acacia trees would be completely depleted of leaves and probably all dead a long time ago.'

David let me photograph the giraffes from all angles before he continued in a subdued tone.

'In fact, the thorns have been developed by the acacia trees as one of many defence mechanisms against overgrazing. This did not seem to deter the giraffes enough though, so over the centuries the acacias have developed another sophisticated chemical mechanism used as a highly effective deterrent. They have found a way to communicate with each other and warn other acacias in the vicinity that giraffes are eating in the area.'

I stopped photographing the giraffes and began to look at all the acacia trees surrounding us with new eyes.

'Once an acacia tree is fed on by a giraffe, it is a matter of time before it begins to release tannins, which taste awful to the giraffes and interfere with their digestion. Ingestion of too many tannins can be lethal to the giraffes, and they know it.'

We looked on in silence as the giraffes crunched on more leaves. David continued.

'The giraffes stop eating the leaves of that tree as soon as the chemical compound is released. Not only that, but acacia trees within 50 yards react to the release of the tannin by their neighbour and immediately emit their own tannins. The tannin released by all neighbouring trees slows down the greedy giraffe's appetite.'

'So, what do the giraffes do next?' I asked, fascinated.

'The giraffes know what the trees are doing and as an adaption, they travel upwind to those trees which have not yet caught on the wind.'

The giraffes continued eating the acacia leaves peacefully. What I had thought all these years to be such a natural phenomenon of the African savannah plains, was in fact a complex game of survival between flora and fauna. It was fascinating. I never dreamed that I would one day find myself in a place where the trees talked.

On that magical day in the Tarangire Park, we saw cheetahs, baboons, monkeys, joyful families of wild pigs with their tails pricked up, herds of elephants, zebras, impalas, eland, and buffalo. The variety of birds was astonishing, as Tarangire Park was home to the largest amount of breeding species of birds on the planet. We could only spend a few hours in the park as we had to cover the distance of 200 kilometres to our next destination, the Ngorongoro Crater, before dusk. The first twenty kilometres were leisurely and relaxing as we sped on the main road of the Great Rift Valley amongst the savannah plains. On the twenty-fifth kilometre, we unexpectedly propelled all the way to the car ceiling, before plummeting down just as unexpectantly back onto our car seats.

'What on earth was that, David? Did we hit something?' I asked, massaging my painful head. Harry woke up. The Panadol had kicked in a long time ago, and he had fallen asleep.

'No, of course not. Just a little pothole, that is what it was,' David answered, with a reassuring smile.

From then on, for the next 180 kilometres, we lurched, jolted, and plummeted as we negotiated our way amongst the hundreds of other 'little potholes' strewn randomly all over the gravel road. During the four-hour drive, Harry, fully awake, found ample time to accuse me of generating the idea of going on a crazy safari like this, as apparently, he would never have had that idea on his own. We had, by then, been married for over a year, and it was Harry's idea to go on the safari, which had been my lifelong dream, as a belated honeymoon. Fortunately, after exhausting that topic of conversation, Harry turned his wrath onto the producers of the Jeep and all cars in the world in general. Apparently, according to him, they did not put enough foam inside the car seats, which was outrageous. It would have been particularly painful for Harry, as he envisioned the mounds of soft foam laying idle in his factory, while there he was bouncing up and down on a piece of foam, 'the thickness of a sheet of toilet paper,' he assured me repeatedly.

Eventually, we evolved a series of simple and highly synchronised movements, aimed at relieving the growing pain in our spine. We sat on one side of our rumps and then on the other when the cars bouncing was too painful. It was better than no strategy at all, although the relief was only momentary before it was time to switch sides again. The good thing was that it took our minds off all the other discomforts we were experiencing. Or so I thought.

'I will throw up. I am not feeling well. All this bouncing is making me car sick...' moaned Harry.

'You are not car sick, you never were. Just try to concentrate on the beautiful landscapes we are passing. Look at this landscape. This is Africa at its finest, it is the most beautiful thing I have ever seen.'

Harry obediently looked through his window and lost himself in the idle contemplation of the boundless yellow arid grasslands, stretching into the distance as far as the eyes could reach. That inspired sight had the effect of instantly sparking his imagination.

'I feel that I have a fire in my stomach...' he announced dramatically after a couple of minutes of staring through his window.

'What?'

'I have a fire in my tummy. I am telling you, it feels like burning down there.'

'You sound like a bloody dragon Harry. Stop moaning!'

'I need water, I'm thirsty! I have a fire in my tummy!'

'Harry, we are all thirsty and we have no water because you selfishly drank it all when you were dying in Tarangire Park. Even David gave you his! Now have the decency to stop whining and wait until we get to someplace where we can get more. I am sure there is such a place somewhere around here, right David?'

'Of course, there is! The only petrol station on this road is coming up in fifty kilometres. It is a genuinely nice petrol station. Lots of water bottles there to buy,' David replied, eyes glued to the road despite going turtle speed, carefully avoiding eye contact with me or Harry. 'It will still be open if we hurry a little bit,' he added, as he glanced nervously at his watch.

He accelerated slightly and we all bounced up into the ceiling as we emerged from yet another pothole. David slowed down again to turtle speed.

'You see? Only a few more kilometres. We are almost there!' I said to Harry.

'A few more kilometres? Didn't you hear what he said? At this speed, it will take us two hours to get there! I will die ten times before then," Harry whispered histerically. 'Fifty kilometres! I have a fire in my stomach, I am telling you. Oh, the pain...'

Unfortunately, despite his promises, Harry was still very much alive and talking when we rolled into the petrol station over an hour later. Without waiting for the car to arrive at a complete stop, Harry jumped out and ran for the door. Relieved to finally have a moment of silence, David parked next to the pump to refuel. I saw a circle of beautifully dressed Maasai women selling beaded handmade artefacts standing nearby and made a quick beeline for them. I had wanted to buy local jewellery since we landed in Arusha, but had had no opportunity of doing it yet.

Ten magical minutes later, having giggled, poked, and been poked in return by the lovely beauties interested to see if my pale skin felt as ugly as it looked, I had made friends with all the Maasai women — which resulted in a rare and impromptu free photo opportunity.

I was by then also attired in about a kilogram of colourful Maasai necklaces and countless bracelets to match. Long stunning earrings drooped from my ears as I looked around trying to locate Harry. I was just in time to see him emerge from the petrol station, swaying under the weight of an entire crate of water bottles he had bought. Behind him, David followed, morosely carrying two big shopping bags.

'What on earth have you bought?' I asked, staggered by the crate and the shopping bags bulging in products.

'Corned beef, local biscuits, bread, tinned cans of sardines, local lollies, and chewing gum. I even managed to get two cans of Coke. It's warm, but it will do. That's all they had,' announced Harry proudly.

'Why did you buy all this? We are going to a luxurious five-star lodge, where food is provided, at great cost I might add. Remember how much we paid for the three nights stay, food included? Also, we don't drink Coke.'

'You never know. We are in the middle of nowhere here. For all I know, there may be no lodge there at all. Nobody will find us if we run out of fuel or if the car breaks down. Better safe than sorry.'

David, who at first was startled by my sudden transformation, only shrugged his shoulders and carried his heavy haul to the car. Harry did not notice my Maasai attire. He began consuming his newly acquired water supply immediately, as we drove off from the petrol station. David and I sat quietly, patiently waiting for what would happen next. We both knew we would be elaborately informed of all of Harry's successive symptoms in the exact order and severity of their appearance.

David had caught on to the fact that Harry suffered from verbal diarrhea, interrupted only when he dozed off from the effects of the meds he was on. As expected, we didn't have to wait long.

'Oh, it feels so much better already, all I needed was water, lots of water. I think I was just thirsty after all,' he informed us, after slurping his way through a litre of lukewarm water.

For the next half an hour, Harry sat quietly, sipping the second litre of water. It looked like he was finally enjoying the sights of the approaching Rift Valley mountains, the Maasai men picturesquely standing guard over their herds of cows, and the beautifully shaped umbrella trees, mixed with whistling thorns and yellow fever bushes. As we approached the shade of the Ngorongoro Crater hills, the vegetation became greener, and the landscape hillier. We passed a few little village settlements with friendly Maasai, who waved us hello as we passed by.

'After this village David, could you please stop? I need to step out of the car for a minute.' That was our first indication that the effects of water were making their way through Harry's body. David stopped the car as asked, and Harry hurriedly stepped outside to relieve himself.

We subsequently heard that same request every ten minutes for the following two hours. Harry relieved himself at the 'bottom of that hill' and 'on top of that hill please,' under a huge baobab tree, under a thorn bush, and on the side of the road with no trees at all. He urinated in a forest, under the wrathful eye of a group of unimpressed olive baboons, which being highly territorial, did not take nicely to the blatantly aggressive territorial marking by such a big, ugly, intruder. Harry micturated amongst 'those rocks over there David, please,' and, in desperation, right amongst some intrigued Maasai herders passing by. We were silently grateful that he did not urinate in the car, which was a strong probability in the state he was in, having drunk his way through a third of the water crate.

We finally arrived at the magnificently located Ngorongoro Wildlife Lodge. It lay strategically perched on the rim of the giant caldera and overlooked directly into what is referred to as the Eighth Wonder of the World, offering breathtaking panoramic views of the 'Garden of Eden,' some 600 metres down below. The whole side of the lodge overlooking the crater was just a glass terrace. Looking at the misty landscape scintillating with the last sparkles of golden sunset was breathtaking. I instantly glued myself to the telescopes located on the balcony, offering swooping panoramic views of the Ngorongoro Conservation Area and beyond, intent on locating at least one elephant on the distant floor of the crater.

Harry, on the other hand, drifted straight to the reception desk with a muddled gait of a plastered customer, without even a glance at the magnificent lounge or the breathtaking view outside. He had been uncharacteristically quiet on the last half hour of the road.

Unsympathetically, I let him deal with the logistics of signing in all by himself. After a while, I reluctantly tore myself away from the contemplation the crater views and looked around trying to locate him. He was long gone. I asked the receptionist for our room number and gingerly made my way along the long corridor in search of our quarters. When I opened the door of our room, I was instantly taken aback by the expansive grandeur of the incredible setting. An entire side of our room was a giant window covering the whole wall and stretched in front of my eyes, was the Eighth Wonder of the World in its full golden glory. I stood speechless at the door, momentarily incapable of further movement, so fascinating and magnificent was the loftiness and transcendency of the sublime sight.

'Oh, finally, I'm so glad you are here! What took you so long? I have been waiting here for half an hour. Close those curtains, will you?' Harry moaned from the huge bed in front of the window. I had not even seen him there.

'What took me so long? Well, let's see, I was only taking my time looking at the most beautiful view I have ever seen in my life!' I said, trying to remain calm. 'And you chivalrously left me there without even telling me our room number. I am not closing the blinds! Have a rest, but I do hope you will be well enough to escort me to the dining hall soon. I have smelt amazing things in there on my way and I am starving.'

Harry did escort me to the dining hall after his bath. Barely twenty minutes later, I escorted him back to our quarters. We had just sat on the outdoor balcony of the lodge, lit with warm fire pits in the freshness of the beautiful African night, when Harry changed colour and almost passed out. I decided a hasty retreat was in order.

The next day, after a sleepless night, Harry had deteriorated again. He was barely talking and refused to have breakfast. I decided it was time to seek medical advice since as per their information booklet, the lodge offered the services of an in-house doctor. At the break of dawn, we hurried to the medical centre located on the first floor of the lodge. We were the only people in the whole vicinity and, judging by the surroundings, had been for years. The deserted waiting room displayed two plastic chairs, smelt of stagnated air, and had a reassuring layer of dust covering every surface. It looked like everyone was always healthy at the Ngorongoro Lodge. Except for Harry. The nurse behind the reception desk looked as surprised to see us in her domain, as we were to see someone alive in such dead surroundings.

'We wish to see the doctor,' I explained after we had all stared at each other in stunned silence for over a minute.

'The doctor?' she stammered, looking bewildered at such a strange summon.

'Yes, the doctor. I read in the booklet there is a doctor here at the Lodge?' with my finger I showed her the word *doctor* printed in black and white.

'Oh...the *doctor*...' she finally said hesitantly, eyeing the word I was showing her.

'That is what I said. The *doctor*. Can we see *them* please?'

'I feel very sick...' Harry said, swaying melodramatically, rubbing his tummy, and suggestively belching while trying to vomit. That finally had the desired effect on the nurse.

'Yes. You can see him. I will take you to his room.'

She ushered us to a big, dark, and dusty room, with drawn curtains. An interesting smell of medication, mixed with vinegar, antiseptic and stagnant air hit our nostrils. The door closed softly behind us, and we were left alone. Harry sat in the chair opposite the desk. I preferred to stand. In the semi-darkness, I suspiciously took stock of the bizarre surroundings. Apart from a diminutive old-fashioned wooden medicine cabinet filled with yellowed thick glass jars, evidently made in past centuries, I distinguished a few African artefacts on the walls. There was a buffalo skin on the floor and a life-size wrinkled leather statue of an ancient man sitting on a chair next to a window. *How interesting*, I thought, as I moved closer for a better look.

As I stood there staring, admiring the exquisite, detailed handiwork of whoever had sculpted the leather masterpiece, the statue stirred, opened its eyes, and looked at me accusingly. I jumped up, shrieked, and ran backwards at full throttle. My flight was abruptly interrupted when I landed on Harry's lap.

'What is wrong with you?' he hissed in my ear, as he tried to dislodge my tangled body from his. I clung on to him for dear life.

'The statue... that old leather statue over there... it moved. I think it is alive!'

Holding me tightly against him as a human shield, Harry stared, stupefied, at the statue which had begun to stir more, eyeing us dejectedly. Harry and I huddled together like two baboons.

'So...' said the leather statue. It cleared its voice, after the effort of the short sentence. Evidently, it was as surprised to hear its voice in the lugubrious surroundings as we were.

'So...' the statue began again, 'how can I help you?' It slowly got up from its chair and laboriously shuffled towards us.

'We would like to see the doctor,' Harry whispered, still holding me tight.

'Yes, how can I be of help? I am the doctor,' the statue sat down behind the desk facing us.

'Oh, of course, *you* are the doctor. Most unusual place you have here, doctor. I am sick you see, and I need some medication to get me through my trip.'

'Why do you think you are sick?'

'Well, I have totally lost my appetite — every time I eat, I am nauseous, and I feel generally unwell. On top of that, sometimes I shiver from cold and sometimes I am boiling hot. I am also constipated. I have a funny tummy and I am very weak. I think I have malaria, but the malaria pills seem to have done nothing to improve my condition. If anything, I feel worse. Maybe it is the side effects of Nivaquine I am feeling?'

The doctor listened, nodding his head thoughtfully. Without a word, the old man consulted an ancient black leather-bound booklet, the only thing laying on his desk. I had been eyeing that intriguing object for a while, thinking it was a genuine ancient testament from centuries past. After consulting the medical bible thoughtfully, the wise old man smiled.

'You do not have malaria, and these are not the side effects of Nivaquine. It is the change of weather that is affecting you. Weather in Africa is different from the weather in Europe, and your body is violently reacting to that change in temperature zones.'

'But I do not live in Europe! I live in Nigeria, with similar weather conditions to here. It must be something else than the change of weather doctor.'

I giggled, positively entertained. The old man didn't listen to Harry's vehement protest. He opened a drawer and took out a handful of tablets, without even a glance to see what they were.

'So, let us see what we have here,' he said. 'An antibiotic, that is very well, this will cure whatever it is you may have,' he said brightly, handing it over the desk to Harry. He helped himself to the next box of pills on the pile he had created with a shaky hand and read the label, holding the box close to his eyes.

'Now, that is Paracetamol, that should help for the pain,' he handed it out to Harry. 'Hmm, this one is for digestion. It may help with constipation... and let me see, oh, this one is Valium. That should help with the lack of sleep. Take all of them three times a day with food.'

Seeing the look of incomprehension on Harry's face, the good doctor misread it for disappointment. He enthusiastically fished inside the pile again.

'You can also take these pills. They may help with nausea. And if you feel you need to vomit, these ones will hold your stomach...'

Two more boxes were handed in quick succession over to Harry. He was sitting in front of a mound of medications, while the little wrinkled man in front had only a couple left on his side. He had obviously finished his consultation, and exhausted by so much talk and movement, closed his eyes and reversed to his previous statue condition. Within seconds, his eyelids drooped, and little snoring sounds confirmed that he was sound asleep.

For some time, I had stopped giggling and anxiously watched the ancient medicine man. I observed his every move, ready to bolt at the first opportune moment. At the same time, I tried to discreetly pull Harry into a standing position, but to no avail.

'Come, let us get out of here, quickly, before he wakes up and gives you more medication,' I whispered and jumped to my feet at the sound of the first salutary snores. Harry reluctantly stood. It was glaringly evident that he was not happy with the medical assessment and was seriously contemplating shaking the old man awake for a desperate second opinion.

'And do not think I will let you swallow any of those pills!' I whispered as I saw Harry sweeping away the medicine loot from the desk. I pushed and shoved him forcibly towards the sanctuary of the door, and the world of the present century with living people on the other side.

I do not know how or when Harry managed to ingest all of the medication — Valium included — before we climbed into the car for our Ngorongoro Crater drive. By the time we sighted our first zebra herd on the flat savannah of the giant crater, Harry was in a drug-induced stupor, his face plastered with a permanent silly lopsided grin, and saliva dripped from one corner of his mouth. His body was flaccid, he did not talk, and he stared with great concentration right in front of him, where there was absolutely nothing to sightsee, except great expanses of empty savannah plains.

David looked genuinely concerned and was as silent as a tomb. He had long stopped trying to behave as a tour guide and knew he had to get rid of us as quickly as possible. With his teeth clenched, and hands tightly gripped on the steering wheel, he maniacally sped across the Ngorongoro plains, without a glance towards the magnificent herds of African buffaloes, elands, gazelles, spotted hyenas, or hippos — which I saw for the first time at breakneck speed.

'Was that not a serval, there, on the side of the road, David?' I asked tentatively after we had covered half of the crater without slowing down once. I knew servals were a rare sight, and this one was right next to the road, hunting a juicy rat.

'It was indeed. He is gone now,' David answered, revving up the engine to scare the animal away, with a polite glance in the rear mirror to ascertain that this was the case. The animal had indeed disappeared in the thick black exhaust fumes emanating from our car. We drove on in icy silence.

'Oh, look, wild pigs! How beautiful!' Harry exclaimed suddenly.

He was grandly pointing in the direction of a mud-caked family of startled warthogs, tails up ready to flee. Known as one of the ugliest and stupidest animals on an African safari, the sorry bunch represented the species with flying colours. The car skidded and screeched to a sudden stop, as David pressed the brakes, stunned by the sound of Harry's voice. It was the first time we heard it all morning.

As we stood in the dust and the sudden silence, Harry ecstatically stared at the wild hogs, which stared right back at him, not quite sure what to make of us. In all probability, they had never been the centre of attention before, as most tourists preferred to look the other way when they made visual contact with their unattractive appearance. Finally, the mother hog gave a few angry grunts, and tail indignantly perched up high, fled through the low grassland, followed by her unsightly tail-perched piglets. Without a word, David sped off again. We only stopped once more. We had driven in circles around the crater since morning, through the swamps, past the lakes, through the lush rainforest, the open grass savannah and the arid desert plains, all part of the beautiful and varied scenery of the immense and majestic Ngorongoro Crater. David had, until then, skilfully avoided all prime areas of animal sightings — which was easy enough as there were always a few cars assembled when there was something of interest on the horizon.

It began to rain, and as we approached the same swamp we had already circled a few hours earlier, I spotted some lions sleeping lazily on its banks. I tapped David's shoulder in silence, as Harry was by then comfortably asleep. The Valium had taken full effect. David stopped the car reluctantly. We watched in gloomy silence as the pride consisting of three females and their cubs slept peacefully, undisturbed by the rain. After having waited so long for my first sighting of lions, it was anti-climactic to watch those big cats doing absolutely nothing, and after a few minutes, I whispered to David to drive on.

Towards the end of that long day, we left the unforgettable Ngorongoro Crater, which was only 18 kilometres long and 16 kilometres wide, having avoided all of the 25,000 large animals permanently living there. It was a skill David probably did not know he possessed, and probably never needed to use again in his career.

We arrived at our next destination, the Manyara Lodge, named after the adjacent lake, within two hours. Harry went straight to bed, informing me that he was feeling hot, cold, nauseous, dizzy, had no appetite and had a nasty headache. I ate dinner by myself and went to sleep early.

The next day we went down to see the lake, renowned for its thousands of flamingos and tree-climbing lions. I do not know if David did some homework and chased all the flamingos away before driving us down to the lake, but we did not see a single bird. And although there were thousands of trees, we did not see a single tree-climbing lion sleeping in any of them. Maybe David did, but he certainly did not share his sightings with us. He was locked in doleful silence. After two hours of driving us around lake Manyara, relieved to the point of almost kissing his steering wheel in silent thanks, David finally spoke.

'It is now time to go back to the airport in Arusha.'

We had plenty of time to stop at a beautiful little hospital in Arusha, where we arrived hours before our scheduled flight — compliments of David, who, I am quite sure, reached some sort of track record on the treacherous dirt road of the Rift Valley. The hospital was a small, whitewashed bungalow, pleasantly surrounded by pink bougainvillea bushes. Harry stormed out of the car before it even arrived at a screeching halt on the gravelled path. He ran inside, me closely behind. A nurse welcomed us with a warm smile from behind the reception desk. She was neatly attired in a freshly starched nurse's cap, with a black line in the middle signifying her status as a registered nurse. I stood in the doorway bewildered, feeling I was being transported into a century-long gone. Harry, however, was in no nostalgic mood. Without any chit-chat or even a hello, he demanded to have all sorts of blood and urine tests performed on him. Immediately, without any delays.

'I think I am dying,' he whispered persuasively to the smiling nurse.

Without losing her lovely smile for a second, the nurse invited him to the adjacent room, where all Harry's fluids, vitals, organs, and body systems were duly checked. He emerged from the room, clearly satisfied that the cause of his imminent death would finally be uncovered, pre-mortem. We sat in the tiny waiting room in complete silence. The various test results came back within twenty minutes. We were mesmerised to see such state-of-the-art service, as we stared at the four pages of printed computer graphs. The smiling nurse explained that all the results seem to indicate that there was nothing wrong at all — there was no malaria, no infection, no inflammation of any sort. Harry was in fact perfectly fine. She suggested the symptoms he was experiencing pointed to IBS. We stared at her uncomprehending.

'And what does IBS stand for?' Harry asked.

'It stands for irritable bowel syndrome, brought on by excessive stress,' answered the nurse.

In short, Harry was constipated due to his angst at being in the most beautiful place in the world. He was instantly cured after hearing the diagnostic.

Years later, we took our children, Adalia and Chris, to the place where the trees talked. That time, we visited the Kenyan plains of Maasai Mara. Africa left the same impression on them as it did on me. A part of that wondrous place will always stay in them, and I am grateful for that.

Above
Cycling along
the pristine
Zanzibar coastline.

Left
The famous carved
wooden Zanzibar doors.
Some of them are
centuries old. In the year
of our visit, they became
listed as World Heritage.

These Zanzibari fishermen went out to sea every morning on their old wooden dhow and sold their catch on the Zanzibar Fish Market. They told us that they had been doing this for generations.

Above and below
The sights of Zanzibar.

Zanzibar's coast is filled with beautiful mysterious stone caves.

To this day, the Zanzibar dhows are used to transport charcoal, timber and fruits from the Tanzanian mainland to Zanzibar.

Sailing on the dhow with a friendly Zanzibari fisherman.

Above
Rooftop view from a restaurant in Zanzibar.

Below
Ground view from a beautiful cave on the beach.

Changuu Island, just off the Zanzibar coast, is renowned for its giant tortoises, the longest living animals on the planet, reaching a lifespan of over 200 years.

On a beach in Zanzibar.

Above
My first view of the Ngorongoro Crater at dusk.

Below
The morning drive at the bottom of Ngorongoro Crater. The escarpment of the crater is the backdrop.

Above
A herd of African Buffalos.

Below left
My first Masai photograph.

Below right
Harry in front of the giant baobab next to our tent at the
Tarangire Park.

Above
Heavily sedated Harry asleep on our first safari.

Below
The Masai continue to live in the Ngorongoro Crater, despite the lurking lions. All they carry with them is a wooden club.

Above
View from the opened roof safari car driven by David.

Below
A herd of zebras at the bottom of the Ngorongoro Crater.

Above
The baobabs of Tarangire Park.

Below
Giraffes amongst the iconic acacia trees at Tarangire Park.

Eye to eye with a giraffe in the park.

Above
Walking with the giraffes at the Crescent Island Sanctuary with my children, Chris and Adalia.

Below
Zebras in the Masai Mara.

Above and below
Masai Mara.

Above
Adalia and Chris on Crescent Island.

Below
Masai Mara.

Somewhere on Crescent Island with Chris hiding in between my legs for safety. There are no predators on the island, where scenes from the movie 'Out of Africa' were filmed.

Above
A stroll on Crescent Island.

Below
This is why strolls are not recommended on the safari plains in East Africa. Lions camouflage so well in the grass; it is possible to walk straight into one without seeing it.

Above
Adalia surrounded by very curious young Masai ladies in the Masai Mara village.

Below
Chris jumping with the Masai warriors.

Two giraffes and two humans on an unforgettable day in Kenya.

Chapter 20

FAREWELL TO AFRICA

Ten years after arriving in Nigeria for just a 'couple of years,' I knew it was time to leave. I had spent all my young adult life in a country far away from my family and the luxuries of civilisation. As soon as I found out that I was pregnant, I announced to a stunned Harry my intention to leave the country permanently. We had been married for over two years by then and I needed a home. A real home.

It was time to go back to Australia.

'What is wrong with having a baby here?' he asked, perturbed both by my announcement of pregnancy, and my imminent departure because of it.

'Are you serious? You want me to have a baby in a local hospital in Nigeria?' I asked.

'And what is wrong with that?'

'Everything is wrong with that!'

It was decided that I would return to Australia by myself, and Harry would stay back, indefinitely. As soon as I made up my mind to leave, with a very set deadline of six months at the most, I was instantly propelled into action by an unstoppable premature nesting instinct. I began to pack everything in sight, knowing what a Herculean task lay ahead of me. Our African collection had been steadily growing in wooden artefacts, carvings, statues, paintings, terracotta and bronze figurines, furniture, leather chests and drums. It was my job to pack it all, ready for shipping to Australia.

Ten years of my life had just gone so quickly and unexpectantly. I was an entirely different person from the young girl who arrived in Nigeria all those years ago. There was a feeling of sad finality in the air, and although I was happy to return home, I knew I would always leave a big piece of my heart in Africa — where I now had so many special memories, as a child, and as a young woman.

The organisation of the container to take our items all the way to Australia was Harry's job. After thorough research, Harry found a reputable and affordable shipment company and arranged for a moving date. The plan was for the company to deliver to us the container and later a truck to transport it to the port. We were to load the empty container onto the truck, which would only arrive on the moving day, to pack the container with our belongings. Harry arranged for a forklift and a driver from his factory to load the container onto the truck. The forklift was also meant to load all the heavy crates into the container, while the lighter items were to be carried manually.

On the eve of the truck's arrival, a message came to us from Harry's factory, which was five minutes away.

'Sah, there is a fira at the factory. Come quick quick, everything is burning down!' said the frightened messenger.

Harry went immediately and helped coordinate the desperate efforts to mitigate the fire, as foam is a very flammable material, and the intense blaze was spreading quickly throughout the factory's rooms and warehouses. The fire extinguishers could do nothing against such an inferno. An hour after it was called in, once half the factory had burnt to the ground, a rusty fire engine arrived at the breakneck speed of 20kph. The fire truck itself was a mobile fire hazard. It arrived enveloped in its own haze of black smog, emanating from its burnt outer layer. It stopped at a safe distance outside of the factory gate, and the doors slowly opened.

Unhurriedly, the sleepy firefighters set about their task. Eventually, and with great difficulty, they deployed their contorted firehose and pointed it expectantly at the flames from an optimistically safe distance. As it turned out, distance was not to be a problem at all. It immediately transpired that there was no water in the tank of the truck, and not a drop came out from the hose. That development did not seem to bother the firefighters. In fact, they looked very much the image of people who had completed their job successfully. They enthusiastically joined the crowd of hundreds, who had by then gathered to watch as the fire continued to burn, unhindered. It eventually subsided by itself in the early hours of dawn, when there was nothing left to burn.

Harry arrived home at six in the morning, having spent the entire night watching helplessly as his factory burnt down. He was smeared with black ash and looked unrecognisable from grief. He stayed just long enough to have a quick cup of tea and rushed back to work, or what was left of it. Our personal life was all forgotten for now.

That left me to deal with the packing all by myself. I'd had a sleepless night too, worried about Harry. I was therefore ready long before 7 am, the scheduled time for the truck to arrive. The container had already been delivered a few days beforehand, but we needed to load it on the truck before we started packing it.

At 10.30 am, when the truck had still not arrived, I grew slightly worried. Even by Nigerian professional standards, it was a long time to be late. There was nothing left to do but wait. At 3.45 pm, when I had given up all hope of ever seeing the truck, Harry called, informing me that the truck had arrived at his factory.

'The problem is that the truck does not seem like it can start again. In all honesty, I don't know how it made it here in the first place. It is in a shocking state of disrepair.'

'Well, can't they send a second one to us? It is their responsibility. They need to provide us with a truck for transport of the container.'

There was a long silence on the line. Then Harry cleared his throat.

'Well, it would appear that this *is* the second truck already... The first one expired a long way from here. Hence the seven-hour delay. They do not seem to have any other trucks available.'

I was speechless.

'I will try to find some workers to push the truck and maybe it can cover the distance to our house,' Harry concluded.

It almost did. Twenty workers from the factory pushed the truck along the scorched factory ground, and onto the main road. There, in a final effort, the truck reluctantly ignited, and made it all the way to the last corner before our house — there, it expired again. The driver made his way on foot to inform me that he was '*almost here, madam*,' and that he was 'stationed' around the corner, and he only needed to change a few tyres.

I was too appalled to ask any questions. I sent all of my workers, who had been ready since 7 am, to help him change the tyres and I waited. It was almost 5 pm. In the meantime, the forklift arrived from the factory, ready to begin the process of loading. It overtook the truck on the last corner and arrived amidst a bellowing cloud of smelly exhaust smoke and an engine roar loud enough to wake up the dead. The driver parked the forklift in the middle of our backyard without switching it off. After ten minutes, I gathered enough courage to approach the forklift driver. I only had one question.

'Excuse me, could you tell me why you are not switching the engine off? It is very loud,' I yelled over the noise.

'*Na Madam, if I goh switch the engine off, it no goh not start again. Do you want me to switch it off, madam?*'

'Oh, no, do not switch it off at all, please!'

I wished I had not asked. Before, I was only curious, but now I was on the verge of a panic attack. We waited some more. By then, the whole neighbourhood waited and watched us, and the enterprising pedlar boys sold peanuts and water to the growing crowd.

When the truck finally arrived, enveloped in a diesel cloud, Harry had arrived from work. It was past 6 pm, and the night was slowly setting in. The idle forklift driver went straight into action, only to discover that his deafening hoisting machine was too powerless to lift the two-tonne container. The spectators clapped with glee at its unsuccessful attempts to lift it off the ground.

'*I dey need to go get de bigger one!*' the forklift driver shouted straight into our ears. He quickly disappeared, and was back within twenty minutes, with the heavier machine — which lifted the container effortlessly off the ground. The truck immediately sunk down by a good fifty centimetres as the air escaped from its brittle cracked tyres. The truck driver's helper was ready for that occurrence — in anticipation, he had already started a vociferous automatic pump, its only function to prevent the truck from collapsing.

Every time an item was forklifted onto the truck, it sank more to the ground. I watched mesmerised as more items were heaved onto the container, expecting everything to collapse at any moment. The totem figures were too heavy for the forklift to push all the way inside. The problem was resolved with typical African resourcefulness. A long metal pole was used as leverage, while ten people pushed the clangourous forklift forward, propelling it centimetre by centimetre to push the heavy load all the way to the back of the container. The noise, the pollution, the swearing, the shouts, the sweat, and the chaos of what had become a late-night operation was too much to bear. I could only stand and watch helplessly as somehow, with no logic or reason, things slowly advanced.

Towards the end, we became insensitive to the noise and the exhaustion, and no one saw or heard anything anymore.

The noise coming from our generator — as of course power had gone — mixed with the forklift's thunderous roar, rhythmically reinforced by the sonorous beat of the automatic pump keeping the truck upright, and the wheezing engine noise of the expiring truck was uproarious. That pandemonium was supplemented by the screams, the shouts and the orders coming from all sides, which no one could possibly hear or cared to listen to. To round up the calamitous atmosphere, visibility was close to null, as we were surrounded by thick smoke emanating from the different machinery. It was pitch black and approaching midnight.

But this was Africa.

In the western world, such a scenario would have doomed the whole operation to fail, but the same elements held all the keys to success in Africa. Organised chaos had the effect of producing the most innovative and spontaneous outcomes. Somehow, things just happened, and before midnight — in classic African style — the operation was finalised, and every item was packed. I don't know how the truck made it to the port or how many stops it had on the way to inflate the tyres.

Now that my African chapter was about to close, all I had left to do was make it back to Australia for the delivery of my first baby. My flight was scheduled on September 12, 2001 — the day after 9/11. That flight never came, because the plane was on the ground in transit at a New York airport. The US shut their National Airspace following the attack, and flights were grounded, diverted, or returned to their home countries mid-flight. I waited for my rescheduled flight to arrive, and three days later I was finally on my way home.

I arrived in Australia in September 2001 to a changed world.

Milton Keynes UK
Ingram Content Group UK Ltd.
UKHW051111210823
427021UK00011B/19